RIDING WITH GHOSTS

BY GWEN MAKA

eye books

Challenging the way we see things

This Eye Classics edition first published in Great Britain in 2010, by:
Eye Books
7 Peacock Yard
Iliffe Street
London
SE17 3LH
www.eye-books.com

First published in Great Britain in 2000, as *Riding with Ghosts* and
Riding with Ghosts: South of the Border

Copyright © Gwen Maka
Cover image copyright © Bryan Keith

Cover design by Emily Atkins/Jim Shannon
Text layout by Helen Steer

British Library Cataloguing in Publication Data
A catalogue record for this book is available from the British Library

ISBN: 978-1-903070-77-2

Note on terminology:

While writing this book I have been conscious of the current pressure to be 'politically correct' in the written and spoken word. In the case of North American tribal peoples I believe that 'Native American' is currently politically correct among white Americans. However, not only did I find this at times clumsy and impersonal, I also, in my travels, never met any individuals who used this term about themselves. Rather, they used tribal names or, more generally, 'Indian' or 'American Indian'. I also found this the case in books.

When I read of a prominent Oglala Sioux (Lakota) proclaiming that 'Native American' reminded him of the repressions practised against the Indian, and of his belief (and of others too) that 'Indian' does not – as commonly stated – come from Columbus's belief that he had found India (which at that time was called Hindustan) but from the gentleness of those aboriginals encountered by him, so that they were 'una gente in Dios' – a people of God, then I was satisfied that these terms were not offensive in any way.

Therefore, in all cases historic I have used the tribal names or 'Indian'. When referring to native people of the current era I have again used the tribal name where this is known and relevant, and interchanged Native American, Indian, American Indian, tribal peoples and Native people, when talking more generally.

ACKNOWLEDGEMENTS

For Ethan and Savannah.

Thanks to Dan Hiscocks of Eye Books for taking the risk of a new edition and accepting my wish to do a vastly revised script – and for his inspiring ideas and advice. To Helen Steer at Can of Worms Enterprises for her hard work and patience at my many script revisions.

Thanks to John and Jane Snow, Linda Raczek, Linda of Coeur d'Alene, Selina, Martha, Armin and Maria, and many others, for opening their homes to me. To all the wonderful people I met along the way who constantly humbled me with their many kindnesses and who never showed any resentment of the fact that my 'pains' were personally inflicted and voluntary. Their ability to keep laughing in the face of immense daily difficulties filled me with admiration, brought colour to my days, and made me realise that you can have nothing yet still be generous with kindness.

My special thanks to Julian, for his endless inspiration and for still being out there somewhere – still cycling. He made it seem quite normal to get on a bike and cycle for a year.

But above all, I thank all those solo women travelling alone in every corner of the world – by foot, bicycle, train, bus, canoe, car, whatever – with confidence and courage and flagrantly defying those doom mongers who are always warning us what a dangerous place the world is. In my travels these solo women always provided intelligent companionship, however short, whenever I met them. Christy Rodgers (who, when not travelling, publishes the radical journal 'What If...' from her home in San Fransisco) deserves special mention for her unassuming passion of quietly trying to make the world a more 'thinking' place. Such women can truly motivate the rest of us and show us that women alone, of any age, do not have to stay at home, whilst the older among us can dream, not of what we **can't** do, but of what we **can** do – or more specifically, of what we can **try** to do!

CONTENTS

"History... creates the insidious longing to go backwards. It begets the bastard but pampered child, Nostalgia. How we yearn... to return to that time before history claimed us, before things went wrong. How we long even for the gold of a July evening on which, thought things have already gone wrong, things have not gone as wrong as they were going to. How we pine for Paradise. For mother's milk. To draw back the curtain of events that have fallen between us and the Golden Age."

Graham Swift
Waterland

Riding with Ghosts

Seattle to Mexico

MAP: SEATTLE TO BAJA

Cycle route: ----

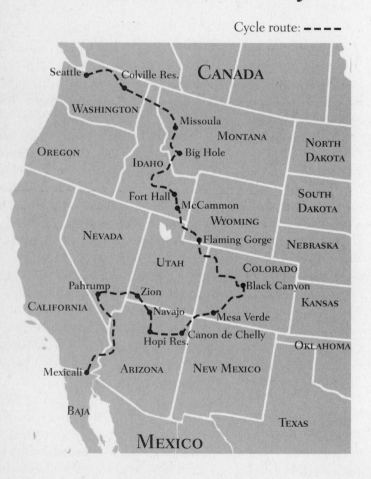

INTRODUCTION

I really didn't know it would be like this! As I sweated and cursed my way up the never ending hill which culminated in the Loup Loup Pass I wondered how on earth it was that in a lifetime of cycling I had managed to reach the age of forty-five without learning that cycling uphill could feasibly kill you.

And in all these years why didn't I know that wind wasn't only something that gently swayed the tree tops, but was really a malicious and vindictive spirit whose sole reason for being was to hurl me under the wheels of any passing articulated lorry or sling me into the deepest muddiest roadside ditch, and whose buffeting blasts could quickly reduce my world to a swirling maelstrom of humourless hell?

After all, since being a child I had often seen cyclists loaded down with luggage, pootling leisurely up steep hills without breaking a sweat, even having the energy to wave at me as we passed by in the car, so I already knew how easy this bike malarky was! How envious I'd been of them when they erected their cosy little tents next to my parent's caravan, and lit their cute little cookers as they sat on the soft green grass and watched the burning sun go down. I would watch them jealously, embarrassed by my indoor luxury. I mean, cycling tourists always had fun, didn't they?

So it was that for years I'd been longing to set off on my own Grand Tour; it was something that I knew was going to happen *some* day. I just had no idea how or when or where. And as my parents refused to go abroad ('there's plenty to see in this country') and as I was always financially challenged, I was thirty-four before I finally got beyond Britain's shores on a bus to Brussels for a weekend demo.

For many years the travelling idea got stuck in the cobwebs of daily survival; I was a single mother trying to juggle what had to be done without the means to do it. I remember thinking of life as a hurdle race – I would just get over one hurdle when I had to prepare for the next one, which I knew was just around the corner!

Then, one day, as I returned from the supermarket on my bike, laden down with six precariously wobbling carrier bags of food for my three teenage sons, an idea began sneaking into my mind. It was like a virus which had lain dormant for years, and suddenly it burst forth into a fully fledged outbreak....

I would go cycling!

Why did it take so long for such an obvious idea to form? Why hadn't I thought of this before? So convinced was I by this revelation that over the next few months I bought four Carradice panniers, a beautiful silver Dawes bicycle, and booked myself onto a Teaching English as a Foreign Language course – I thought it might come in handy. The panniers went into the waiting room of my airing cupboard, the TEFL was done in my summer holidays, and the bike was stolen twelve months later.

After my children had more or less left home and my little dog Flossie was no more, I decided it was time to use my TEFL skills to see a bit of the world and hopefully raise some cash for my 'one day' cycling trip – wherever that may be. Sticking a pin in a map to make the decision of where to go it landed on Turkey, so I left work, jumped on a ferry and after a month arrived in Istanbul. Once there I thumbed the local yellow pages, knocked on doors and soon found work teaching English to spoilt little rich kids and polite attentive big kids and settled into a happily chaotic life in that addictive metropolis.

In the end it was Justin who was the catalyst. My days were floating dreamily by in the smoky haze of nondescript cafes and drifting conversations with a variety of carpet seller friends – lazy conversations dominated by petty gossip; the perpetual elusive carpet sale; how to get home at midnight on fifty pence; which tourists wanted the weed; and always, always, the lack of money. Heady stuff!

The reason it is his fault is because one mellow, yellow day he turned up at my current hostel on his bike. Justin, I should mention, is one of the untamed of the twentieth century – a truly natural traveller;

a meanderer on the planet who is vaguely circling the world, but with diversions that are long and fascinating. He arrived from Russia complete with donations of three large glass jars of bottled preserves, several pounds of potatoes and piles of butter – all the heaviest things you can imagine – determined to defy those dedicated lightweight cyclists who decimate everything from toothbrushes to gear levers in order to reduce their weight as much as possible without personal physical amputation. He argued that as he wasn't carrying it, it was no problem. I was to discover that this was not a logical statement.

With financial considerations taking top priority we decided to share a room for the winter. The result was a fourth floor room with huge corner windows which fully encompassed the magnificent vista of the Blue Mosque, like a glorious three-dimensional Walt Disney screen. This scene flooded our senses daily, and for the remaining months we constantly had to remind ourselves that we were not living in a fairy grotto, or in the white witch's wonderland.

One hot afternoon Justin was out and I picked up his mini world atlas. Of course, it was obvious, I would cycle from Seattle to Panama. A quick decision.

And yet, not really so quick. Ten years earlier I had visited the United States where I had spent six weeks in my tent, studying development on the Rosebud and Pine Ridge Sioux reservations of South Dakota – the homes of the Brule and Oglala Sioux. This trip was undertaken with a staggering combination of ignorance, stupidity and such a lack of funds that the Greyhound ticket seller in New York got fed up with me asking,

"How much is it to go to x, or y or z?"

"Where do you actually *want* to go?" he eventually asked.

When I told him, he just gave me a ticket and said,

"Just give me what you've got."

Following a combination of camping, hitch-hiking, starving and a whacking dose of luck, I left America very much thinner but also very much wiser. I had gained a greater understanding of the harsh realities of life on the reservations, of land distribution, social problems, education, intra-tribe conflicts, etc.

I was also wiser about my own survival. Things such as how to return the seventeen hundred miles to New York in three days with only four dollars; how to live with my own company; learning that I never again wanted to travel with a dependence on others – I needed my own transport; learning how to take unavoidable risks and accept the possible consequences; to be adaptable, to trust my hunches.

But the most overwhelming emotion I left with was a powerful confirmation that my previous imaginings of 'how America was' were correct. It felt how I thought it would feel but even more so, because no written words can express the magic which hovers over those wonderful wide open rolling plains, nor can they convey the vibes of the past which shimmer in the golden air and permeate the land.

And most importantly, I discovered that when travelling alone, and in dire straits, an internalised need really does become an external reality, just as the philosopher Karl Jung said – I believe the word he used was synchronicity. Thus when things get tough, the niches for survival open up, like another dimension. You learn to 'live between the lines', to see them, so not only do things turn up just when you need them, but you begin to feel almost an instinct about any situation.

I remember one night camping in my tiny tent on the open prairie outside Rosebud village.

I was hungry, lonely and a little depressed. It was evening, and the sky filled the world – so huge and so blue. I went to the brow of a nearby hill and watched as from the west an enormous fluffy cloud came floating through the blue – a thunderhead. It was a great billowing mass, and within it a magical thing happened – as the lightning flashed and thunder crashed that cloud flickered on and off like a bright light in a white tent.

It was a revelation for me, who had never before seen a storm contained within a single cloud, surrounded by a clear sky. In Europe a lightning storm means low grey clouds that smother your head, the lightning comes from an unidentified source, and the world is enclosed in a fierce, murky onslaught of darkness and close horizons. But that evening on the Rosebud nothing happened in the clear blueness of the sky beyond that South Dakotan cloud, and it drifted sedately on its way across the heavens – all the energy and the drama remaining within itself.

I found some wild choke cherry, lit a fire and cooked them. I made a cup of tea and continued my reading of *Black Elk Speaks* and read of how, more than a hundred years before, the medicine man Black Elk had also camped on the Rosebud at a time when he was unhappy about the fate of his people, the Sioux. I read of how he went to the brow of a nearby hill, and as he sat there a thunderhead passed, and thunder crashed and lightning flashed within it. As he watched the great cloud pass he felt at peace once more and knew what he must do.

Some would call this coincidence. I call it synchronicity.

Yes, in those lands everything felt alive – the land, its history, its rocks, the people who have passed through. A vibrant tactile thing emanates from the earth and wraps itself around you, draws you safely into its warmth. And so, planted in my mind was a desire to return.

The idea of just packing your bags and leaving is an attractive one, but in practice few can do it easily, for even without work or family commitments the accumulation of age is almost invariably accompanied by a parallel accumulation of cumbersome life debris, although desperation at the passing years can sometimes lead to a ruthless eviction of some of this.

I recall a wonderful down to earth Australian friend, Jan, who regularly threatened her two wild teenagers that if they didn't toe the line and make her life less stressful, then one day they'd come home and find she'd fled to Timbuktu. And indeed, one day they came home and found she'd fled, not to Timbuktu, but to Istanbul, where I met her. She was making good money teaching English which she proceeded to pass on to a series of dubious boyfriends who fattened up nicely under her benevolence, until four years later she returned home to her, hopefully, now contrite children.

I only had two months to prepare for America. Of that, one month was taken up with completing some outstanding work, and two weeks were to be used for a final visit to my three now grown-up sons who lived in Mallorca. This left two weeks to find someone to live in my house, deal with bureaucracy and, most importantly, equip myself for my trip, including the main item of buying a suitable bike to replace my previous stolen one. But I still had my panniers which had been waiting patiently for me these past ten years. With great ceremony, I lifted them out and attached them to my spanking new bike, another Dawes, green and elegant and already loved.

Then, at eleven o'clock one night, a day and a half before abandoning my house, there was a knock on the door. There stood Justin. He had cycled from the ferry at Felixstowe to Norwich without stopping (seventy miles) and now informed me that my twenty-one gear bike was no good for the Rocky Mountains. The gears were not low enough and needed replacing.

"Blimey," I asked him, "how big *are* those hills?

"Big!" he replied.

By this time I was in a state of total exhaustion and confusion, as every day produced yet another long list of tasks to complete. I hadn't even had a chance to think about the journey at all; I'd made no plans whatever; I was just going to jump in at the deep end and go. If I'm honest though, I knew that it wasn't *only* that I hadn't had time, it was also the only way I could do it; it was the way I worked. If I'd thought about such a massive undertaking then I would have been be forced to face all the things that could go wrong; all the reasons *not* to do it! It was just too scary!

I know many people plan for months, even for a trip in Great Britain, and I imagine *everyone* plans for something more adventurous, especially if some degree of self-sufficiency is involved. But I believe that if I had started researching (and internet wasn't widely available at that time) then I'd never have set off, I would have been too daunted by the scale of the whole thing and would have chickened out. By simply making the decision to go, and booking a ticket, it was done, I *had* to go. The result was that my US map was just a road map with very little detail, (so I hardly even knew where the mountains were); I had very little money; knew nothing of the climates, geography or potential dangers. In fact, all I really knew for certain was that I would be starting in Seattle with the aim of getting to Panama – or wherever I ran out of money. I'd just get over to America first and take it from there, a day at a time, and see what happened. And that's what I did.

What really got me wound up and frantic was the work involved in actually *getting* away, not worries about the trip itself.

"I can't stand it! I just can't do anymore," I whined.

"It's okay. You're already there. You've already done it," said Justin.

And yes, I had. I had let my house, organised bills, bought a one year return ticket. I was ready to go. But on a night of one too many beers I had also agreed that an ex-work colleague could come with me for the first month and I was having serious reservations about this. But as she had presented me with a *fait accompli* when I returned from Turkey, and not wanting to disappoint her, I agreed, telling myself that it might ease me gently into the start of my otherwise solitary journey.

Not having been on a long bike journey before it was a bit of guess work trying to decide what was essential equipment and what wasn't. All the planning in the world won't get it exactly right, especially when it comes to things like bike spares. It is only *in situ* that you learn to distinguish between essentials, usefuls and waste of spacers. A long trip (either by time or distance) is made considerably more difficult as climatic and/or seasonal zones will be crossed. So for example, whilst lots of clothes may be a must for the first months, you don't want the extra clutter when the temperature starts to rise.

In theory items can be shipped home but travelling on the economic margins does not permit the flexibility of buying new gear and shipping out old. As I was calculating on a paltry five or six dollars a day (it was go with this or not at all) I had nothing over for emergencies or luxuries.

In spite of lots of experience in camping, I made three major errors in my choice of equipment, all of which were totally inexcusable.

The first, and biggest, was in not replacing my three season down sleeping bag with a five season synthetic one. I really didn't imagine it *could* be so cold as it was during the long dark winter nights in the Arizona desert (research?!). I was going into the unknown and turning a bike ride into a survival expedition.

My second mistake I blame on the iconic long distance walker Chris Townsend who gave an impeccable review for a light weight, single skin Gore-Tex tent which he claimed to have used in the hurricane conditions of his two thousand mile walk through the Canadian Rockies. This tent deposited lakes of condensation on me in any conditions damper than the Sahara Desert (he subsequently wrote another review where he completely reversed this initial verdict). It also took ages to dry. I would never buy another single-skin tent however tempting they may look!

Another mistake was buying a very expensive multi-fuel cooker which caused me many tantrums over the months. At times I had to wait a couple of days until I had calmed down sufficiently to deal with its eccentricities in a reasonable manner.

The moral of all this is not to buy untested equipment when embarking on a long journey, *and* to do some research into weather conditions.

Finally, because my decision to undertake the trip had been a quick one, I had not had the opportunity to train. Not that I would have anyway. I reasoned that there was little point in cycling hundreds of miles a week when I could use the trip itself to train. As a consequence my first days reached a pathetic twenty-five miles a day. After a month I was up to fifty and gradually increased until I stabilised at around eighty with a maximum of ninety-five on a day of mountains in Mexico. (I was flabbergasted by those cyclists who claimed mileages of up to two hundred miles when loaded up.) But I wasn't in a hurry; wild camping is a great pleasure for me and my great satisfaction is to stop early in the day and spend the remaining daylight hours enjoying my surroundings.

LEAVING SEATTLE

On a sunny day the Puget Sound must glimmer and glisten around the islands and headlands like a jewel, and though the day was grey and damp it was, for Seattle, a good day; the sun had only been seen twice this year, I was told. Given the abysmal lack of summer throughout the country I could well believe it. I had imagined mid-August to be a late start to my ride which would mean rushing in order to reach the Rocky Mountains before the snows of winter fell. But as it happened, 1993 had been a freak year of unquenchable deluges resulting in widespread flooding of the Missouri floodplain. To travel earlier would have been misery.

Seattle was my introduction to the 'skid-row Indian'. These much maligned urban down-and-outs are tragic figures who cannot cope soberly with what history has thrown at them and their heritage. Chief Seattle, after whom the city is named, realised that the unstoppable tide of whites would eventually destroy his people. In a long moving speech (now thought to have been sexed up by the media) he said:

"When the thicket is heavy with the smell of man... then it is the end of living and the beginning of survival."

Sadly for many of his descendants, survival is found at the bottom of a bottle. Whilst present-day Native Americans may not have direct experience of 'what once was', they have, I believe, a culturally inherited memory of what they have so recently lost. This memory remains strong, and it is one which can either eat away at the spirit or be directed into positive energy and determination.

A Maori friend spoke of this to me once. I had been to see a violent but excellent film about inner-city Maori culture, called *Once Were*

Warriors. I asked him about its accuracy and how such alienation could be avoided.

"That was a road I could have gone down," he told me. "In the short term it's the easiest way. You can either direct your energy negatively, screwing yourself up with all the wrongs that have been done to you, or you can say, 'They aren't going to beat me; I'm not going to let them ruin the rest of my life,' and channel your energy productively."

When I visited the Rosebud and Pine Ridge Lakota (Sioux) reservations of South Dakota twelve years ago, the initial scene was one of cultural desolation. Wife and child battering, alcoholism, dependency, tribal government corruption and conflict, racism, violence and unemployment; it had the lot. An old man lamented that nobody had visions any more. He didn't know why.

The following day, three unemployed men (two Sioux and one Navajo) sat in a shabby living room with the television blaring out; simultaneously a cassette was playing. Nobody was listening to either. As I looked on this depressing scene they suddenly began playing their drums, shaking a gourd and singing traditional songs, totally oblivious to the parallel chaos. I did a retake on my first impressions.

Later, a pony-tailed man showed me the scars on his chest and back and explained that they were the result of his participation in the Sun Dance. This is an ancient ritual practised with variations by tribes throughout the country. It usually involves painful ordeals of body piercing in which hooks (originally eagle talons) are inserted under the muscle into the chest or back and attached by a line to a cottonwood pole or heavy buffalo skull. Gradually the hooks are torn out by the force of body weight against the pole. The ritual is variously described as being for self-sacrifice and prayer, the acquirement of power, the giving of thanks to Wakan Takan the creator. It was banned in 1881 and for many years went underground. Happily it is now enjoying a revival – with some changes in method – and this particular year a ten year old boy had undergone the ordeal.

In his autobiography Lame Deer, medicine man on the Pine Ridge reservation, says that some of the older generation criticise the present-day participants of the Sun Dance, saying; 'they don't go underneath the muscle,' 'it's only the flesh,' or 'the young men have gone soft,' and so on. Lame Deer gave his response to this criticism:

"These dancers work for a living... in a few days they must be fit to pitch hay, drive a tribal ambulance or pick beets. One did not need money in those old days. While a dancer's wounds healed, the hunters brought him all the meat he and his family could eat.

No, in many ways the dancers of today are braver than those of days gone by. They must fight not only the weariness, the thirst and the pain, but also the enemy within their own heart – the disbelief, the doubts, the temptation to leave for the city, to forget one's people, to live just to make money and be comfortable."

When earlier generations took part in this annual ritual there had been little to induce doubts in the ancient belief system; the American Indians believed totally in their world of mystery and spirits and visions were their everyday life. In these days of high-tech and internet, how much harder it must be to hang on to traditional ways.

When more than two hundred men, women and children were massacred at Wounded Knee, South Dakota in 1890 Black Elk wrote:

"And so it was all over. We did not know then how much was ended. When I look back now from this high hill of my old age, I can still see the butchered women and children lying heaped and scattered all along the crooked gulch, as plain as when I saw them with eyes still young. And I can see that something else died there in the bloody mud and was buried in the blizzard. A people's dream died there. It was a beautiful dream...."

Although the Cascades do not reach the elevation of the Rockies and the passes are relatively low at around four or five thousand feet, nevertheless they are rising up from sea level. In western Colorado even the valleys may be at seven thousand feet so the rise to an eleven thousand feet pass may still only be a four thousand feet climb. In other words, the Cascades were tough for a beginner.

The moss-covered forest allowed few grand vistas, just tantalising glimpses of eerie shrouded spires of rock and – where the land opened out along rivers – the incredible translucent blues of mountain waters.

In addition, this was black bear territory and the business of hoisting our gear up trees at night was not only a nuisance, it was impossible. After many failed attempts to throw a line up the tangled trunks of massive droopy conifers we lowered our standards to a point where a coyote pup would have had no trouble reaching our goodies.

At the top of Washington Pass I was horrified to see snow drifting to the ground. This was August, for heaven's sake, how can it be snowing? I had visions of dying a cold lonely death in the Rockies in October. But then the sun came out, and it was a glorious fourteen miles downhill, the temperature and morale rising with every bend in the road.

Suddenly I burst out from the darkness of the forests and into golden-flecked, sun-bathed, rolling grasslands. Cattle and horses grazed in meadows of wild sunflowers; it was dry and sunny and I could see for miles. I felt a great sense of relief as the cold wet nights of the Cascades were left behind and my spirits soared as I bowled into the museum town of Winthrop.

Hockney Landscapes

Looking back over my diary entries, the most common introduction to each day is variations on the theme of, 'My god, what a day!' The first such entry occurs on August 25th.

Enjoying the ease of riding in the pleasant valley of gentle hills which surrounded the close-knit communities of Twisp and Winthrop I was suddenly confronted by a signpost indicating that this sharp turnoff was mine. Apparently this was the Loup Loup Hill, which culminated in the Loup Loup Pass, the one that made me wonder what the hell I was doing here. Anywhere you see the word 'Pass' be prepared for a slog – I had learned that much – but the easy valley had lulled my body and mind into dreamy lassitude. I had my amazing little computer telling me everything I wanted to know about speeds and distances and things. On bad days it told me things that I didn't want to know, on good days it motivated me to better things. It was a bit like the proverbial half cup of tea – is it half full or half empty? A bike computer is the same. On a good day it tells you how far you have gone, on a bad day it tells you how far you have still to go. The real beauty of it though, is that it allows you to psyche yourself up and pace yourself for the distance you intend to go that day. There is little worse than thinking you have ridden at least forty miles, and then to find a sign that informs you that you have done only twenty. It is enough to make a plodder like me give up at that point. A huge gumption deflator.

For some reason I did not even know the Loup Loup existed, and in my still unfit state it nearly killed me climbing that mind-numbing hill – simply because I did not know where the bloody top was. Now I know that a miserable little eight miles can go on forever.

I suppose every long-distance walker, jogger, sailor and cyclist develops her or his own strategy for coping with physical and mental stress. In these early days, hills and mountains were stress. My strategies for coping varied from mentally ticking off the distance on the computer in ever more tiny amounts – until I was counting tenths of miles – to counting pedal revolutions, so that every down-pedal on the right foot counted as one. After each thousand of these I thought I must be making headway. I also counted telephone posts and made up stupid songs.

One of the most wonderful moments in the life of an unfit cyclist in the USA – to which nothing can compare – is that exquisite moment when a yellow sign appears at the side of the road showing a little black lorry going downhill instead of uphill. This will be a few yards from another sign which says Such-and-Such-a-Pass Summit. After repeating obsessively to yourself: 'I can't do it. I must be mad. I can't do it,' you reach the top, breathe deeply, and gasp; 'I've *done* it!!'

And the Loup Loup Pass was only a hill, for heaven's sake.

In the Colville Reservation border town of Okanogan, my riverside searches brought me into contact with Sue, in whose garden I camped that night. She was later to play a brief but volcanic role in my life, but at this time I thought she was just a friendly local, and not the wacky person she turned out to be. I should have been suspicious when she declared that the large bird which had landed on a tree across the river was a sign that I'd "been sent". When I returned three months later I discovered that this was its nightly roosting tree.

She also professed to have regular conversations with her dead grandfather who, she said, had been a lawyer and a medicine man. I could have accepted this more readily if she hadn't been one hundred percent white.

It seemed to be a common phenomenon for whites to claim some Native American blood and to have tribal paraphernalia around their homes – tastefully (or not) integrated into the interior design of the home. If all those who boasted Indian heritage did indeed have it, there must have been some pretty fecund natives around in the last three hundred years.

This desire to have a Native connection suggests a certain spiritual disillusionment with white culture. To know that you have an Indian big toe must make you feel a bit more exotic than old droopy-drawers over the road. I know that I'd dredge the sewers for that roving cell if I knew it would enable me to imagine a strand of my ancestral line galloping across the plains having a whole load of fun.

The next day we reached Nespelem, the tiny capital of the Colville reservation. I had particularly wanted to come here because it was the place where Joseph, war chief of the Nez Perce tribe, spent his last years and where he was buried in 1904. Joseph is commonly held up to be the epitome of the noble savage – with the added prestige of being regarded as a military genius. His skills were exhibited during the fall of 1877, when he turned what was for his tribe a desperate flight and fight for survival – women, children, the old, tipis, horses and all – into a masterly rearguard action and withdrawal. His tactics are still examined *ad infinitum* at the Big Hole museum in Montana which I would later visit.

On their trans-American route-finding expedition of the early nineteenth century Lewis and Clark had been impressed by the friendly, intelligent and good-looking Nez Perce, who bred the spotted Appaloosa horse, farmed their ancestral lands in Wallowa Valley, Oregon, and hunted during the summer months in Washington, Idaho and Montana.

Up to the time of their flight the Nez Perce had lived peacefully with the whites for seventy years, and were still trying to do so with the settlers who were invading their valley in ever increasing numbers. To the everlasting shame of the government but consistent with their many callous decisions regarding the 'Indian problem', it was decided that the Nez Perce should be moved elsewhere and that whites should have access to all their lands.

Even then the tribe did not resort to war – merely asking that they be allowed to stay long enough to gather their scattered livestock before moving to their new reservation. This was refused, the outcome being that a group of young warriors were unable to control their justifiable anger and frustration. This led in turn to a skirmish and some deaths. Joseph said afterwards:

"I did not want bloodshed. I did not want my people killed. I did not want anybody killed…. I said in my heart that, rather than have war I would give up my country. I would give up my father's grave. I would

give up everything rather than have the blood of white men upon the hands of my people."

But it was too late. The tribal leaders knew that the killings would bring down on them all the wrath of the army, so they quickly gathered what they could and set out on what became their epic four month, seventeen hundred mile journey. Their aim was to reach the sanctuary of Canada, where Sioux chief Sitting Bull was already taking refuge following his defeat of Custer the previous year, and where he had founded a community of displaced Sioux.

During the course of that tragic journey the Nez Perce were hounded mercilessly by the army, the cold being so severe that horses were killed so that young children and babies could be put into the warm carcasses. The tribe was finally apprehended at Bear Paw, less than forty miles short of the Canadian border, mistakenly believing that it had outdistanced the pursuing soldiers and reached the safety of Canada.

Small though this story may be in the vast annals of an often scandalous and shameful western expansion, it is nevertheless one that pulls strongly at the heart strings with its pathos. Joseph said afterwards:

"I am tired of fighting. Our chiefs are killed... it is cold and we have no blankets. The little children are freezing to death. My people, some of them, have run away to the hills and have no blankets, no food. I want to have time to look for my children and see how many of them I can find. Maybe I shall find them among the dead. Hear me, my chiefs. I am tired; my heart is sick and sad. From where the sun now stands I will fight no more, forever."

Uniquely amongst the Indians of the West, Chief Joseph and his Nez Perce won the respect of the entire American nation at the time, unlike Sitting Bull and Crazy Horse, whose present glamorous reputations owe much to hindsight and a change of attitude. The Nez Perce were admired as much for their humanity and chivalry as for the fact that for a while (despite three quarters of them being non-combatants) they consistently outmarched, outwitted and outfought the United States army.

Of course Chief Joseph eventually made peace, unlike wicked old Geronimo who fought like a tiger almost to the end in the southern deserts of Arizona and New Mexico, still technically a prisoner of war when he died in 1909. He has therefore always remained wicked old Geronimo – leader of the murderous and sadistic Apaches.

Looking today at the faded old photographs from that era, one is struck by the contrasting auras projected by the different tribes. The Nez Perce look out with intelligent, sympathetic eyes which comprehend those human conditions and emotions which we recognise – sadness, warmth, mischievousness. They are 'of us'.

In contrast, the intense wary faces of the Apaches are alien to our air-conditioned lives; in them we see minds and bodies finely tuned to the harshness of desert living, and revealing nothing of the softness of comfortable living and easy choices. They are ancient and untamed; they speak to us of the primeval, of watchful predators, giving us a glimpse back to a wild pre-Columbian past.

But above all, the faces which stare at you from those old photographs are the faces of shell-shock victims, stunned by the tragedy and awfulness of their new alien lives, faces mourning the loss of a wild, roaming freedom and the lingering death of what must surely have been the most beautiful life lived by anyone, ever, anywhere, in the world.

In Nespelem I was told by a local woman that whites were not permitted to visit Joseph's grave as it was also the general tribal graveyard. Later I was told that his head was not in the grave but in the Smithsonian Institute, together with the skulls of other 'interesting' Native Americans.

The feeling that history is alive and vibrant in the outback of America, and that if you are silent the ghosts of the past will speak to you and may reveal themselves, is at times overwhelming. When you meet Oglala Sioux children who ask you in all seriousness (as if it happened last week) if you think they were right to wipe out Custer and the Seventh Cavalry at the Little Big Horn, then you have to do a double take on the date. When someone points out the route along which the parents of Crazy Horse took his body to be buried in an unknown grave, and shows you the site of the 1890 Christmas massacre at Wounded Knee, you realise that those days are still powerful in the minds of the tribe. The present recedes from prominence and becomes simply the time we are going through at the moment – neither more nor less relevant than the past.

It is as though you stand before a translucent veneer which almost allows you to see the secret treasures on the other side; you glimpse vague shadows and shifting forms – to anyone who can stop and listen, the deafening noise of silence can be heard.

Not only does this massive land carry its Native Indian heritage within it, it also enters the psyche of the white American people. It pervades American art, music and literature; it looms huge in good and bad westerns; road movies can't exist without it; small-town scenarios rely on it for their background atmosphere; poetry exudes it. Even when you can't see it on screen or canvas or in words on the page, you can feel its presence in the unseen and unsaid.

The following day my mood was subdued. I had had a great time at a local dance the night before and wanted to remain at Nespelem a little longer but at this stage of my journey I was still imprisoned by the need to keep to a schedule, even though I didn't know what that was, other than to get to Colorado before the snow.

Just as we were leaving the reservation, a man presented me with a feather from the protected bald eagle to protect me on my journey. I attached it to my handle bars and there it remained for the following twelve months.

Passing Davenport and the Grand Coulee Dam a new landscape approached. This was a landscape to be appreciated by the artist, not the ecologist. Devoid of trees, enormous undulating fields of rich, dark, freshly turned soil interspersed with acres of swaying and swishing yellow wheat. And yet the clean-cut lines which divided the large blocks of contrasting colours made it a land of striking beauty. The empty road meandered with the hills and an occasional tractor interrupted the emptiness, leaving a trail of dust. Overhead, the massive cloud-free sky was of the purest and most delicate blue. This, plus a golden orb and the occasional white tailings of unseen planes cutting across the heavens, brought vividly to mind the simplicity and clarity of David Hockney's shimmering sunlit paintings.

In landscapes of such silent grandeur, events and characters often assume a greater significance than they would in a more cluttered world. Maybe it was the focus of my mind on more ethereal things which transformed the ravens, standing in pairs like conscious beings, into the spiritual guides assigned to them by traditional tribal lore. Certainly in those still days it was possible to believe anything.

Such mystical sentiments are smashed as soon as the local whites are encountered. They are of tough, uncompromising pioneer stock and, since their ancestors were obviously cut from the same unyielding cloth, it is no wonder that peaceful co-existence between whites and natives proved to be impossible. Nevertheless I found their down-to-earth, no nonsense matter-of-factness both refreshing and amusing. As I sat in a café in the heart of these wheat lands, an immaculate and extremely good looking woman in her seventies greeted a neighbour:

"How y'all doing?"

"Oh, not so good. Only firing on three cylinders today."

"Well, shoot! You'd better get the fourth one operatin'!"

Stopping at a roadside coffee and cake stall down the road I found a similar attitude to life. The stallholder had buried her husband of fourteen months only the week before:

"No point sittin' around," she told me cheerfully.

Minutes later an RV, a car and a gang of Harley Davidson boys pulled in. A very thin and elderly blue-rinsed woman stepped from the RV, a middle-aged Seattle couple got out from the car, and the bike boys jumped cheerfully from their steeds. I was overwhelmed by the friendliness of this surreal combination coincidentally brought together in this lay-by. Blue-rinse reminded me of a virulently racist Afrikaner I had seen on television, until she smiled and told us about her dear late husband who, she said, had been part Indian. She was an avid reader of all things Native American.

She beamed at the bike boys. They beamed back. It was wonderful.

These Harley lads took me back to some heavy bike boys I had met on the plains of South Dakota back in 1982. As I was erecting my tent on a small-town site I was approached by six bearded and burly mountain men who were returning from a bike rally. They shyly asked if they could put their tent next to mine. I said sure but what was their problem?

"We don't have the six dollars site fee. If we camp with you maybe we won't get caught."

The camp manager was a small, frail elderly woman.

"But why don't you camp wild?"

"It's too dangerous," these giants replied, "We might get 'rolled.'"

We approached Spokane nervously, our first city since Seattle, and stopped several miles before entering its suburbs. Corey came over on his mountain bike. He told me that cities are legally obliged to permit camping in their parks and he knew a nice one where we could stay. We followed him the fourteen miles into the centre. From the high outskirts of the city it was hard to believe that the wooded valley below hid a high-rise metropolis of hundreds of thousands of inhabitants, only revealing itself as you descend.

We arrived at our peaceful city park and as the sun went down it was hard to convince ourselves that we were not taking part in some real-life Camberwick Green. Firemen would soon come and rescue a meowing kitten from a tree, and a cute little train would chug-chug round the corner. There were the usual joggers, picnickers, aerobic walkers and cyclists. Then out came the dog training class, oblivious to all but their furry companions. As the trainer barked out her orders, cheerful white-haired ladies carried chairs to a spreading cherry tree and sat in its shade to listen to the points of their club's Annual General Meeting. The sun slipped, darkness fell, friendly disbandment took place and all was tranquillity.

I drifted into contented sleep, dreaming beautiful dreams of ageing into one of those inspiring, energetic, silver-haired ladies.

At midnight loud firecrackers shattered worryingly close to my tent until the offenders ran off at my angry emergence. I slept again until woken at dawn by thunderous rain. After several minutes I became confused by its regular repetitious nature. Cautiously I peeped out. I was camped directly over an automatic grass sprinkler. Everything was soaked and I was lying in a lake.

The next day was a hard one. My unfit body was finally reacting against its demanding new routine and protesting that 'OK! Fine! But enough is enough and now it's time to go home.' The miles were long, my lassitude total. Fortunately we found a nice bike path which took us all the way from Spokane to Coeur d'Alene. As we stood there straddling a junction, uncertain which direction to take, a car pulled up, the driver checked our problem and immediately drew off with strict orders to follow the car.

And so we met Linda. Sad, 'crazy' Linda. In the three days we stayed with her we were never sure how much of her wildly erratic and eccentric behaviour was due to her natural eccentricities and how much to a neural condition. After seventeen years of marriage her husband had abandoned her. He could no longer cope with the public embarrassments caused by her behaviour and was about to take off for Saudi Arabia with their teenage daughter and his girlfriend.

In this town of pastels, sneakers and immaculate casuals, Linda walked out with her jogging trousers ripped up to her knees and with large ragged holes elsewhere. This indication of her rebellious and liberal mind was misleading however – on seeing the only punk in town, she announced:

"My god, I'd kill any daughter of mine that went 'round like that."

With her friend Melanie, we were dragged off to the lake in order to satisfy Linda's urge to jump in. Reluctantly, Melanie, Jill and I jumped into the icy water.

"Well come on then," we shouted, "you were the one who wanted to do this!"

"But – I can't swim," she whimpered and remained firmly land-bound as we shivered, soaking, back to the house. Back home she donned one red shoe and one blue shoe, pushed us into the car and headed for town: "We're going to eat!"

Armed with her cheque book, she bought us pizzas in the Pizza Hut (where she walked out with five plastic cups hidden between her thighs), ice creams in the ice cream parlour, burgers in the burger joint, and sweets and shakes in the confectionery. Only when we had a sit-down demonstration were we finally able to stem this gluttonous extravagance.

We were told that before we left we had to go over the border to Canada, we had to go white-water rafting, and we had to meet Linda's adorable daughter.

So we did go to Canada (the incredible street murals in the border town made this a well-rewarded trip) and we did go on a drunken white-water debacle. When we finally got to meet her daughter we encountered a surly, rude child who deserved to be left to her fate in Saudi. As she got into the car with her father and his girlfriend, Linda stood in front of her floor-to-ceiling windows, pulled down her knickers and mooned her large, flabby, white bottom to the outraged group.

The following day, massive rows took place on the telephone over the incident. The daughter had been humiliated and embarrassed. Linda grovelled, whined, apologised. With tears in her eyes she passionately declared her love for her child and begged forgiveness. Suddenly, her face brightened, her eyes twinkled and all vestige of remorse vanished.

"Yes… but… what did they *say* when I mooned them?" she asked. And with that she doubled up in an uncontrollable fit of giggles.

BIG HOLE BATTLES

The road became smaller and quieter as we progressed southward following the valley of the Bitterroot Mountain Range which lay to our right. Whilst lacking the grandeur of peaks and great mountain vistas, it encompassed such a variety of miniscapes that it was endlessly interesting and comforting.

This was also Chief Joseph territory. The Nez Perce had hunted here in the summer months and had passed this way in their flight to Canada. Lewis and Clark had also passed this way crossing the Lolo Pass with great difficulty in their search for a cross-country route to the west.

Thomas Keneally writes that it is dangerous to think of an old country as new – the New World is only so from a white perspective. Many would justify the displacement of native societies by white invaders as part of a continuing process – arguing that they were only doing what American Indians had themselves been doing for hundreds of years beforehand. One result of the belief of America's newness is a need to create history – white history. Pre-1492 is not white, therefore it is often not recognised as history. Only with the first symbolic step of Columbus's buckled shoe upon its shores, was America born. For the American north-west, history started much later with Lewis and Clark.

An indication of this need to emphasise their own history is the plethora of historical markers which are scattered over the landscape like confetti: 'Lewis and Clark stopped for lunch two miles down the road.' 'Clark pulled a hang-nail on this mountain.' Well, okay, I'm exaggerating, but not by much.

I wish I could have been a member of their incredible expedition in 1804/5 as they struggled to find a way to the Pacific coast. Seeing landscapes and tribes unpolluted by white intrusions; coping with forests swarming with grizzlies and choked with undergrowth; sweeping down rivers; battling under, over and through mountains.

Even tamed, the Bitterroot Valley is still exquisite. Grasslands, meadows, wetlands, ponds, creeks and forests mingle in irresistible lushness. Buzzards and golden eagles soared and the vivid little bluebirds made their first appearance. They would accompany me most of the way to Mexico. Wherever there were roadside fences they hopped and fluttered ahead of me, the electric blue of their plumage flashing in the sunlight. My winged companions were always a constant delight and their dynamic company never allowed loneliness to invade.

This was horse country. Horses were everywhere – strong, short-legged and deep-girthed quarter horses. Weekend rodeos are still popular events and great fun; the loose skills of single-handed American riding contrasting sharply with the stiff back formality of the English rider. Weekend cowboys or not, the competitors rode as one their mounts, wheeling and skidding as their horses responded to the lighter touch.

The second treat of the day was coming across the most fantastic roadside stall. Combined with the familiar bric-a-brac were the added excitements of saddles, bridles and a myriad of unidentifiable leather goods which I longed to possess. And there were knives: penknives, flick knives, Bowie knives, survival knives, skinning, gutting and splicing knives. And guns of course! I have wanted a rifle since I was a teenager, and in Montana I wanted not a rifle but one of those handsome weapons of the Old West; one that my hand fitted snugly around as it slotted smoothly into its leather holster.

Whilst I disagree with the rights of all citizens to carry arms and with the arguments against control, I fully understand the resistance to disarmament. Those that say they need guns to protect themselves and their families are deluding themselves; they are merely trying to present a logic – where there is no logic – which is acceptable to modern society. But it is not a matter of logic. In reality the white history of America *is* the gun, and Americans are joined with their weapons at the heart, not at the head. They love their guns!

At the start of the hunting season not only do the urban cowboys prove their manhood when they make their ritual annual trip to the hills with their pickup, their six-pack and their rifle, but they also make the backward psychological link to their ancestors who fought and struggled to maintain a stake in the land.

Legally, of course, you have to be resident in a state for six months to qualify for ownership of a gun, but there would be no problems buying one at a roadside stall. I asked the stallholder what he would recommend for me.

"Lady, ya travlin' alone so ya gotta havva gun that's gonna kill first go. If a guy comes into ya tent in the night a pistol ain't gonna be no good 'cos ya cain't be sure of a good hit. Ya gotta git that fella first shot, else he's gonna blow y'all away. Now, with a sawn-off shotgun y'ain't gonna miss; it don't matter where ya point the goddam thing that guy's gonna be fish-food a mile around – and ya ain't gonna have *no* more trouble lady."

Wow!!!

As I turned I came face-to-face with a real-life nineteenth-century mountain man – long white beard to his waist, black cowboy hat pulled low down over his eyes, braces holding up ragged baggy pants, dirty bandanna around his neck; on his leg was a large knife. It was good to know there was another Montana, an old Montana, away from the highway and the RV's.

The starry skies of Montana are infinite. They carry you into other worlds. This night the vast unfathomable reaches of the solar system were revealed to me.

In my youth, when light and air pollution was less, I remember we used to get excited over those clear nights when the Milky Way stretched across the sky like a sparkling tiara. Now tragically it is no more. But just as the memory of bluebell woods, cowslip glades and buttercup meadows fade from the mind, so too have we become accustomed to the loss of our stars; so much so that we hardly even bother to raise our heads any more. Our heritage slips easily away and with little fight, even from those of us who profess to care.

In Montana the skies are full of a thousand Milky Ways – skies which draw you deeper and deeper into their infinite depths and which fill the head and heart with long forgotten memories.

That night we camped in a beautiful meadow; the mountains silhouetted behind. I lay outside and watched the sky and allowed myself to be entertained. I thought of the obsession of the compulsive traveller to glimpse such moments as these; to gain a peek into another older world – desperately seeking a brief time in one of the dusty niches where the inevitable onward progression towards universal uniformity can be delayed for a few precious minutes. The obsession to discover places where the hand of man has touched only gently or not at all.

The road moved southward; traffic lessened. As the road narrowed I thought of the thousands of years during which the Indians had meandered through this lush wilderness, camping in the meadows, bathing in the creeks, just as I was doing. Camping one night on a small National Forest campsite towards the narrow valley head near Sula, I took a walk up the craggy, wooded hill nearby. Even on that small climb I could begin to appreciate the difficulties of Lewis and Clark; it was hard work. By the campsite a historical marker announced that they had camped two miles downstream, *"…where Indians had camped two days previously."*

It was time for a detour to the Big Hole battlefield. This was the site of a dawn attack on the retreating Nez Perce by a large detachment of the Seventh Infantry commanded by Colonel Gibbon. The date was August 9th 1877. As the road was temporarily closed to cyclists we had to take the steep, switchback gravel trail up and over Gibbon's Pass. With lots of swearing I reached the top of the pass where the willow scrub and short grass bordering a shallow stream made an idyllic camping place. Animal tracks crossed the area and a sign announced that this was the very route taken by Joseph and his people. Jill was too nervous to camp in the isolated spot and so headed to a National Forest site twelve miles away. I lit a fire, visualised Joseph's ghostly tribe passing quietly by, and had an undisturbed night.

The track to rejoin the road passed through wild expanses of marshland and bog, glorious swaying grasslands bordered by forest, and huge meadows of magnificent purple flowers. All that was needed was a herd of bison to complete the scene of Eden.

The rolling mosaic of grass, scrub and forested slopes continued to the site of the battlefield. This arrangement of ecological zones creates such an attractive landscape that it remains ever pleasing to the eye, satisfying some basic need for particular combinations of colours, shapes, textures.

Americans do nothing by halves, and historical signs are backed up by thousands of excellent museums and tourist information centres which are found at sites of geological and historical interest. But the Big Hole battlefield museum left me feeling uneasy. I tried to examine the cause of my unease. To begin with, where were the Indian employees? The whole show was run by several staid elderly military men, and in my cycling paraphernalia and jingling attachments, I was drawing disapproving looks. I suspect that if the star of their show – Chief Joseph – had turned up, he would surely have been evicted as a filthy vagrant.

I also found it obscene that the Big Hole 'battle' was presented as a fair fight entered into voluntarily by two sides who were equal in all respects – warriors fighting warriors. In reality this was a desperate but determined group of men, women, children, babies and the old, forced by white greed and racism to flee for their lives; forced by the government policy of systematic removal and murder of a people who had persistently expressed their peaceful intentions and unwillingness to fight.

Afterwards, the soldiers would go home to families and villages. They would not see their culture and way of life smashed; they would not be sent into exile to a foreign land; they would not have to pick the bloody bodies of their children out of the mud. This was a dawn attack on a sleeping village. Eighty-nine bodies were counted at the site, the majority women and children, with others dying later. Colonel Gibbon wrote:

"Few of us will soon forget the wail of mingled grief, rage and horror which came from the camp… when the Indians returned to it and recognised their slaughtered warriors, women and children."

And yet in the end this was, for what it was worth, an Indian success, from which they yet again reorganised and escaped – until the next attack.

The murder of women and children is ignored at the museum. Exhibitions, talks and videos show it only as an exciting war drama. The video I watched finished with the final insult to the Nez Perce by stating that it was not until 1885 that Joseph and his people were allowed to return to their homeland. In fact the tribe was divided and none were ever allowed to return to their Wallowa Valley, even though Joseph fought for this until his death.

Edward Abbey, the guru of wilderness enthusiasts, says that we cannot imagine the awfulness of disinheritance until we have seen it. This I believe absolutely! We can never begin to feel the almost unbearable alienation of soul, the incalculable loss of spirit and the crushing despair when the Indians were dragged screaming from their ancestral lands!

Down the hill below the centre a group of *tipi* frames had been erected by the river where the Nez Perce camped that fateful night. It was a perfect spot with good grazing for the horses, timber for *tipi* poles and firewood, water for cooking, washing, fishing and game for hunting. I tried to visualise it buzzing with noise and activity as, relaxed in the belief that the soldiers were far behind, the camp prepared for a peaceful evening. Children shouting and racing, women raising the *tipis* and preparing the meals, horses whinnying, dogs barking.

I walked in the shallow river where the horses had drunk after their long trek. In the clear shallows, mica caught the sun and glinted like silver. Before dawn a woman was seen collecting water, hesitating at a sound from the hill opposite before dismissing it as unimportant.

Within the *tipi* village I felt little. There were no ghosts lingering here. The twentieth century had eradicated them all. On re-entering the centre, the ranger was giving a talk to a small audience of men in camouflage fatigues. The talk was on the role of the howitzer in the Big Hole 'battle' and its capabilities. Time to leave!

We cycled the eleven miles to the little town of Wisdom. One hundred and fifty contented souls, ('we all just love it here!') two bars, an art and craft gallery, a garage and a store for everything else. After downing a couple of beers, we retreated to the American legion ground to pitch our tents on the edge of the village. This was just an ordinary football pitch and Wisdom was nothing to write home about, yet I was mesmerised – by the sunset, by feelings of contentment, elation, and whatever else carried to me on the cooling breeze. I still think of that evening as a very special one in my life, when everything felt exactly *right*. The sun sank in a burning glory of gold, amber and orange. The stars came out!

Next day my peace of mind was shattered as I crashed, bashed and rattled my way down thirty miles of gravel track to rejoin the road at Gibbonsville. All started well with surreal scenes of abandoned ancient Chevys and derelict barns, the trail crossed the state border into the Salmon National Forest of Idaho. I stopped and washed at a wayside stream and felt clean and fresh. Shortly after, I came across evidence that the lowest IQ in Montana had been at work here: some bright spark had installed a cattle grid the wrong way round. I winced as my wheel slipped between the grid and the derailleur crashed onto the metal.

As I came round the next corner I came face to face with a huge Charolais bull which stood square in my path protecting his small harem. Slowly I withdrew into the trees and the anxious bull slowly led his women away. Further down the track I discovered that I had left my highly prized binoculars behind in the trees. As the thought of struggling back along the rough track for miles was unbearable, I sacrificed them to the Charolais spirits and continued grumpy and bad-tempered as my bones, bike and brains rattled down to Gibbonsville. I had stopped having good thoughts about anything except the bliss of stopping. Eventually I met up with Jill and found that she had got us into a proper campsite complete with bar and café. After a couple of beers my humour gradually restored itself.

I was slowly learning that it was no good moaning about mistakes brought about by my own carelessness and lack of concentration. I must take responsibility for my actions and be more diligent; this would be especially important when I was travelling alone and negligence could have dangerous consequences. The secret was always to keep things in the same place, never vary it, and always to put things away when they have been used, so that anything missing would be immediately noticed. Being methodical was vital. My mistake had been to put the binoculars down on my handlebar bag, from where they slipped to the ground while I was watching the bull, instead of wrapping them around my hand grip where they normally lived.

At North Fork we joined the main Salmon River, and the cosiness of the Bitterroot gradually gave way to a bleaker, more dramatic scenery. Velvety, pleated brown slopes swept majestically down to riverside cottonwoods, broken intermittently by towering faces of pink and buff rock. I rested by the river, feeling the sun singeing my skin, and wanting to savour this untamed place a little longer.

Crossing the 45th parallel halfway between the Equator and the North Pole, Jill celebrated by taking a pee by the signpost; nearby was our first porcupine experience – a fresh road kill.

Dead roadside animals were to be a significant feature of my journey. Every day the stink of deer, antelope, elk, coyotes and dogs would greet my nostrils as they lay by the road in varying states of decay. I had read that two hundred black bears are killed monthly in Pennsylvania alone, and hundreds of thousands of deer and antelope die each year in this sad carnage.

The American west is also littered with evidence of another kind of death. The sight of old log cabins from a former era collapsing slowly and romantically into the ground complemented the barrenness of the Salmon River Valley superbly.

As I wandered through the rooms of these derelict cabins, I had to acknowledge that although the Indians had been forced to accept the end of a beautiful era, these pioneers had also had a tough time in their struggle to escape poverty and persecution. The small, dark, tomb-like rooms and the earth floors conjured up a vivid image of the grimness which must have encompassed their lives in this bleak land, so bitter in the depths of winter and so unresponding in the fruit of summer.

CRATERS OF THE MOON

Travelling through the harsh Salmon River landscape on September 2nd 1805, Clark wrote with his idiosyncratic spelling:

"... proceeded on through thickets in which we were obliged to cut a road, Over rockey hill Sides where our horses were in perpetual danger of Slipping to their certain destruction and up and Down Steep hills, where Several horses fell, Some turned over, and others Sliped down Steep hill Sides, one horse Crippeled and two gave out, with the greatest dificullty risque etc we made five miles and Encamped."

In a two year journey such entries were significant. If God was in a sullen mood when he made the sun-scorched mountains of eastern California, then he must have been in a rage when he made the hills of the Salmon River, where the long stretches of steep, barren, unstable slopes are simply tipped willy-nilly around the place. It felt like a landscape from the beginning of time, an oppressive wilderness alien to life. Nature had looked at the piles of brown and grey debris and shunned them. No gentle, green mantle softened their starkness – the passage of time had gone unnoticed.

The wind screamed through the narrow river gorges, forcing me to walking speed. I found a gentler spot where yellowing cottonwoods sheltered the river, and drifted to sleep to the sound of hundreds of geese honking their way southwards through the dusk. The exciting gut-wrenching yelps, howls, yips and yaps of coyotes rang across the hills. Everything was as it had been for hundreds of years.

The village of Challis snuggled beneath the brooding rocky nodules of this primeval landscape. It was a pleasant oasis, providing pancakes and cinnamon buns to sustain us for the rough, wet and windy ride to Clayton. In my ignorance I had imagined the Salmon

River Mountains to be sparse in wildlife, but in the cosy café of Clayton I met my first real-life hunters and learnt otherwise.

Being by nature and culture averse to the idea of killing for fun, I was predisposed to find in hunters the most unpleasant of characteristics. But these guys were not run-of-the-mill; they did not pick their prey with a telescopic lens at five hundred yards. They were the elite of the hunting elite – hunters by bow and arrow in the Indian way. In order to have a chance of catching their prey they had to be skilled enough to get within thirty yards of it.

They bought us a beer and explained the skills required for their sport. To give them a chance of success, their hunting season commences one month before the guns are allowed in. Never, they told us, did they leave an animal injured, unlike many of the urban cowboys who swarm the countryside in the hunting season, paying $450 for the privilege of killing a single bull elk. They said that the likelihood of me cycling to Mexico without a puncture was greater than them actually bagging one.

My anti-hunter bias was somewhat mollified by meeting these civilised and, dare I say it, sensitive men. I hoped they were representative of the hunting lobby generally. In any case, can we judge the American hunter by the same criteria as his English counterpart? In this country the progression from hunting for food to hunting for sport has been imperceptible and, by tradition, it has always been a man's right to carry arms.

The end of the day saw us entering a kinder domain. It also saw the start of frosty mornings and frozen water bottles. Since leaving the forests of Washington we had mostly been blessed with perfect weather – blue cloudless skies and star-filled nights – but now the season was drawing in.

In Sunbeam I encountered my first hot springs. The continuing geological activity of the Rocky Mountains means that the American West is scattered with the miraculous phenomena of clean water flowing from hillsides at temperatures too hot to put your hand in. America provided its early inhabitants not only with the necessities of life, but also the luxuries. As the streams enter the river at Sunbeam, a variety of pools have been formed and you can select one with your own temperature preference, the multitudes of heat-adapted fish dashing round picking delicacies from your body.

Given Jill's apprehension of the potential dangers abounding in this 'dark continent', I watched amazed as she emerged naked from one of the roadside pools, put on her short, bottom-revealing T-shirt, washed her clothes, then climbed bare-bottomed up to her bike. Standing by the road she started leisurely to hang her washing on her bike. I was flabbergasted. I think that passing motorists must still be regaling open-mouthed friends with the tale of the bare-bottomed cyclist.

Being a child who used to hide my toes because I thought they were odd, I realise that my exhibitionist tendencies are somewhat inhibited. Not for me the jolly, unabandoned romp in the school changing-room showers – it was a quick five-second dash. So I know I should have said: 'Oh what fun' and frolicked alongside Jill, bare bum wobbling in the wind; I knew that I should stay cool about other peoples' behaviour. But I couldn't. Instead I bristled crossly and just hid down the bank until, thankfully, the bum was finally covered.

A few miles on I turned a bend and suddenly the magnificent, jagged, snow-covered peaks of the Sawtooth Mountains soared up before me. The beauty of using road maps, instead of geographical maps, is that you never know what is round the next bend – everything is white and flat. You are never prepared for mountains, even though 'Horrendously Steep Mountain Range' may be printed in six-inch letters across the map. But in America, hills are called mountains, and mountains hills, so that doesn't mean a lot. So when you travel in the assumption that the earth is still flat, the sudden emergence of ten thousand feet summits is like a miracle:

'Blimey. Where the heck did *they* come from?'

As the months passed, I learnt to lose some of my dread of mountains, and actually came to prefer them to a day of hills. You know where you are with a mountain. Firstly, you psych yourself up. Then, you trudge slowly up one side, see the picture of the little lorry with its tail in the air, and sail gloriously down the other side. And, because mountains are usually several miles long, they give you the chance to get into a steady rhythm and to pace yourself. Hills do not do this; they can grind on and on forever. Up and down they go; up and down, up and down; slowly wearing away your reserves of energy. 'Make your mind up,' I would cry, 'What's the sense in going down, if you only have to go up again?' But that was on a bad day, and on the whole American hills were pretty well-behaved.

In the Sawtooth village of Lower Stanley I continued my week of 'firsts' and met my first gold and silver miner. He was that priceless American character, the eccentric. Jed was a rejecter (and a reject?) of what can easily become the suffocating conformism of American society. He spoke with restrained venom of the plastic people 'down the road'. 'Down-the-road' was the tourist ski-haven of Sun Valley, and the many enthusiastic recommendations we had been given about this place were the sole reason I'd chosen this route. Linda had told us back in Coeur D'Alene:

"When you get to Sun Valley, you won't want to leave."

Jed was not impressed. Probably in his late forties but badly worn, this Vietnam veteran was the archetypal dropout, sporting shaggy beard, scrawny frame and a faded leathery face. His mountain-man image was complemented by his habit of regularly slipping from his normal voice into a deep, rolling, gravelly growl. It was great! He survived (barely) by working a single-pump garage three days a week and working his silver mine the rest of the time.

"Winters reach minus 60°F round here," he told us, "so then I head for Arizona and pan for gold; nobody knows my place. Last year I got three ounces, and one day I'm gonna to hit the big one."

Jed showed me that a livelihood (albeit precarious) can still be made from the land and the rocks, but characters like him must concentrate on the practical issue of survival rather than on the head trips which are often the privilege of the British New Ager.

By now Jill was not enjoying the ride; she was homesick and needed a constant hearth and more social contact. She didn't like wild camping and the daily move was aggravating her need to resolve matters which she had left unresolved back in England; her holiday had run its course. We decided to part at a convenient place so she could spend her remaining time with friends in San Francisco. We identified a place on the map called Sage as our separation point from which Jill could cycle directly down to Salt Lake City and take a bus to the coast; but equally, we selected it because we liked the name and imagined it could be another Wisdom.

Sun Valley was a huge disappointment. After all the hype I was expecting big things, and to be fair it may have been more striking covered with snow. It was pretty enough I suppose, but any attraction it may have had was deflated by the gaggles of giggling girls, posturing boys and unfriendly shop assistants. The hills were simply the playground of the rich, the famous and the groupies. Definitely not my kind of place.

My only aim was to get out as quickly as possible, so we headed out to Bellevue where we discovered Rita's Thrift Shop which was all the more refreshing due to its contrast to nearby sophistications. In a country where a brave punk spawns outrage, and where materialism and modernity are gods, the tracking down of the stubborn eccentric is a very special prize. Thus, the Ritas of the world (resplendent in bright pink jeans, cowboy hat sitting on grey hair) are to be admired for their individual philosophies which lead them to create such idiosyncrasies as Rita's Thrift Shop.

When I first visited America I reasoned that as we spoke the same language, and because we have a history in common, we would be on a similar mental wavelength. I was wrong. In much of the country there is little similarity in the thinking patterns between us – America has a very different mentality and attitude to life than the British and I was frequently thrown off balance when I realised how contrasting were our thoughts and ideas.

But America is designed to confuse, and the visitor quickly learns that it is a land of contrasts and contradictions, and as soon as you expect one thing, the opposite will happen. One day I would be amazed at the crushing rudeness of someone, and the next some kind, lovely person would open their home to me.

With memories of our night in Spokane still fresh, we avoided the temptations of the town park and headed riverside – Jill to the roadside campsite and me to struggle through the woods to find a perfect shingle beach beside a clear flowing river – my favourite camping place. The opposite shore was a tangled cottonwood and willow wilderness, backed by the darkening silhouette of the Sawtooth foothills.

Noticing the flood level of the river, and the large amount of material caught high in the branches during previous floods, I hoped that the first drops of rain, which fell whilst I erected my tent, would also be the last. Although I understood the basic dynamics of flash floods, I was totally ignorant of the physical factors involved: how much rain has to fall, for how long, at what distance and on what type of rock and soil, for it to become a flash flood.

Of course the only rule to follow in the face of such unknowns is not to camp in washes or any place which shows evidence of previous flooding. These also happen to be places which are frequently the most convenient and often the prettiest. But common sense should also prevail and if it hasn't rained for a month and the sky is clear, then go for it. If it rains hard over the nearby mountains in the night then you may be in for a sleepless night for, just as ignorance can be bliss, it can also make you imagine dangers where none exist.

Until now, my aim of cycling to Central America had invariably been greeted by expressions of horror. *Bandidos* would rape me, the Mafia would murder me, guerrillas would execute me, robbers would rob me, and finally, if none of these got their hands on me, the homicidal drivers would surely flatten me. People who had been there would say: 'Yes, but we wouldn't go alone.' Those who had been alone would say: 'Yes, but I wouldn't cycle.' Those who had cycled said: 'Yes, but I would not go if I was a single woman.' Cyclists who had cycled in America said they would not cycle in Mexico, whilst those who had cycled in Mexico said they would not cycle in Guatemala. And so it went on.

Then Jill struggled through the woods to bring me the heartening news that the campsite owner's friend spends eight problem-free months in Mexico every year; he loves the country and the people. Oh, thank you for positive and informed people. I slept to the sound of water rippling over stones.

By the time we left the wind had risen, black clouds were speeding across the sky, and thunder and lightning threatened to engulf us in a watery deluge. We headed for the last house for miles and begged shelter in the barn. There we met Laurie – not looking a day over twenty-six but with a brood of six delightful children between the ages of one and twelve giggling around her.

I was still waiting to meet the infamous precocious American 'gimme, gimme' child which makes us so proud of our own less sophisticated offspring, but with Laurie's brood I was once again pleasantly disappointed. Her children had learnt to walk the tightrope to which we aspire for our own children. Like Shaun, a sensitive, intelligent boy I had spent several hours with on the Colville Reservation (who had showed me the ways of ants and beetles), they had developed an articulate but modest confidence, whilst still hanging onto a childlike honesty and innocence and an ability to take pleasure in simple things. Their young maturity enabled them to talk to adults as comfortably as with their own peers and they had none of the stuttering, lowered-eye shyness so often exhibited by English children when addressed by, or having to converse with, adults. You really could have an intelligent conversation with eight-year-old Robbie or eleven-year-old Shaun.

Laurie's husband, Spencer, had about one thousand acres of mostly poor hill land. He was also the state president of his church. After marriage Laurie had left her hometown of Seattle to live in this desperately lonely spot. I asked how she liked living out here.

"I was so lonely when I first came out here. The isolation was terrible and I spent the first two years crying. It wasn't until I had the children that I gradually got to know people, through school and that, and now I love it and wouldn't want to live anywhere else."

To pay for their children to go to college, Laurie and Spencer bought and sold two or three calves each year. Later they wanted to work overseas as missionaries. I thought of all the tragedies that could have been avoided if all missionaries had practised their form of gentle and tolerant Christianity.

It was with great difficulty that I finally erected my tent. I was besieged by hordes of adorable barefoot toddlers and tail-less cats and kittens, none of whom could quite believe this new opportunity for fun and harassment which had suddenly entered their lives. The evening fun involved chasing the calves around their meadow. Afterwards they licked our fingers while little Robbie told us of his love of the countryside, and how he enjoyed going to the hills alone and pretending to be an Indian. With his junior gun he exhibited his shooting skills and explained his dilemma:

"I like to go hunting with my granddad, but I don't like seeing dead things." He went on, "My father is a good hunter because he doesn't like to leave things hurt, so he always tries to kill them with the first shot. He hates seeing things suffer."

At breakfast I was too embarrassed to confess my atheism and knelt meekly around the table with the family as Spencer asked God to protect and guide us on our journey.

That day he protected me across the wide flat valley of the Craters of the Moon in a violent lightning storm. The well named Craters are a vast barren area of jumbled, tumbled piles of shattered volcanic basalt, ash and clinkers deposited as recently as two thousand years ago and which gave the pioneers of 1864 a tough time as their wagons were smashed to pieces crossing them.

For the first time in my life I was afraid of a thunderstorm. The rain slashed down and the lightning crashed to earth immediately above me as I pedalled frantically, a solitary figure on the straight, never-ending road of this huge valley. I was the only moving thing and the highest point in this treeless terrain. Over and over I repeated my monotonous mantra:

"You will not get me, you will not get me!"

My mantra worked, or Spencer's prayers, and it was with monumental relief that I passed safely beneath the storm and arrived cold and sodden into the town of Arco (the first town in America to get electricity). With nowhere to camp and feeling in need of the small comfort of a lawn and the warmth and dryness of a local pub, I knocked on the door of a motel and begged for a space on the lawn for a couple of dollars. I was greeted by a tight-lipped and tightly-permed elderly harridan – sour-faced and stern. She scowled disapprovingly at my bedraggled figure, slowly running her gaze from head to foot, and foot to head. Suddenly her face erupted into a bright smile.

"You can camp for free," she said.

I grovelled my thanks. Then Jill arrived; shivering, soaked, purple with cold and miserable. This was enough to melt even *my* heart. The gentle harridan looked at her silently, then walked over to a motel room and opened it for us.

"You can have this!"

"But we can't pay for it," we said.

"There's no charge," she answered.

She went on to tell us happily about the day last year when dozens of Harley Davidson boys had descended on her.

"They were such nice boys," she told us. "I let them camp on the grass and they were no trouble at all. I really enjoyed having them around. It was real fun." Such kindly souls lurk beneath the most unlikely skins. Murderers live in blue-eyed boys and angels lie behind warped faces.

Well, we salivated over the cooker and luxuriated in front of the TV; we crooned as we turned the taps on and nearly burst with ecstasy in the shower. The only blot on the evening was that we shared the room with millions of tiny black flies which crawled over the sofa, galloped up and down the walls and did the Grand National across the floor. (The next morning revealed a world outside absolutely swarming and heaving with these tiny insects – the grass, the flowers, the paths, the roads – all moved as if alive.)

Of course, there was only one thing to do when having the rare luxury of a key to a room – find the pub. So we did. I have vague memories of being bought, and downing, lots of vodka, and having a long inane conversation with a man about cows whilst in and out drifted the drifting women and men of this small town. Small town American bars are often such soulless places and very unlike the more social British bars where you go for a drink, meet your pals, take your family, and have a meal, a chat and a laugh. Small-town bars really did seem to harbour sad, lonely people trying to prop up sad, lonely lives.

At 6.00am I was throwing my guts up in the bathroom and dying. I continued to die until two o'clock when I finally managed to crawl weakly onto my bike.

"Let's go."

Atomic City is probably one of the weirdest places in the USA. It was Jill's need for security that led us off the road to it. As usual I wanted to stay out of town, so it was with a grumpy face that I followed. I was glad that I did. In this surreal dead-end, one-horse town of empty trailers and boarded-up bungalows we camped on the village green. The only signs of life were in the bar-cum-store across the road (also called Atomic City) which was run by an assortment of more elderly sour-faced spinsters – it must be the long, lonely days which produce such bitter expressions. Our experience of the previous day had taught us not to be deterred by exteriors, and sure enough the soft underparts were soon exposed. I was asked:

"Aren't you afraid cycling alone and camping?" (Two women together are classed as being alone, two men together are not.)

I looked at the headline spattered across the local newspaper in front of us:

LOCAL COUPLE MURDERED IN THEIR OWN BED

"Well!" I answered, "If this is what happens when you stay at home around here I reckon we stand a better chance on the road."

We spent the evening watching the horses galloping around in the field behind us and musing on how great this place would be for an episode of the Avengers – a half-empty town with the surreal name of Atomic City, controlled by elderly spinsters, set in a sagebrush desert by the lava beds, humming to the sound of rattle-snakes, sinister nuclear plant silhouetted ominously on the horizon.

I lost Jill in Fort Hall Indian Reservation (home to the Bannock and Shoshone tribes) so decided to head onto the next town. Suddenly, after two miles, eight vicious dogs shot after me from the garden of a nearby mobile home, splitting into two and attacking me on both sides whilst their owner sat in her garden and watched. I had brought a horsewhip with me against such confrontations but it was too short. Like Indiana Jones, I careered down the road, frantically trying to outride them as they snapped at my heels. I swished my whip from side to side, kicking out with both feet until finally I outrode them.

I stopped further along, shaking with anger and shock and vowing to find a better replacement for my whip – one which could smash a killer dog's brains out if need be.

While I was dicing with death, Jill had found us a good camping place in the garden of Mary, a reservation schoolteacher, and her husband, Dave. Dave was a Bannock, and his forbears had shared Fort Hall with the Shoshones since the 1860s. Fort Hall was the main centre for the spread of the Ghost Dance movement, born of despair as native people saw their lives and cultures destroyed. A Piaute Indian called Wovoka visited different tribes telling of a vision he'd had which said that if enough Indians did the Ghost Dance then white people would all vanish from the earth, dead Indians and buffalo would be resurrected, and all would be as it had ever been.

The Ghost Dance philosophy was not a violent one, but its sentiments were clearly threatening to white Americans. As the movement spread the whites panicked and over-reacted wildly, believing there was going to be an uprising. The culmination was the dreadful massacre on Christmas Day 1890 when hundreds of surrendered Sioux were slaughtered in the snow by Hotchkiss machine guns at Wounded Knee, on the Pine Ridge Reservation of South Dakota.

So the Ghost Dance died as an unfulfilled dream, the buffalo still in the earth with the ancestors. And Big Foot achieved immortality as the Oglala Sioux photographed twisted and frozen in death on those treeless white plains.

It was hard to find a track through Dave and Mary's house. Where there was a space it was filled. After climbing through and stepping over mountains of papers, books, clothes, food, rubbish and dogs, I made a nest in the middle and listened open-mouthed as Mary told me true horror stories such as 'How to dress in America if you wish to be regarded as a human being.'

'Thou shalt not wear tracksuit tops/bottoms.'
'Thou shalt not mix winter whites and summer whites.' (....Sorry?)
'Thou shalt not mix blue and green.'
'Thou shalt not adopt any individual style of dress.'

I was dumbstruck: "And what happens if you break the codes?"

"Everyone will look down on you. You will be thought of as a very low class person."

"But it can't be like that on the reservation. Aren't the Indian people more relaxed about such things?"

"No *way*! They're no different to white Americans in this matter."

Maybe it was the same in England and I just didn't know about it; after all it was not until middle-age that I realised that the smooth legs of women were not due to genetic chance but were achieved by daily shaving! How did I not know this? (Allegedly in Australia it is far worse. An Australian girl told me that if you go onto the beaches unshaven you are likely to have men shout 'Neanderthal woman' after you. Her own brother-in-law had rebuked her one day for not having shaved her legs.)

We had a lovely barbecue of steelhead trout caught by Mary's quiet husband. He talked about Indian fishing rights on the reservation. Being, I assumed, closer to nature than most, I asked him what the red-tailed hawks which I had seen in the area were called. He tried 'rook', then 'crow' and finally admitted to ignorance. Later I found out, surprise, surprise, they were red-tailed hawks – serves me right for making assumptions. Mind you, red-tailed hawk *was* an easy one.

And so, the last night with Jill. Until now the journey had not presented a challenge other than the physical one, and problems had been shared. I had become accustomed to the cosy ritual of our roadside cafe stops and had not had the chance to cope with loneliness or daily difficulties alone. For the next eleven months I would be talking to myself.

The biggest change though, would be the switch in emphasis from people and places to the land. Although we had mostly camped wild, frequently our daily journeys had taken us from village to village. This was not the emphasis I wanted. I wanted my days to start and end *between* villages! My resting-place at the end of the day would not be a village park or an official campsite, however small and wild – it would be a secret, off-the-road nook, where the moon and stars and the animals that roamed nearby would be my sleeping companions. I looked forward to it with anticipation and excitement.

SHOOTING STARS

So Jill and I parted. I felt nervous at our separation, but I also felt elated and relieved. Now the ride was truly my own; I could follow my own inclinations, impulses and desires. I knew my days would be lonelier but I relished the thought of the silent days to come.

That day the omens were good. As I rested by a lake under glowering skies, I watched hypnotised as a pair of white pelicans floated soundlessly down to the still water. With such quiet, patient grace they gently soared back and forth in perfect harmony. Slowly, slowly they descended – like white feathers on a windless day. And as if this were not perfection enough, their ghostly descent was accompanied by Neil Diamond singing "Love on the Rocks".

These were extraordinary moments, still as clear as the day they happened – memories to be held forever, existing in their own right irrespective of my creation of them. I became aware of another dimension which we rarely glimpse but which exists before, behind and within the world we see and know.

I remembered listening to an American anthropologist on TV once. He talked of humankind's search for happiness through religion, and the impossibility of 'taking on' the religion of another culture. The happiness which all people seek in their life, he said, is in truth a simple thing, simple but elusive. It could only be found by experiencing the reality of the moment, a reality such as I had known watching the pelicans descend, when I had been aware of my place in the world. All animals live in their moment, and it is our consciousness of time which also condemns us to discontent, our compulsion to dwell in the past and visualise the future.

And this is the magic of America! This was why I had been so easily seduced. Because America is not mean; it offers its secrets so generously and readily that little effort is needed to find them, and if we are receptive, to experience the joy they can give as we enter into America's heart; into its power and fragility.

Yet such glories also bring with them an overwhelming nostalgia for what we have lost in our separation from our primeval past. We feel disgust at ourselves as a species for having soiled our own nest; we become homesick for the earth's prior unsullied state. Our contemplation of the infinity of time also confronts us with the painful reality of how very finite we ourselves are.

On the 24th September I left Idaho, passed into Utah and entered the southwest corner of Wyoming. A brisk tail wind carried me swiftly through the peaceful towns of Georgetown, Bennington, Paris and St. Charles to Bear Lake, quiet Mormon settlements of old values, slow days and a pleasant, slightly worn veneer. Historic signs point out that the early Mormons settled here in the belief that they had reached their chosen state of Utah – only later did they discover their mileage shortfall, but I guess they'd had enough of the Mormon trail by then. After descending from the blaring, harsh desolation of the Wyoming sagebrush into the sudden green and blue shelter of Bear Lake Valley I can well believe that they fell on their knees to God, believing they had reached the Promised Land.

And they made a good decision. The valley is an oasis of charm and comfort, especially compared to the searing deserts of Utah, where those who got their navigation right ended up. I am sure Bear Lake residents are grateful for the lack of diligence of their ancestors.

As the autumn sun settled behind the low hills of my canyon campsite, the foliage burned in shades of orange, red, yellow and gold. Every evening I thought I had found the perfect place to end my day and every evening I found perfection again.

I cycled leisurely alongside the azure blue of Bear Lake, which straddles the borders of Idaho and Utah, and at its end I entered a steep narrow gorge up which the wind howled so powerfully that I barely needed to pedal. As I left its confines I was confronted by a vast expanse of open space and huge heavens; the geographical transformation was scarcely credible. It is good to leave areas of such desolation but it is even better to come back to them again. The green cosiness of Bear Lake valley may have been lovely, but it is the desert which makes the guts lurch and which gives a sense of liberation and freedom.

My diary shows a happy day's ending:

"It's wonderful here. The sun has gone. Long horizon flaming orange over the hills behind, massive silver moon rises over hills in front. Cloudless sky."

My late morning starts and early finishes were keeping my mileage low, but once on the road I felt I could cycle forever. I stopped many times during the day just to look around me and rest my bum. Even on a bike the sound of the breeze and the movement of the bike exclude the silence needed to hear total stillness. The mornings were cold now, and my water bottle was frozen solid in the mornings, but the continuing good weather kept my spirits high. It was the rain which I dreaded, not the cold.

This was open ranch country, so secret off-road camping was not so easy to find. Feeling exhausted by the late afternoon I turned off down a rough track to a ranch and asked permission to camp by a nearby creek.

I found a creek-side spot and bathed in the swirling water. I felt a tremendous sense of well-being as I stood there. Life had been reduced (or raised) to a level of such sophisticated simplicity that I could only revel in it. I had become attuned to its daily rhythm and routine; the packing and unpacking, watching the world from my tent, simple meals (usually involving an egg), natural sounds, the movement of sun and moon, the changing sky. I felt the movement of the pedals turning and watched the road passing speedily beneath my feet; I was conscious of the bike beneath me and the sound of its parts gliding smoothly and efficiently. I would change gears and they would click satisfyingly into place.

I was proud of my bike. It was a beautiful and efficient machine which moved faultlessly day by day through the space it opened up before it. Clicking, clunking and whirring when it was supposed to click, clunk and whirr. I was aware of myself moving through space and time. In the evening I felt myself sitting on the earth, making firm contact with its solidness. I was a flexible, bending and blending element in my right place, cradled in the soft firmness of my environment. Trying to analyse my sense of balance and harmony, I kept coming back to the word 'freedom'. I was free to stop or go, free to think – or not. No one imposed on me wishes or words. I looked proudly at my packs – I had all I needed, no more, no less. True, I needed the little money I had, I needed to move to buy food. I was no hunter, the ultimate in self-sufficiency.

Some time after returning I received a letter from a cyclist friend of mine who was living temporarily on a boat in Guatemala. He asked why, in the end, freedom is not enough. Why, ultimately, there always develops the need for an aim, a purpose in life; why is it not enough just to **be**? Why, even when we have made our lives the ideal in simplicity, we still have the compulsion to invent problems, and to live in a fictional world born of our imagination?

He had been on the road a long time when he wrote this. As a beginner I had not reached that stage yet (if it was an inevitable stage) and still wallowed in my lack of a grand purpose and in my freedom.

There was mining in the area, and that evening I watched the trains snaking slowly, slowly round the hills. In Europe goods trains speed by; in America, with their mile-long carriages, they saunter across the land. With evocative names like Santa Fé and Union Pacific they meander round, through and over the plains, hills and mountains. Never in a hurry, and looking as if they have always been there. It is ironic that the instrument which hastened the demise of American Indians and wildlife alike now seems such an old and integral part of the land.

That night the sunset tried a new theme. As the day ended the sky was transformed into a translucent silver sphere which changed imperceptibly into the subtlest and most delicate shades of lemon and rose, before intensifying to its usual routine of yet another flaming horizon. As the great moon rose, the world evolved into a globe of blue light and black shadows.

I had not realised until I prepared for sleep that I was sharing my large brush-covered site with livestock, but in the dark I could hear them huffing and puffing in nervous curiosity around my tent. I had visions of being flattened by a terrified cow as it became tangled in my guy ropes and fell on me. Periodic slaps on the tent sent them scattering for a while to a safe distance.

Preparing my breakfast in the morning, I looked up at the sound of rustling and heavy breathing. My heart stopped! Facing me, a mere thirty steps distant, surrounded by his womenfolk, stood a glossy black, muscle-bound Aberdeen Angus bull. Now, I am not an expert on bulls, but I had heard that Aberdeen Angus are a beef breed (and therefore less docile) and the bulls are given to unpredictable behaviour. They wandered away and I breathed again and decided to skip breakfast. There followed the quickest packing of my trip.

I nearly made it. All was on my bike and ready to leave when Angus, his harem and five horses returned. He reduced his distance to fifteen steps and stood four-square and solid, staring with unblinking little eyes at this impostor who had dared to enter his domain. (I noticed that I was also next to their watering place which probably didn't help.) The cows got bored and left, followed by the horses. But he remained, unmoving and transfixed only by me. I gave thanks to whatever it was that told me to camp on the water's edge and planned my escape.

Talk about experiencing the Reality of the Moment! If you ever feel the need to do so, try standing eyeball to eyeball with a miffed bull. It may have blown the theory that it brings happiness but it certainly concentrates the mind superbly!

Finally, he decided it was time I took the hint a little quicker, so he roared. How he roared! I had never heard a bull bellow before, and even in those precarious circumstances I had to admit that it truly was an awe-inspiring sound. He roared his almighty bellow to the cow gods in the sky and then proceeded to paw the ground, sending clouds of soil over his glossy back. Then he roared again and tossed his head. It really seemed as though he meant business.

I decided it was time to quit the scene. Fully-clothed, I leapt off the three foot bank into the waist deep muddy water and there I crouched for twenty minutes, while he bellowed and pawed his heart out, confused by the vanishing trick of his morning's entertainment. I doubted that he would attack my bike, and it was unlikely that he had the intelligence to work out that I was in the river so, eventually, he slowly ambled away, stopping every few steps to look around and have another bellow. As soon as his rump had disappeared into the bushes I belted for my life across that endless field and escaped. Recovering my shattered nerves on the other side of the gate I turned and saw that he had returned once more to the site. I chose not to grumble at the negligence of my guiding spirits and thanked them instead for allowing my escape from what could have so easily become a mangled morning.

In Green River, the barren landscape gave me my first glimpse of the butte scenery so characteristic of Utah. The daytime temperature was also becoming more Utah-like – it was *hot*. In the tourist information office I was told about the spate of attacks which had recently taken place on tourists in Florida. From this, my informants deduced, with some logic that I could not follow, that it would be unsafe for me to travel through Mexico.

As I paced myself for the long, slow climb out of town in the shimmering, treeless heat a mirage whizzed by. It returned and plonked itself in front of me. My god, it was Captain Whats-His-Name from *Thunderbirds*! All blond hair and tanned, and wearing the latest psychedelic cycling gear. Seemingly oblivious to my stressed, sweaty state he came straight to the point:

"Would you like some company for a little while?"

"No thanks."

"I'm a trained masseur from Florida. I could give you a massage."

"I think it's a bit hot for a massage."

"It would relax you."

"And where do you propose this massage should take place?"

"You could put your tent up along the road."

"Have you ever been in a small tent in the hot sun?"

"It would be okay."

"Er... no, it wouldn't."

"It wouldn't be a problem."

"Yes, it would! Because I do not *want* a massage, thank you. Goodbye."

I must have looked desperate. (Boy, did I look *that* desperate?)

I struggled on in the heat, still trying to absorb what I had been told by the man in the tourist office. Three inches of snow in Colorado! Colorado was only a day's ride ahead for heaven's sake. It could not be possible. I had not yet learnt that the predominant factor in temperature was elevation, and most of Colorado was at least seven thousand feet.

Hills are hard enough at the best of times for weaklings like me, and in scorching heat the difficulty increases exponentially. But sometimes Not Very Nice People decide to lay nice, new, soft tarmac, and strip the vegetation for fifty feet either side of the road. I ploughed through, leaving tracks in the melting road, and feeling as though I was towing a ton on soft tyres. The sun was reflecting blindingly back in my face and the lack of surrounding greenery exacerbates the conviction that this is what it must have been like when the oil started to warm up, in the days when they used to boil people in the stuff.

Turning off to follow the perimeter of the Flaming Gorge Reservoir, I made a new hill acquaintance. This was The Hill Which Pretends to be Flat. You spend an entire day wondering how you can be so knackered just cycling along a flat road. Later you find that you are actually two thousand feet higher than you were in the morning.

I finally gave up and decided to head down a track and pitch camp for the night at a spot called Squaw's Hollow. There I met the third road surface fiend of the day; it was my old friend – the corrugated, or washboard, surface. This is usually to be found on gravel, sand and dirt roads – occasionally on tarmac. Whilst hot tarmac and flat-hills wear you out, the corrugated track just puts you in a thoroughly foul mood; the level of badness being determined by the distance between corrugations – narrow ones being bone, bike and brain shakers, wider ones allowing at least a bit of rhythm if the speed is slow enough.

Oh the bliss of stopping! The total rapture of laying the bike down, closing your eyes, and breathing, 'Enough!'

As I looked around me, across the emptiness and over the water, I became aware of a total stillness – it was like being in a sealed void. Even away from human noises there is never a complete lack of sound – a breeze may rustle the leaves on the trees and stir the grass; clouds may bring movement; an animal may be heard. Always something moves. I felt slightly disturbed and ill at ease. It was all a little eerie, and I didn't know whether this was due solely to the stillness or if there was some other, as yet unidentified, intangible. After all, quiet places should be peaceful, not creepy. But here, there was not a breath of breeze, there were no trees or plants to rustle, there was no wildlife, no birds flew over the water or floated on its surface, and there were neither boats nor fishermen in this fishing-obsessed land.

Even the adjacent barren hills had a decidedly ominous presence. I looked at my map and my mouth dropped open when I saw their name – Devil's Playground!

Then I walked down to the water's edge and caught sight of something by the little bay. Walking closer I found a tent bag with a good quality tent hanging half in and half out, there was a tin of sauerkraut, an enamel jug, a bag of flour, a dog lead and collar, and a cap saying 'Death Becomes Her'. Everything had been abandoned.

My remaining hours before sleep were devoted to going over all the possible explanations for these items being abandoned. Why would someone start to take a tent out and then vanish? Why would they leave their food unopened? Where was the dog?

During the night every noise I heard was a murderer returning to the scene of his crime, a dead man bemoaning his demise or the devil coming down from his playground!

The long, nervous night finally ended and I was still in one piece. The devil was still in his playground and dead men had not walked. I made a sagebrush fire to cook breakfast (my cooker and I were not speaking) had a bath in the reservoir and left my creepy, wild and haunted campsite. In the village of Manila I informed the police of the mysterious absentee camper and handed over the numbered dog collar; they could trace him from that.

Detouring onto the loop road into Sheep Creek Canyon instantly transformed my world from that of a hot and treeless desert into a beautiful gorge which was a riot of gold and green, of cliffs and towers of rock, which escalated into vast uplifted cliffs of sandstone. The horizontal strata had been so deformed that they now stood vertical, in a blatant exhibition of what Mother Earth is capable of when she chooses. Her power was emphasised by a sad little sign which stood as a memorial and warning to all who are negligent or innocent of her potential. It spoke of how, in this lovely spot of flaming aspens, a whole family had been wiped out by a flash flood.

I camped by a stony, rambling creek in the shadow of a cliff face and wandered to the stream, which I saw was swarming with large sockeye salmon. Having gone upstream to spawn and end their days a few had already died and become lodged under rocks, others had mangy moth-eaten fins.

I had been told that spawning salmon are so greedy that they can be caught easily with nothing more than an empty hook. I had line and hook and sure enough, within seconds a fish snatched it, but it also broke my line and went off with the hook in its mouth. This is my worst fishing scenario so I agonised about it a while and set about devising new tactics. I tried grabbing unwary tails projecting from under rocks, but fishtails are slippery and they all got away.

Then I hit on Charlie! Charlie was my new anti-dog device. After discovering the inadequacies of my horsewhip back on the Fort Hall Indian Reservation, I had been on the lookout for an improvement, and, of course, the roadside had provided a metal rod, about two and a half feet long. Perfect.

After many misses I finally delivered the deadly blow and grabbed my prey before it was swept swiftly away. I was so proud. And of course I ate my prize. I *had* to after murdering it, although with its massive teeth and its grotty, rotted fins and tails I really did not fancy it by the time I had prepared it.

The road curled seductively between the soft buff rocks, and the glorious yellow-gold blaze of the autumnal aspens complemented the dark spires of the conifers. At the end of the canyon I looked with disbelief at the hill which I had to climb to get out. Sometimes ignorance really is bliss, so that one can keep on hoping that the next bend is the last, but here I could see the route of my ascent laid out clearly before me. It zigzagged back and forth in formidable angles suited only to the Bighorn sheep. After two hours I reached the top and with great pride in the evidence of my increasing fitness, I collected wood and lit a fire.

In the colder north a wonderful thing happens at the end of September. That is when the summer season is officially over, nearly all tourists vanish and official campsites close. As the water and toilets are also disconnected it is, in effect, the same as camping wild. However, there is something luxuriously hedonistic about putting your tent up on a smooth flat 'official' surface and having your very own picnic table and barbecue facilities, especially when it's free. So, when I got to the deserted facilty-less Flaming Gorge campsite I set up camp on its rim.

The Green River is the river of the gorge and several people died in its first reconnoitre. It is a spectacular sight. The rich, dark red, tree-speckled cliffs plunge 1,700 feet down to the still, metallic water. Only by seeing a boat far below can you absorb the massive scale of the place. I was glad I had come.

People the world over prefer to camp near others and neither know, nor want to know, how to rough it in 'a backpacker way' (and why should they?). They get nervous off the beaten track and *very* nervous if they are not with, or cannot see, other trekkers. Thus they stay on official campsites and do not move far from their vehicles. Some of the less philanthropic among us may be thankful for this as it keeps the quiet places quiet and unspoilt.

Edward Abbey (*Desert Solitaire* is a must for wilderness lovers) had only contempt for those National Park visitors who only wanted car parks, cola machines and paths, and he raged against the building of roads into these special and often isolated areas. As a Ranger in Arches National Monument before and during its development, he systematically removed the stakes which surveyors had laboriously planted, believing that mass tourism reduced the natural world to a theatrical tableau. Such places, he believed, should require effort to reach if they are to be valued sufficently; we do not have the right to discover them too easily. And although I had followed a road to the creepy Squaw Hollow, the lovely Sheep's Creek Canyon, and now the majestic Flaming Gorge, and maybe they *were* too easily accessible, nevertheless I felt as though I had put enough effort into my arrival to earn my 'right' to be here. I'm sure that Abbey would have approved!

That night the wind roared along the chasm, rose up the sheer cliffs and blasted into my camp. All would be very still until a distant fearful howling could be heard. Closer and closer it would come until it hit my calm spot with a battering of trees, tent, fire and possessions.

Then it would pass on its way and all would be quiet once more. So passed this dramatic night.

Another phenomenon which was new for me was the discovery of shooting stars. I grew up thinking they were a great rarity and remember clearly the only one I ever saw. But in America they zoom around the sky like manic lambs, making the night sky a magic living world. By day, the earth showed its clothes, by night it revealed its glittering jewels. I lay by my tent – reluctant to remove myself even slightly from this night. I had never realised before what we miss in murky climes, and what we lose when we close our doors.

The next day's treat came early. I was peeping out my tent to see a group of mule-eared deer grazing in the early morning mist.

To travel the road from the Flaming Gorge to Vernal is to pass from tree-clad hills into the juniper-spotted desert of deposits which, like those of the Salmon River, look as though one good storm would wash them all into the creeks. I rode into Uintah County at 8,428 feet and at the top of the long hill down to Vernal I finally got my first distant glimpse of Colorado.

The panorama was breathtaking – misty rocks of red, buff, grey and pink stretched far away to the horizon. These bare deposits of sandstones and limestones were laid down when dinosaurs roamed the land and until their ultimate demise about sixty-five million years ago. Subsequent erosion has made their final resting places easy to unearth, and it is impossible to travel in the area without absorbing the knowledge that this is dinosaur land – where else would a town be named Dinosaur?

Camping on a juniper-clad, rock-strewn rise overlooking a sagebrush plain near Dinosaur, I slept to the sound of owls hooting and small mammals scuttling. I was woken in the morning by the sound of gunfire. Scrambling from my tent, I saw that I formed one corner of a triangle, with hunters a mile to my right and antelope a mile to my left. The hunters were shooting (out of season) at the antelope, who (ignoring the shots) were only worried about me. It was me they ran away from, not the deadly fire.

It was always fascinating to see the effect of my bike on domestic animals and wildlife. A group of antelope or deer would be totally unfazed by the largest, noisiest vehicle on the road – rarely even raising their heads. But as I silently approached them they would stare in stunned disbelief, not knowing if I was animal, human or mechanical. Invariably they would conclude that I was some unknown dangerous alien and off they would bound over the horizon. Horses always had a second-sense of my presence in the landscape and would see me coming miles away – staring motionless until long after I had passed.

The road from Dinosaur was uninspiring, although this was made up for by the empty roads. However, it was on this stretch that I discovered Rangely. This unremarkable town offered three special things which make it forever indelible in my memory. First, it had a deserted hunters' campsite under shady mature trees. This was not only free, but it also had the ultimate in bliss facilities – piping hot showers and toilets. I was in heaven. I washed everything it was possible to wash, wallowed in the showers, and celebrated by having chicken for supper.

The second thing for which Rangely should be given elevated status is the friendliness which I met there. This was epitomised by the local policeman. At 9.30 in the evening he pulled up beside my tent. I asked if there was a problem.

"Not at all. I saw you ride into town and thought I'd check out to make sure everything's okay with ya'll."

"Yes, everything's good."

"Say, you're travelling alone; are you carrying a gun?"

"Well, no." (Didn't he know that I couldn't legally have one?)

"Well, you sure as hell *should* have one. It's dangerous for a woman out here alone without any protection. Whatcha gonna do if some weirdo rips into your tent at night?"

"I always make sure I camp off the road out of sight. No one can find me in the places I camp."

"There's always one'll find you. Weirdos get into the hills and all over the darned place."

"I wouldn't know what gun to get anyway."

"I reckon a .380 would be best for you. It's better for a woman 'cos it's a bit lighter and doesn't have such a kickback. But it'd see a guy off just fine."

"What have you got? Can I have a look?"

To my astonishment he took his gun from its holster and handed it over to me. Hadn't he ever heard of the murderous Bonnie? Then he then took out his metal truncheon.

"Well, you should at least have one of these," he said.

He gave me a demonstration on how quickly he could open it. It was a neat little telescopic weapon which a simple flick released it to its full length. I doubted whether he had much use for it in this quiet backwater. I also doubted my chances against a big brute even with such a potentially lethal weapon in my hand, although I was left with a great desire to add one to my belt.

The final highlight of the day was the passing of the biggest, brightest and pinkest shooting star I had ever seen. It arched across the sky like a great burning ember, leaving a tail many millions of miles long to colour the heavens. I slept the sleep of the clean, the full and the satisfied.

Road to the Rockies

Next day I continued along the Rangely road towards Meeker, a town named after an awesomely silly and bigoted man who was agent at the White River Ute Indian Reservation in 1879.

Colorado's Utes were a wonderfully wild people who loved horses, horsemanship and hunting. Their only 'offence' was that they did not want to become farmers and they spent too much time ranging far and wide over their traditional hunting grounds, trying to pretend that what was happening to them – disinheritance – was not really happening at all.

Meeker, whose sense of his own racial and moral superiority was particularly well-developed (even by the notoriously racist standards of the Colorado settlers), ordered the ploughing up of some of the Utes' best pasturage, including the strip they used for racing their ponies, their favourite pastime.

They asked Meeker to stop and when he refused they fired over the heads of the ploughing team. Meeker panicked, sent the troops in and his folly left thirty-seven Utes, twelve soldiers and eight agency workers – including Meeker – dead. After the event Governor Pitkin, the wealthiest of the entrepreneurs said:

"It will be impossible for the Indians and whites to live in peace hereafter...my idea is that, unless removed by the government, they must necessarily be exterminated...The advantages that would accrue from the throwing open of twelve million acres of land to miners and settlers would more than compensate all the expenses incurred."

This was ranch country – small, sparsely vegetated hills with only occasional farms – and it felt bleak and alien. Following the Pioneer

River, I stopped at a house for water. A young woman with several children met me, two were sick. She was pathetically keen to talk and I could only wonder at the loneliness of her life. Childbirth must often be the only antidote to this.

I had thought that the road to the gateway of the Rocky Mountains would be a hard slog, but the seventeen miles to the boundary river of the mighty Colorado were gloriously downhill. Here the river was not so mighty and the colourful villages scattered along it – Rifle, Silt and Newcastle – were quaint and old time-ish.

Throughout the West roadside litter is often removed by local organisations which 'adopt' a two mile section of highway. The names of these organisations often brought a smile to my face. At Silt it was the 'Silt Silly Stitchers' who cared for their bit of road, and I imagined wild, elderly women kicking their heels up as they galloped down the highway – litterpicking stick in one hand and knitting needles in the other. By far my favourite though, had to be 'Theta Zeta Daughter of Epsilon Sigma Alpha Adopt a Highway Litter Control next two miles.'

In Glenwood Springs I camped by the river and railroad under quivering aspens where the peaceful clank, chug and manoeuvring of the engines lulled me as I watched the river swirling in the twilight. And though clouds were gathering, the golden light shed by the aspens made the sun shine, rather like those transparent coloured sweet papers you look through when you're a child.

I recalled my experiences of the day: the storm, the town, the wildlife, a beautiful golden horse. Dazzling bluebirds had fluttered around me all the way to Rifle and ravens had now been replaced by squawking and chattering magpies. Near Rio Blanco two golden eagles had soared over the hills where a group of mule deer watched me.

But the day had also brought the saddest sight of my trip – an antelope whose back legs had become entangled in a barbed wire fence whilst attempting to jump it. It hung, inverted, with the barbs sticking into its soft belly. For days I thought of its painful, languishing death.

And, finally, the mountains! I had seen big mountains before, but nothing had prepared me for those mind-blowing vistas of Colorado. These mountains induced none of that claustrophobia which can gradually seep into the mind after spending time enclosed in the close confines of a concertinaed crust, and which makes you wish for the air of a more open land. In Colorado there was space. *Everywhere* was space; long vistas over huge rolling foothills to the magnificent snow-covered peaks of distant ranges. The dark green of firs and spruces intermingled with yellow aspens, glistening white snow shone on jagged blue summits. I was a little late to see the full glory of the autumn colours, and the great swathes of aspens now had large brown patches; but I had the compensation of fresh snow bringing a crisp, delicate beauty to the mountains. After weeks of burning heat it was like seeing the world for the first time.

It is not easy to select a route through Colorado when you can only have one choice. But when almost every bend in every road reveals a new scene of overwhelming beauty, it scarcely matters which way you go. Nevertheless, the invasion of jetset tourism and ski slopes meant that I did not want to pass through Aspen, however dramatic the surroundings. I imagined another Sun Valley.

My road wound its lovely way to the tiny village of Redstone. Being out of season, it was not bursting at the seams with awed visitors and so it managed very easily to be what it sets out to be – quiet, quaint, and folksy. Vivid autumn leaves covered the gardens of exquisite, pastel-coloured, clapboard dwellings, gardens reared up to meet the rough, steep, rocky slopes above.

I coffeed in the coffee shop, browsed in the arty shops and took photos of the tiny log cabin museum. I 'oohed' and 'aahed' at all the pretty bits, and predictably I envied the wintertime residents of this charming place.

As there was nowhere to camp, I moved on. I started to pull out from the road junction because an oncoming land cruiser was indicating to turn into my exit. I was met with a blaring of horn, a slam of brakes. A sixty-something opened his window and yelled at me.

"Go fuck yourself!!"

"You had your indicators on for turning right!"

"Stupid fuckin' cow!!"

I remembered the lesson that we all learn as learner-drivers – never trust a flashing light. However, in this case, rather than it being for the preservation of one's physical health, it was more to avoid the unpleasant experience of encountering one of those sad characters who seem to have missed the point of life. Having been thoroughly informed of my place on this earth by this piece of rubbish, I left Redstone. It was time to challenge my very first Rocky Mountain Pass – the McLure.

Of course, the McLure Pass was just a baby compared to some I had tackled – only three miles up and a pass height of 8,755 feet, but it sure as hell looked steep to me. Like the hill out of Sheep's Canyon the road was laid out zigzagging in front of me before I had even started. I could see what I was faced with. Also, I knew this was THE ROCKIES – the Real Thing – so I was seriously intimidated. In reality of course, the thing with the lesser reputation often turns out to be the most deviously difficult.

To apply oneself solely to the struggle of the slope in Colorado would be to miss out on much of the reason for being there and I did not want to miss a single thing. I wanted to see every mountain from every angle, and this meant lots of stopping to see what was happening behind me. Up and up, until Sopris and Capitol and all their big babies showed their jagged summits far above tree-line and foothills. Up to the snow-covered pass, and then the reward of a long, fast downhill ride with the vast rippling foothills spreading out to the west until they formed the skirts of other far ranges.

Setting up camp by the river, I was approached by a friendly middle-aged couple from Washington who were just the antidote I needed to the fool of the morning. They were so thrilled to have met their first touring cyclist that they wanted a photo of me to show their family. The husband then asked shyly:

"Would you be offended if my wife took one of us together?" Their departure left a little gap in my day.

In Paonia, rain threatened and I decided to stay in town. Searching for a playing field to camp on, I met an elderly lady who invited me to camp in her garden.

This was Emily, wife of Pete. Emily was a real sweetie who, although she was in her sixties, was still teaching. A reserved, private woman she had learned to assert herself quietly in the face of her husband's patronising authority. He constantly interrupted her in mid-sentence, and she would allow him to over-ride her with an expression of weary patience. When he had finished she would resume where she had left off and so complete what she had started to say. I doubted whether she had been allowed the opportunity for much self-expression in her married life.

Pete spent most of his time in his study, and books on maths and religion were scattered around the living room. On my first entry into their home Emily drew him out and informed him I was staying. Briefly putting his head round the door, he answered: "Surely," and retreated again. Several times he reappeared to deliver orders: "Have a shower!" "Eat at our table!" "It's raining. Sleep indoors!"

In spite of my instructions I slept outside.The rain thrashed down throughout the evening and night. In the morning I breakfasted indoors and was given instructions that I must visit the Black Canyon on the Gunnison River, which according to Pete, was more dramatic than the Grand Canyon due to its great depth compared to its width. It was simply a single great gash into the earth's crust, plunging vertically to the river at the bottom. Pete presented himself for a 'Pete With Bike' photo and I departed.

The towns along this route were all a joy to enter. I had not expected to find American towns becoming a focus of my enjoyment, and it was a pleasant surprise. Hotchkiss was no exception. In spite of having its fair share of cutesy, candy-floss buildings, it had managed to maintain a definite western aura. It had an art shop hidden behind a little bungalow of pink, purple, blue and white spattered walls, there was even a health shop and a second-hand bookshop. Unfortunately, these were all closed. Maybe it was Sunday again – days and times had long since ceased to mean anything. Hotchkiss's final *coup de grace* was its twelve thousand foot mountain backdrop.

I asked the man at the gas station about the Black Canyon. I knew car-drivers' opinions were often not applicable to cyclists and I wanted a second, and local, opinion; was it too incredible to miss, was it worth a three day detour? After all I couldn't go running off willy-nilly all over the country on the basis of any passing recommendation.

An out-of-state woman stopping for gas overheard our conversation and joined in; she called a couple of local lads over to participate in the discussion. Then her sister, husband and brother-in-law got out of the waiting car and trundled over to contribute their opinions. By now, the debate on whether it was 'worth' my doing a detour to the

Black Canyon had been taken out of my hands – it was an open discussion in which my presence was not necessary; I was simply the 'she' of the debate:

"Yes, but she's..." "Okay, but if she..." "Well, I think she..."

The main conclusions seemed to be *first*, that I was going to the Grand Canyon later so would be seeing a gorge of even greater amazement value and so should skip the Black Canyon (first woman); *secondly*, that the Black Canyon is different to the Grand Canyon so the two cannot be compared (gas attendant); *thirdly*, that the point of my trip was to see the country, so why not see it then? (husband); *finally*, the road was a flat and easy ride, both to the gorge and along both sides, so apprehension about the difficulty of the ride should not stop me (local boys). Given my still skinny legs and dubious lung capacity, it was the last point that clinched it for me.

I headed out to meet the canyon. I struggled and huffed. I cursed – oh, how I cursed those boys as I watched my speedometer stuck on six miles an hour. My mood was not improved by the vicious guard dogs which came raging out from yards and gardens, slavering for a taste of biker's leg. I hated the stupid, ignorant owners of those free-range killing machines as passionately as I dreaded hearing the sudden manic eruption of blood-curdling, teeth-baring, hysterical barking as the next Doberman spied me trying to sneak past and shot out after me like a bullet.

It was with relief that I arrived intact at the edge of Crawford. There I did an elevation retake. Hotchkiss had been 5,200 feet; Crawford was 6,800 feet. I had risen 1,600 feet in twelve miles on this 'flat' road. Now that I knew there was a reason for being so knackered it was not so bad. Nevertheless, I was thinking of turning back when I entered the centre of Crawford. Suddenly it was all worthwhile. This delightful, tiny, hilltop village had everything: three stores, a gas station, townhall, lovely views and – the crowning touch – a store incorporating a launderette, a shower (four dollars) and coffee by voluntary donation.

Aiming for *absolute* perfection, the village even had two old men smoking pipes on a street-side bench, *and* a free, deserted campsite on the outskirts. Castle-like pinnacles of rock stood around the village protecting it from outside invasion. I thought I had died of exhaustion and gone to heaven.

I calmed my frazzled nerves by downing three cups of coffee, and went to fill up with cooker fuel at the gas station. I asked the attendant about the road ahead.

"I don't know. I never go past Maher," she replied. My mouth dropped open; I pushed it back into place. Maher was only about five miles away. I felt like screaming at her:

"Do you know how lucky you are? You live in the middle of some of the most beautiful scenery in the world and you're too lazy to get off your ass and see it."

But she was nice so I didn't!

I suppose it is the great American paradox that individual people can appear to be totally static, entirely without curiosity about what is over the next hill, yet at the same time there are so many removal hire vans on the road that it is easy to imagine the whole country is on the move. I was told that in Colorado you are awarded a special vehicle number plate if you were born in the state, and that there are few of those plates around.

Another aspect of the paradox is apparent when you observe American tourism in action – millions visit the national parks every year. The biggies like the Grand Canyon and Yellowstone are buried so thick in tourists that you cannot doubt that Americans wish, at least, to see the iconic sights of their country. On the other hand few visitors stray more than a hundred yards from the security of the road, from the 'official' viewing points or from the safety of their car. Maybe we should be grateful for this. After all, if everyone went off trekking all over the place it would result in a greater disturbance to the ecosystems than already exists, and people like me would be moaning like mad.

In any case it is not realistic to compare the American continent with Great Britain. In my little country it's very easy to put your boots on and go for a walk; we can even get to the top of our highest mountain in three hours. In the American West everything is on such an enormous scale that 'going for a walk' is not really an option, there are no little country lanes to meander down on a Sunday afternoon, no riverside pubs. Everything in the Big Big West is too big for that. That's what makes America grand and awe inspiring, and it must also make 'down the road' (even five miles?) pretty intimidating unless you are an avid outdoor enthusiast with all the gear.

The night I spent at Crawford was noisy. My addiction to the manic cacophony of coyotes was satisfied, and the darkness was made even more eerie and exciting by the hooting and tooting of a pair of owls long into the night. It was a night for witches on broomsticks and bats silhouetted against a huge full moon; but there was no moon – just a starry, starry night.

The following day continued invisibly uphill. Fifteen miles out of Crawford I did another elevation retake at an 8,600 feet marker. Another 1,800 feet in fifteen miles – a total of 3,400 in twenty-four miles. No wonder I felt like I was riding through a muddy puddle. It continued its slow, gentle, exhausting, uphill grind for another six miles or so, to 9,000 feet.

In the late afternoon I found a hidden headland to camp on, with staggering views over the Sopochero Valley to the scrub oak and aspen foothills which rose in folds to the San Juan mountains beyond. I was dumbfounded to realise that I had to *cross* those soaring snow-covered rocky fortresses in a few days time.

But that was for another day, and right now everything had to be worth it for this scene alone. The whole *trip* was worth it for this. All was space, colour, sound, movement. The wind blew strong, whipping the clouds into seething, soft, bubbling masses which raced across the sky, throwing rapidly changing shadows across the landscape. Chipmunks and nutcrackers scampered, chattered and fluttered around me among the rocks and junipers. The soil was moist and organic beneath me. Everything felt so dynamic, so fluid and alive.

That night the cold and the hard rain kept me awake into the early hours. In addition I was on a slope (they always get bigger in the night) which kept throwing me into the bottom of my tent, where I ended up in a scrunched up, uncomfortable ball. It is at three o'clock on such nights that one asks oneself: 'What the hell am I doing here?'

Red Mountain Pass

The morning was dry and the sky had resumed its attempt to look as though it had come out of a Rupert Bear story – large fluffy clouds you could roll and bounce on dashed across a deep blue heaven. The damp air was whooshing up out of the depths of the canyon and forming clouds as I watched before being swept up to the sky.

I was out of food and water and had a great lust for a bacon sandwich, so was looking forward to getting to the village of Sapinero. The road veered high above the Gunnison gorge, giving tantalising views of rocky plunges and sheer drops over which it was scary even to look. Even I, who normally enjoy heights, had to sit, or crawl on my belly, before having the nerve to peer way down into the depths – butterflies fluttering wildly in my stomach – to the gunmetal strip of water far, far below. Otherwise I feared I would be drawn like a magnet into its gaping jaws.

Coming down to the dam the scenery 'disappeared' and rain fell drearily onto the bleak reservoir. Buoyed up by thoughts of my bacon sandwich, I toiled on. When I got to Sapinero it appeared to consist solely of one wooden building, comprising store, gas station and restaurant. This would have been ideal, except it was closed.

When you are hungry, cold and tired, you do things that you would not normally do. So it was that I approached the only vehicle around and asked the lone male driver if he had any water or snacks which he could give me. He delved into his provisions and offered me a packet of biscuits and a tin of pears. I cycled back to a site of deserted caravans, thinking maybe I could find some non-reservoir water and a place for my tent. There was neither. Suddenly my friendly provider appeared in his transit and offered me a lift to Montrose, twenty miles away. Thinking of the prospect of a wet hungry night in this depressing spot I accepted.

I had to pay quite dearly for this privilege however, as it turned out that Grant was a Born Again Christian. As we drove he regaled me with the glory of God and the oh-so-predictable story of his conversion.

The tale of the Born Again male is nearly always the same. You don't need to hear it more than once. It usually involves a long story of degeneration into a life of drink, drugs, crime and women. But, just when things cannot get any worse, God reveals himself and suddenly life has meaning once more.

I remember these revelation stories from speakers coming to my school and Sunday school, and I always found them gripping at first, especially as the speaker was sometimes quite young and trendy and looked like he was still a bit naughty. As he told us a great story of his past badness I would think that this time it might be different – maybe there would be no conversion – it was much more interesting. Inevitably of course, he always came to that line which started: 'And then, one day...' and I would realise with a groan that I'd been foiled again.

Christians seem proud of these converts to their cause, but I am sure that I would be more proud of conversions by people who were strong, and happy with their lives, than the sudden desperate conversion of someone who was hanging onto a straw in a stormy sea.

Luckily for the comfort of our drive together, Grant also happened to be a really nice guy, so I let him talk to his heart's content. When he stopped at a place called Cimaron however (a store and bar), I saw there was an area for free camping and decided to stay there. Liking the look of the area we had passed through, I wanted to cycle the remaining miles to Montrose. It was nearly dark when I finally interrupted Grant so that I could put my tent up (he was talking about the disciples at the time).His parting words were:

"Don't forget, think about God. Don't be stubborn – open your heart and let Him in."

The logic presumably being that if I thought about, and prayed to, this God, then I would believe in him. Does this mean that if I also think of little green men, then I will come to believe they exist also? The possibilities are endless!

Still, if I'm honest, I'm sure I would find it very comforting to believe in a nice God who loved me, and who was guiding and guarding me. Maybe if I wanted to opt for a life as a believer, I could probably brainwash myself into thinking I believed, simply because I wanted to. But the day I start conjuring beliefs from wishes is the time to depart this life.

In any case, for me the wonders of evolution and geology are far more exciting, wondrous and satisfying than any creation story. *Made On Its Own in Five Billion Years* is far more fantastic to me than *Made by God in Six Days*.

As I packed in the morning, I realised that I had left Charlie, my dog stick, back at the previous night's site. This was a blow, as he had become an important part of my equipment by now. Not only was he vital for protecting me against ravaging dogs, but he had several other uses, such as being a prop for my bike where no trees were available.

The next morning I grabbed an innocent motorist at the gas station and begged a lift back to the Sapinero junction. From there, I waited two hours for a lift along the quiet road to my camping place where Charlie was waiting patiently where I had left him. By sheer luck men were working on a nearby pylon. I asked them if they would be heading my way when they had finished.

"No," they answered, "but if you head straight down to the bottom of the gorge, follow the line of pylons, then walk along half a mile, you'll come to a bridge right by where you're camping."

I looked down into the deep chasm and followed their directions with my eyes. Sure enough, in the distance I could see the store next to the camp. I had gone forty miles round by road when there it was directly across the gorge not much more than a stone's throw away. But if I could get down from here, there is no way I could have got up. As it was it took me two hours and many tumbles, cuts and bruises to fight, fall and scramble my way down to the river.

My short ride to Montrose surrendered two badgers, a porcupine, a skunk and numerous deer to the carrion gods in the sky. The gem of the day was a whole gang of brilliant red and black Dennis the Menace caterpillars which I helped across the road before they became a jam sandwich.

The hunting season was about to begin and didn't I know it! Being the nearest town of any size to the western flanks of the San Juan Mountains, Montrose was the initial focal point for hunters entering the area. Clearly the town benefited hugely from their presence and did its best to make them feel welcome. Numerous establishments sported 'We Welcome Hunters' signs, and a large banner hung across the main street. Roadside stalls offered information to hunters, and on Montrose Radio every other word was 'hunter'. If you had anti-hunting sympathies in this town, you would be wise to keep your trap shut.

I had been advised to wear something bright so that I would not be mistaken for something furry on four legs – urban cowboys have nervous trigger fingers. Luckily synchronicity had delivered a bright orange workman's waistcoat among the roadside debris two days before; I now draped it over my panniers.

Everywhere was a frenzy and the road out of town was a nightmare. There was no hard shoulder and a ditch waited to take me to its bosom. Hordes of pick-ups swarmed by as the hunters moved in closer to their quarry, ready for the early morning Blast Away signal; they drove like maniacs. No stupid cyclist was going to make them deviate one inch from their track – even if I was as wide as a motorbike. After nearly being driven into the ditch several times, I decided the safest strategy was to move out into the road a bit, so they would be forced to acknowledge my existence and would have to pull out in order to overtake me.

This was the worst road I had been on, and the drivers the most inconsiderate. The barrage of hooting and abuse being hurled against me was turning my mood black, so I put Queen on my headphones to shut it out. To be fair, Coloradan drivers had been exemplary until now. I put the present road aggression down to the influx of thousands of out-of-state city boys who were probably quite well lubricated, and whose testosterone levels were shooting off-scale as the time for their phallic deer killings drew near.

Finally I was flagged down by a police car. He stepped out unsmiling.

"We've been getting calls in that you're not pulling over."

"I can't pull over for every vehicle and if I keep to the side they're just going to knock me into the ditch. They're not pulling out for me."

"I don't want to be responsible for you ending up in hospital."

"I'm more likely to end up in hospital if I keep over. Anyway they shouldn't be on the road if they haven't the patience to overtake me – they only have to do it once."

"Well, you're the one that'll end in hospital."

Repeat. "I'm more likely to end up in hospital if I keep over – they'll knock me into the ditch. At least now they see me and *have* to pull out – I'm as big as a motorbike and they should treat me like one. Anyway, everywhere else has a hard shoulder – why don't you have one here?"

"Because cyclists don't pay road taxes! Okay, so you're not going to pull over for them... Well... I think we understand one another!"

And off he went! And off I went – with fumes of angry smoke coming out my ears!

The Ute Indian Museum was a potential antidote to my mood but it was, predictably, closed.

In 1863 Chief Ouray of the Utes was a principal signatory on a treaty which signed away Ute rights and access to huge areas of Colorado – eighteen million acres being retained as Ute reservation land. But there was a strongly held view amongst the Utes that Ouray's deals always favoured himself and his own tribe more than the Ute nation as a whole.

In the end whether Ouray was self-seeking or not makes little difference. As soon as the whites found silver, and decided they had left the Ute with far too much land, they broke their promises and the Ute lost everything. When Ouray recognised the end was come he said:

"I realise the state of my people. We shall fall as the leaves of the trees when winter comes, and the land we have roamed for countless generations will be given up to the miner and the ploughshare, and we shall be buried out of sight."

He had good reason to be pessimistic because this was Colorado, the state with the worst record in the Union as far as treatment of the Indians was concerned; where in 1864 Colonel John Chivington and his Colorado Volunteers set a standard of brutality seldom equalled when they murdered three hundred of Black Kettle's peaceful Cheyenne at Sand Creek, near Denver. At the time the Cheyenne were under the protection of the US regular army, and were flying both a white flag and the stars and stripes, so presumed they were safe. The dirty work done that day was too much for some of the witnesses; First Lieutenant Cannon wrote:

"In going over the battleground the next day I did not see a body of man, woman or child but was scalped, and in many instances their bodies were mutilated in the most horrible manner – men's women's and children's privates cut out, etc. I also heard of numerous instances in which men had cut out the private parts of females and stretched them over their saddle-bows. I heard one man say he had cut a squaw's heart out and he had stuck it up on a stick."

President Theodore Roosevelt thought the massacre "as righteous and beneficial a deed as ever took place on the frontier".

When the question was posed to a packed Denver opera house:
"Would it be better henceforth to try to civilise or to exterminate the Indians?" the answer was almost loud enough to raise the roof of the opera house:
"Exterminate them! Exterminate them!"'

My day looked up after arriving in Ridgeway – thanks to the two great women who worked in the Tourist Information Centre. I had intended to cycle on to Ouray, which stood at the very foot of the thirteen mile Red Mountain Pass, my next challenge, but Pat and Sarah seduced me into staying put by offering an exhibition *tipi* to me as sleeping quarters. Unfortunately, the *tipi* was not sealed against the elements and an icy blast whipped under its sides. I compromised by erecting my tent inside.

The *tipi* stood in a field with other replicas, including a Conestoga wagon – huge, heavy wagons originally used mainly for freight. Due to their weight they needed many oxen to haul them. Later they made smaller 'prairie schooners' – to bring pioneer families west; the thought of cramming a whole family in these tiny wagons for three thousand miles of humps, bumps and misery was nothing short of a nightmare.

The entrance to my *tipi* looked out onto the breath-taking and fearsome San Juans'. At only ten miles down the road they filled the sky with their gigantic bulk. I was nervous – how the hell was I going to get over them? – they were just a great solid wall of rock and ice rearing vertically to heaven.

The centre had an art exhibition on which, disappointingly, was another re-hash of the Noble Savage theme. I know there are innovative and exciting artists in North America, but in the rural west there still seems to be an addiction to feathers and Roman noses. There must be few middle-class homes which do not have a Noble Indian picture around the place somewhere.

It would be good, just for once, to see a less romanticised version – maybe just a regular Indian guy in jeans and baseball cap. You could even make him just a tinsy, winsy bit noble – 'Sunset Over Native Baseball Player' – ancient profile silhouetted. I'm sure if I was an Indian seeing all this idealisation of my people by the race that slaughtered and disinherited them, I wouldn't know whether to laugh or cry. I'd want to yell: 'Hey, here I am. I'm still here, but now I live in the twentieth century. But I've still got my noble profile if you want a photo, and I'm in vogue again now – I'm the Third World.'

On my first visit to the USA in 1982, I met a woman who had recently returned from Brazil, where she had visited a museum village of native Indians. She enthused so much about them that I thought maybe her interest might be wider than that particular experience.

"Have you visited any of the Indian Reservations in the USA?" I asked.

"Oh, *no*," she replied, her nose wrinkling in disdain. "The Indians in South America aren't like ours – they are so good-looking and sweet-natured. Ours are dirty, lazy and stupid."

I considered telling her she was a fool – but couldn't get the words out!

Before leaving Ridgeway, I went to say goodbye to Pat and Sarah. Pat was in her thirties, married with children. Her eyes shone as she talked of how she had always longed to travel when she was younger, but thought it was too late now. I told her about Isabella Bird, on the go until just before she died in her seventies. I also told her of an English woman I had read about recently, also in her seventies, who had sold her house to backpack alone round the world. She was just having a three month break for an operation. Such women can inspire the rest of us to really *live*, and to take risks we probably would not otherwise dare to do, confident in the knowledge that other women have gone before, and will come after. No wonder men can achieve such amazing feats when they have the backdrop – and mental backup – of thousands of men before them.

Although it was only ten miles to the tourist town of Ouray, I wanted to stop there for the night. It sits at the very base of Red Mountain Pass and I wanted to get straight into the climb first thing the next day.

There is no messing with these mountain passes; they decide to go up, and up they go – no warm-up slopes, just straight into it. Many people had said to me: 'You can't possibly *cycle* up Red Mountain Pass – especially with all that gear on your bike,' so by now I was pretty paranoid about the whole thing. More scary was that, even though I was literally yards from the start of the incline, I still could not see where the road was, or where it could possibly go. The great mountain just reared up behind the town and gave no indication that it ever let anything through its bulwarks.

Ouray lies squashed up against the base of a cliff, so that it was impossible to find a place to camp wild unless I started out up the mountain. Neither was the tone of Ouray one which would easily thrill to anything so vagrant-like as me. Actually, that is not altogether true, I met some very nice people in Ouray. It's just a certain type of woman with which councils sometimes staff their Tourist Information Offices and who see themselves as the guardians of their town's morals, the front line of defence, and they have their own personal crusade to repel any undesirables. She took one look at me, first in the queue, her lips tightened, and she turned her attention to the other customers. When she was forced to deal with me, because there was no one else left, she endeavoured to be as curt and unhelpful as possible.

Oh, how I hate these ignorant, narrow-minded bigots! Had she seen my bike, her tone might have changed (this would not have excused her behaviour) for I had noticed several times a distinct disapproval from people, until they saw my bike and realised there was a 'respectable' reason for my appearance.

The next day I cycled through the town to my starting point.

"I bet you wish you were going the other way," laughed a hunter.

I thought that was quite funny.

I wondered where all the hordes of hunters had vanished to – it was now so quiet. Then I remembered that the official start to the hunting season was five the next morning, so presumably they had taken up their stations in the mountains ready to bag their quarry. I was told that each hunter was only allowed to shoot one deer/antelope or whatever, and that a tight check was kept on this. I hoped so, but could not help but think that many animals must be left wounded, and die a painful drawn-out death.

I stopped at the foot of the pass, and in spite of the snow which lay on the cliffs I stripped down to T-shirt and shorts – I knew it was going to get hot as hell. I took a deep breath and set off. I quickly got into a rhythm of breathing and pedalling and toiled slowly upwards. After two miles, I passed a woman at the side of the road:

"You're amazing," she said. "Or stupid," I replied.

But I was dead chuffed by her words. That one person acknowledged the difficulty of my task was all the praise I needed, and it spurred me on to the top. And actually it was one of the easier hills I had tackled, maybe because I was so psyched up to it. There were also wide expanses of bleak, marshy bog in the high valleys which eased the ascent. Anyway, the beauty of the mountains would have made all but the most jaded open their eyes and wake up; it certainly boosted my adrenaline and let me know that life is good. For most of the thirteen miles to the top I remained open-mouthed.

The aspens were gone, but in more than adequate compensation the huge, lumpy slopes were mantled in the most subtle shades of mellow golds, tawny and brown-greens. These warm shades were randomly speckled with the dark green spires of conifers – and the whole was given a generous dusting of snow. I longed to explore the ravines and creeks that disappeared into the mountains.

The pass crossed over at 11,018 feet. The snow lay deep and it was too cold to linger so donning every item of clothing that I possessed I began the descent. The loveliness of the land made me reluctant to enter the town of Silverton even though it was only five miles away, so I camped in a wide, open, sloping valley, golden beneath its swaying cover of winter grassland. At the end of the valley the giant cone of what I guessed was Sunlight Peak (14,059 feet) stood proud and awesome in the sunset. The last rays transformed the snow-covered, rocky slopes into pure copper.

Words such as 'happy' cannot describe my feelings as I watched the sun descend from my 10,500 feet Shangri-la. More practically though, it was bitterly cold and the first priority on stopping was to take steps to prevent the cold getting a grip; once you've let the cold in, it's hard to get it out. I thought any local black bears must be hibernating by now, but decided it was better to be safe than sorry just in case the odd insomniac was wandering around. I had already found a dead trunk close by which had suspicious looking fresh scratches on it, so I followed the usual, tedious bear safety code and hauled my gear up a tree.

I woke to a bright, white world; untouched and unsullied by the hand of man. My tent and bike were buried under three inches of snow. It was staggeringly beautiful. As I prepared my porridge, my heart was beating hard and the simplest task took a mammoth effort. I worked in slow motion. Loading my bike was the hardest thing I had done in months. My visions of heart failure faded when I realised that at this height I was probably feeling some slight altitude effects.

As I set off the snow fell heavily in a wild, swirling blaze of giant flakes, freezing my fingers and blinding me to everything except the delicate white-laced branches and the silence of the world. Everything was hushed, and the universe had shrunk to a few square metres around me.

WINTER WONDERLAND

I descended on Silverton like Amundsen arriving at the Pole. I was wet and frozen and longed for a bit of warmth and comfort; I really did not fancy a night out in the snow. Resignedly I searched around and located a camping place in willow scrub on the edge of town. (Two months later I was browsing through my 'odd bits' notebook and found that I actually had the address of a youth hostel in Silverton.) Then I went in search of a launderette. I threw into the drier almost everything I possessed, including tent and sleeping bag, wondering how on earth other travellers manage in wet and cold conditions when they do not have the luxury of a launderette to fall back on. Camping for me is one of the great pleasures in life, but when it is cold and raining and everything is soaking, with no possibility of drying, it is undeniably miserable and depressing.

As its name suggests Silverton used to be a mining town, not only of silver but also gold, which was mined there until two years ago. There were still a lot of small, privately owned mines in the area which gave an equally small, erratic income to any who still bothered with them. Since the end of the mining industry the population has fallen as people have left in search of other work, and the place has a distinct feel of a town at the end of its boom time. Although it had its quota of tourist shops, and probably buzzed with camera-toting visitors in summer, it still retained a down-to-earth atmosphere, and had down-to-earth people, many of whom had been there for years.

It was definitely my kind of town – gritty, slightly worn, *real*. Historical but not museumified. Tweeness and quaintness are nice to look at, but they quickly pall when you see there is no substance beneath the pretty veneer.

A steam train runs daily between Durango and Silverton. In the past this served the mines, but now it was a scenic tourist ride. The heavy snow meant that I might not be able to get out of the valley the next day – the railway could be my only way out. Luckily, the train was in the station so I asked the driver how much it cost.

"$26.75," he said.

"Oh dear," I answered, and briefly explained my predicament. He winked at me, and smiled:

"If the weather's still bad tomorrow, come back and we'll see what we can do."

I discovered a small café, run by an eccentric old couple. They did good high-cholesterol food – home-made burgers, chips, cakes – bliss! I met Leo, a teacher from Texas, in there. Fortyish, bald, interesting, and very un-American. He criticised his government, particularly its destructive foreign policy; he bemoaned the lack of culture, and the trash which was rammed down the nation's throat. He was house-sitting for a friend and debating whether or not to buy a hill with a silver mine on it.

"I saw you coming into town," he said, "and I thought there's one tough lady. She must be Austrian."

I did not know solo Austrian women had a reputation for cycling through blizzards in the Rockies. Still, I was flattered.

"You see cyclists coming into town in twos and threes," he went on, "or with a back-up car. But only very rarely do they travel alone without any safety net."

"Sunny days and launderettes are my safety nets," I replied.

The next day dawned cold and blue and the snow lay thick but no more had fallen. Cars were being instructed to use snow-chains in the mountains. As the sun was bright I decided to go for it; besides, it would take me so long to get up to the high passes that the snow and ice should have thawed by then.

After my triumph of the previous day I was feeling a little complacent about the two smaller passes to come. The seven mile climb to the Molass Pass (10,910 feet) and the three miles up to Coal Bank Pass (10,640 feet) should be a jaunt, or so I thought. But as a punishment for my complacency, the ride up over the top of this winter wonderland was tough and though the views were fantastic, it was again far too cold to hang around (especially as I had become saturated, plunging into waist-deep snow when going for a pee) so, donning three pairs of gloves and balaclava, I began the long, freezing descent to Haviland Lake which Leo had recommended as a nice place to camp.

It was a good site; quiet and peaceful. Conifers grew around the banks and the short, soft grass made an ideal mattress. Across the lake long grasses were reflected in the smooth water. As I brewed my coffee I was surprised to hear the soft tones of Spanish guitar music drifting from the shore. Soon, a young Californian girl – all blond, tanned and disgustingly healthy looking – strolled over. She told me how she always liked to find beautiful places to practise her music in – only then could she feel inspired.

"It must be so wonderful doing what you're doing," she said dreamily. "You must really have *found* yourself. I would love to do something like that so I could really get to *know* myself."

As she was young, friendly and enthusiastic, I did not disillusion her by saying that I had never really lost myself in the first place. It is a commonly-held illusion that by going on long journeys alone a great introspection takes place, tremendous truths are made clear, the real self is exposed and a new perspective on the universe is gained. Well, it was nice to imagine that I was maturing into a female sage, but it was highly unlikely. I was more concerned with getting up the next hill than with becoming a Better Person.

The Californian Dreamer left and it was quiet.

That night was biting cold and, in spite of the addition of a warm sleeping-bag-liner *and* most of my clothes, I shivered through the dark hours, again cursing my failure to buy a warmer sleeping-bag. Nevertheless I felt satisfied. I had come over the Rockies – my biggest hurdle, or so I thought – and had not found them the overwhelming obstacle I had expected.

The following day, sitting outside a supermarket just before Durango, I felt a change in temperature. Now I had come over this great mountain range and down into the valley of Durango there was warmth in the sun once more and it felt good. On the way, nature had provided a roadside hot spring beneath which I washed hair, body and underwear and went on my way thankful for the unbidden bounties of this land.

At the supermarket I met Trev. He was a hobo who hung around Durango and its mountains. I wondered how he survived in the predominantly middle-class milieu of the region, but doubted whether he would care, or even notice, if he was ostracised.

Trev had become the recent proud owner of a bike, but the main source of his pride were the many torches which were strapped onto his bike wherever it was possible to attach one. They even had batteries in them, and he ran me through a commentary on each light, its purpose, power and limitation, although I doubted whether he used the bike much – day or night – and think it was just for carrying his gear. He had no home, but possessed seven blankets and a piece of polythene as a shelter. These were all stacked high on his bike. He boasted that only once had he ever got wet.

"I was sleeping in a cave. It was thirty below freezing, the ice thawed in a crevice above me and the water came down on me," he explained.

As well as changing the temperature at which ice melts he had also made a new speed record.

"I did seventy-five miles an hour once going downhill," he said.

My forty-three miles an hour record paled into insignificance; I must have shown some scepticism.

"Well, I did have a tailwind," he conceded.

Five miles beyond touristy Durango I found a beautiful, huge meadow slung between two hills; it sloped gracefully down to a tree-lined stream. I had a spectacular view over a vast expanse of grasses waving in the dying rays of the sun.

As I cycled the dragging seven mile hill out of the Durango valley, the rotting carcasses were more numerous than usual and now included dogs and cats. The stink was nauseating. A grotesquely bloated bull elk lay with feet sticking stiffly out in *rigor mortis*. And then I arrived at Mancos.

I immediately had a good feeling for this fantastic little town, especially as it had everything I needed to succour myself. I didn't want to camp wild that night; I wanted to be nurtured by all the friendly cosiness and comfort of which small-town America is capable. And Mancos certainly excelled in welcoming out-of-towners. It had a small park which not only actively encouraged camping, but did it for no charge. Benches and tables were provided, there were toilets, and even a suggestion box for comments.

I was aiming for Cortez, where I was going to stay with the friend of a friend back in England, and I needed to make contact. The woman in the hardware store offered me the use of the shop's phone and then gave me a free pot of coffee to take back to my tent. I bought a bag of chips at a take-away (tomatoes thrown in free) and sat at my table enjoying my luxuries and thinking nice thoughts about the people of the town.

Alvin came along. He was overweight and in his forties. Speaking quietly, he recounted a fantastically outrageous tale about a very rich English lord who used to raise sheep nearby. In his spare time he would prospect for some Spanish silver treasure which was supposedly buried thereabouts. Before he died, he told Alvin of this secret treasure, and he has been searching for it since then. He said he had been surviving (barely) for twenty-five years mining for silver and still lived in hope of hitting the Spanish jackpot. I loved these larger than life tales; American ones are so much more dramatic and exaggerated than our piddling little English ones.

Mancos also had the paranoia of most small American towns about drugs. 'This is a Drug-free Zone' signs stood outside the school to warn would-be pushers off their kids. Turn up at any one-horse town and the residents will assure you in grim tones: 'We have a serious drug problem!'

I never found whether these fears were real or assumed. Whether they were based on what residents *expected* to happen, or on actual evidence. Maybe one or two kids had been caught smoking marijuana. I found it difficult to imagine that these sleepy little towns were seething joints of crack and heroin consumption, dark figures pushing children into a life of ruin.

I suspect, though, that there is tremendous pressure on American teenagers to be unwaveringly wholesome and God-fearing and any deviation from this, rather than being seen just as normal teenage rebellion, is often seen a major problem which has to be *dealt* with, and it can easily become hugely exaggerated. As a consequence many of the young do not have the opportunity to be healthily obnoxious before getting it out of their systems and becoming 'normal'.

Mancos had other delights; a disgustingly expensive hat shop full of achingly desirable handmade cowboy hats, and across the road was Joe's workshop, where he made his wagons and carriages. He was in his thirties, heavily bearded, Stetson on his head. He told me that he was self-taught and made everything himself except the wheels – he employed an apprentice girl for that. His vehicles were used in Westerns and he was currently repairing a stagecoach that had been damaged during the making of a film. They were all exquisite pieces of craftsmanship.

Reluctantly I left this great community. I had passed through some lovely villages in Colorado, but Mancos I could have made my home – its unassuming friendliness; its un-prettified charm; its relaxed tolerance; its shops. Nothing fancy; just a nice place. I left a note in the suggestion box, thanking Mancos for being what it was, and at midday I got on my bike and rode away.

Mesa Verde

I hate tourist haunts; well, not the haunts themselves, just the tourists. (Me? A tourist?) They swarm around like noisy bees preventing you seeing what you came for. In spite of this, my next stop was a real tourist trap – Mesa Verde National Park – site of the abandoned 13th century cliff-dwellings of the Anasazi Indians, and part of the Ute reservation until it was taken from them in 1906. As my road to Cortez went past the entrance, I felt it somehow indecent not to exercise some historical curiosity and join the queues; I was glad I did.

It is a pity that the park does not put out a more welcoming hand to the humble cyclist or hiker, as the expenditure of energy and determination which I put into the visit almost sent me to join those long-deceased ancestors. The vacation industry in the States is so focused on the more profitable Recreational Vehicle (RV) that any encounter with low-tech travellers requiring small spaces closer to the sites of interest, low-tech facilities, and low-tech prices, sends it into apoplexy. Compromise is not an option. How can it possibly do anything so simple as adapt camping procedures and prices without a rule from on high?

At least there was a bike-reduction for actually getting into the park, so I paid my three dollars and went in. Being a National Park, wild camping was not permitted and the campsite was a couple of miles from the entrance with a fixed fee of eight dollars. I explained that I only had a bike and my tent took up as much space as a sleeping dog, so please could I pay less than the thirty-foot hotels-on-wheels (plus accompanying tents and vehicles) which surrounded me.

"No! It's eight dollars for everyone."

"Couldn't you give me a *bit* of a reduction?" I begged.

"Eight dollars it is, and eight it stays. Take it or leave it!"

Miserable old bugger! He couldn't even do me the decency of looking up from the book he was reading.

My high-minded principles (poverty) came into play:

"Okay then, I'll leave it!" As though he gave a toss.

I stormed off, furious and disappointed. Of course, this left me with a problem. You couldn't camp wild and it was thirty-eight miles to the ruins and back; plus another six-miles for the loop road around which the extensive ruins were located. The road was uphill and tiring, and the viewing alone would take hours.

Why couldn't they have just a small area for cyclists and hikers nearer to the ruins? There were already car-parks, cafés, tourist information centres and gift shops; a site for half-a-dozen tiny tents wouldn't make much difference. They should be encouraging non-polluting people like me; people, moreover, who are prepared to put a huge effort into seeing the country, and who should be appreciated. I could have given up, but now I had paid my entrance fee and I was damned if I was going to turn back.

The ruins were situated on the very top of a plateau, and in the caves of the sandstone gorges which criss-crossed it. This meant a steep climb upwards, and then following a road which wound up and down, and round and round, for ever; through a long black tunnel where you prayed that nothing else would come through while you were cycling invisibly in the dark. I was not going to make it so late in the day. Deciding that my impact on the environment would be zero if I camped off the road, I decided to flout the rules and find a hidden spot. As I rested by the road, a Ranger drew up and asked what I was doing.

"You're not going to make it, you know. The ruins close at five," he said.

This was another blow. I had thought you could just wander round at will, and time was not an issue.

I began to get the idea that somehow the culture and philosophy of the thirteenth-century Anasazi and that of the American leisure industry may not actually have a lot in common. There did not appear to be total synchronisation of ideals.

I tried to be reasonable. This was an era when The Tourist was so numerous that it had to be trained, guided, force-fed and organised so that it behaved according to the rules, without even being aware of it. After all, if everyone decided to stick their campers all over the place and tramp all over ancient ruins willy-nilly, then where would we be for heaven's sake? If it were not for such protection the holiday-home real-estaters would have got their hands on some of the most special real estate in the world. And that would have been that.

Well... yeah... okay... but... I was tiny, I was tired, and I was miffed. Sod it; as soon as the Ranger was gone, I would find a teeny-weeny spot for my teeny-weeny tent, and I would leave my bed exactly as I found it. It was their own fault for being so inconsiderate and bolshie to those of us who move at a slower pace.

But I hadn't yet learnt that a ranger is not to be played with.

"I'm too tired to go all the way back," I pleaded. "And I can't make it before dark."

Besides, I had no desire to be on these black, silent roads – and especially not in that tunnel – after dark. I had a definite sense that the spirits would be out and about, doing whatever spirits do. There's still debate over what happened to those mysterious Anasazi – one night on these roads and I might find out.

The ranger replied: "That's your problem; but you can't camp out here!"

"And if I do?" (Oh, silly silly question!)

"All the rangers know you're out here," he grumped, "and if we don't see you heading back tonight, then we'll get you on the road tomorrow, and you'll be in jail."

Well; that certainly told *me*. He was driving an empty pick-up; it was worth a try:

"Couldn't you put my bike in your car and give me a lift back?"

"No, I couldn't," he answered. "But there are some cyclists with a van on the road. If you see them, ask if they can take you back."

Meanie! I amused myself with mental replays of things he *would* have said if he'd had a touch of Edward Abbey in his soul:

'Yeah, honey, *sure* I'll give you a lift. It's tough on you cyclists I know, and I'm glad to be able to help. We need more people like you in the world. Jump in love.'

I got to the central tourist point ten minutes before it closed. I looked in the gift shop and bought a coffee. Then I spied them; the cyclists. They were an amazing family, travelling in a large, scruffy van and camping. There were ten of them altogether, including parents in their sixties, and various sons and daughters and their spouses. The grandchildren were a delightful wispy blonde hippie-girl of four, very aptly called Daisy; and a seriously physically and mentally handicapped older girl who had to be carried everywhere. I envied them their energy and happy companionship, few families can enjoy the pleasure of a communal hobby with such apparent enthusiasm.

I told them my problem. They held a conference on who wanted to cycle back, and with great difficulty my bike and gear was squeezed aboard.

We arrived at the campsite at twilight. I was cursing that I might as well have paid in the first place and had a relaxing day, now I had to do the same route again. Fortunately, Miserable Minnie had clocked off by then so I got in without paying.

As the dark settled a large black and white shape came sniffing round my tent. It was a skunk – absolutely fearless and totally unconcerned about my presence. But then, why should it be? Presumably, like myself, everyone got out of its way as quickly as possible and let it scavenge the larder to its heart's content. Anything to avoid startling it into stinky action. Not knowing the first thing about skunk camp-loafers, and whether they were more or less likely to deposit their perfume than a more backwoods one, I backed off quickly and quietly. It moseyed around a while and then took itself off into the darkness.

I rose in the dark at five, and with great difficulty breakfasted and packed by candlelight. At seven I left the still unmanned site. The disadvantage of such a furtive escape was that yet again I had to do the trip with a loaded bike. I considered hiding some luggage by the road but couldn't make up my mind what I might need, so I ended up keeping everything. I suppose it would have been easier to kill myself quickly, rather than struggle through the arduous day, but it was worth every gasp.

The ruins, the whole park in fact, exuded an all-enveloping peacefulness. Mule deer grazed among the low growing pinyon pine, the russet oak scrub and the scented juniper which covered the mesa tops and lined the gorges.

Although earlier, more primitive pit houses were built on the plateau tops at Mesa Verde, it is the cliff dwellings for which the Anasazi Indians are renowned. These incredibly intricate tenements were built in the twelfth and thirteenth centuries. Throughout the sandstone regions of the southwest natural erosion has gouged massive bow-shaped caves from the rock; smooth, elegant, sweeping structures of infinitely pleasing shape. It is in these formations that villages were built and communities lived, in perfect harmony of form and tone with all that is around them.

So large are the caves that some of them housed up to a thousand people living in room upon room behind room, all linked with a complicated system of steps and ladders, and totally invincible to invaders. Ladders and footholds gave residents access to the plateau top, whilst underground *kivas* were built for secret religious ceremonies.

The great mystery for years has been that after all the time and effort put into building their cave houses, the Anasazi only occupied them for between seventy and one hundred years. So sudden was their departure from Mesa Verde that the large and beautiful Sun Temple was abandoned only half-built. Drought has been the main suspect for driving the Indians out, and certainly there was drought at that time, but it was not only Mesa Verde which was abandoned – all cliff dwellings throughout the south-west were evacuated round about the same time. This has led some researchers to suspect invasion by outside tribes as the prime cause.

The strange thing is that the Anasazi did not move so far away. After leaving their homes some set up camp in New Mexico to become the Zuni and other Pueblo tribes. Others took over the barren mesa tops of Arizona where their descendants, the Hopi, still live. The transition from those soft sandstone canyon homes to the bleakness of Hopi land must have been a hard one – the kids certainly couldn't play hide and seek any more. I wondered if the oral history of today's descendants included a story of the great migration of the thirteenth century.

I liked this park. There is something very soothing about a juniper/pinyon pine/sandstone combination. The great rolls of sandstone which hide the tenements are stained black and purple from thousands of years of weathering and organic wash-down from the overlying vegetation. The great shadow cast by the cave roofs makes the sandstone dwellings very hard to see – more so as they are miniaturised by the distorting scale of the canyons. Even the largest and most well-known – Cliff Palace – looks like a model when viewed across the gorge.

As the sun shone down into these tranquil gorges, I think I got an inkling of what life must have been like here. Certainly the Anasazi had their problems of survival, but I felt they really had got it all just about right. I envied them their past. I envied them their life in this lovely place and, for reasons that may be hopelessly daft, Mesa Verde induced in me a wish to simplify my life when I returned home.

Indeed, simplicity was the word that stood out for me, which I took away with me. I was glad that I was able to meander away on my bike after my visit and watch the moon rise, and not immediately have to be confronted by mod. cons. and television. Now we must pay to come and see where the Anasazi lived, and not even my tiny nylon house could be allowed to pollute this holy shrine. I wonder what they would have thought about that. I like to think they would have made a place for me among the junipers; but maybe that is wishful thinking, maybe they'd just have moaned: 'those pesky cheap-skate cyclists – never spend any money and think they should be allowed to camp all over the darned place.'

The slog back was easier. Before the long final descent from the mesa top down to the plains of northern Arizona I sat and brewed a coffee. I looked far over the flat lands of the Ute and Navajo reservations. I could see Cortez ten miles away, looking as though it were at my feet. A car hooted and I turned to see the cycling family waving from their van as they left for the next stage of their journey. I was exhausted, but glad I had come to Mesa Verde. An hour later, I knocked on a white door in Montezuma West, Cortez, and was welcomed by Janie and her daughter, April.

HITCHHIKING DETOUR

Janie used to be a hippie, and it showed. Very thin, with long, dark, braided hair to her waist, she looked as if she had just stepped off the sixties Indian trail after eating carrots for six months. Like many ageing hippies, Janie was resourceful. For three years she had worked as a lawyer on the Ute Mountain Indian reservation adjacent to Cortez, and when I visited she was struggling to make a living as a writer of children's stories. She had an adopted Ute daughter named April, who was a bright, golden-skinned child of nine.

As soon as I stopped at Janie's I developed the most ravenous appetite, and spent an inordinate amount of time at the shopping mall trying and failing to resist roast chicken wings and Danish pastries.

In between chicken and cake I went to a 'Sweat'. This is a purifying American Indian ceremony performed in a lodge where, not surprisingly, you sweat. Traditionally a sweat lodge would have been made of branches bent to form an igloo shape and covered with buffalo hides, but nowadays anything available will suffice – polythene sheeting, mats, canvas – anything which ensures pitch blackness inside. Large stones are heated on a fire outside the lodge and when they are red hot they are brought in two or three at a time, and periodically cold water is thrown on them, sending great gushes of scalding steam into the darkness. When it becomes unbearable the entrance is thrown open and everyone goes out to cool down before the next session begins.

There were eight of us present: our host, his wife and daughter, Janie, April and myself, and two young Ute men who were students of our host at the local college. He was not Indian and I was astounded that he should feel comfortable hosting a sweat where native people were present.

I believe anyone is free to borrow from the religion of another culture but I do not believe that a totemistic one such as that of the American Indian can ever have the same value or meaning to a person brought up in a totally different religion and culture. The religion of the Indian is far older than Christianity, having developed over thousands of years, and though middle-class whites may like the *idea* of playing Indians, I fear they are merely chasing chimeras and daydreams. I don't think it is possible to absorb such a massive and ancient inheritance into their own lives, however much they may desire it. Even many modern Indians have problems with that!

This isn't to say that someone should be criticised for participating in a sweat simply because it makes them feel good – either internally or externally; it's the taking on of all the religious paraphernalia which is so dodgy. Dancing around fires and hollering is fine so long as you have created your own spirits to shout to, and don't pretend to have 'become' Indian, or to have tapped into the essence of whichever tribe turns you on.

Before the ceremony an altar was set up near the lodge and various rituals involving eagle feathers and tobacco took place. (Tobacco is a purifying herb in American Indian religion.)

I don't know what prayers normally take place in sweats, but I had imagined there would be a glorifying of Mother Earth. Maybe it used to be, and maybe it still is. This one was more like a group therapy session.

Inside the lodge our host did most of the talking – about what a load of crap his life was, what a bastard he had been and how he was trying to be a better person. (His wife stayed silent!) One of the students asked for help on a trip he was about to take, whilst the other talked about what a load of crap his life was, what a bastard he had been and how he was trying to be a better person.

Having said all that, and in spite of the gulf between white and native cultures, and the fact that I approached it as an *experience* rather than as an attempt to *get into* Indian culture, I must confess the sweat was a very moving experience. The heat, the thick blackness and the voices became part of a living semi-solid thing. Neither one's own body nor anyone else's could be seen, and the voices existed as disembodied sounds growing out from the black heat. Although we were all in such intimate closeness, at the same time it was very anonymous. Voices without faces, heat you could touch, blackness like a blanket, all enclosing you in this space that had become the universe.

So in the end I was very pleased that I had experienced it and surprised that even though I have no religion (unless you can count what Edward Abbey described as 'earthism') it had been a sort of spiritual experience for me. But I would not try to pretend that it had anything to do with Indians!

The Rough Guide to the USA says that you should never, ever, ever, *ever* hitchhike in North America; basically hitching counts as a suicide attempt. I did not read that until I returned or I might have had second thoughts. As usual, I was jumping in at the deep end and choosing to deal with things as they arose; besides, I was feeling so confident in my invulnerability that I was sure I could survive anything. How silly is that?!

I had made the decision to visit Stan, my Salish Indian friend from the Colville Reservation back in Washington and also to visit Sue in Okanogan, in whose garden I had camped. Conveniently, Stan and Sue lived around the corner from one another.

Leaving my bike and gear at Janie's, I took only a fleecy sleeping bag liner and a few extra clothes for the trip. Janie took me to the truck stop on the edge of town and had a coffee with me to give me a little moral support. Even though I hadn't read the *Rough Guide's* advice, I was nervous as hell. After an hour I was on my own, and I stood in the car park outside. Soon, a truck pulled into the stop and Dave leaned out his cab window.

"Where ya'll heading?" he called.

"Washington State," I answered.

"Well, you'll never get a lift here. You'd be better going down to Albuquerque."

"But that's in completely the opposite direction."

"Yeah, but there's a real big truck stop there. Drivers go out everywhere from there. If you wait half an hour, you can come with me."

Half an hour later I jumped into Dave's cab.

Five minutes later I had my doubts about both his mental stability and his ability to keep calm in a crisis. At the slightest irritation or amusement his voice rose quickly to hysteria pitch as he became gripped by excitement. He handed me the map.

"You be navigator," he instructed me.

Now, I don't think that geography could have been Dave's best subject at school. Or maybe it was, which was why he liked to choose the complicated scenic routes instead of the straightforward interstates – he seemed to have it in his head that the best way to get from A to B was to find the longest, squiggliest and most hazardous route possible. Throw in a mountain pass and a snow blizzard and you get the picture. Unfortunately neither his driving skills nor his nerve were up to this, and there was no way he was going to get rich driving the highways of America unless he underwent a fundamental change of character.

"Which way are you going?" I asked. He explained.

"What?" I gasped.

Not only would his choice of route add more than a hundred miles onto our journey, it would also take us on small bendy roads back up into the San Juan Mountains and over Wolf Creek Pass. I could see this was going to be a long trip.

"But why don't you head straight down to Gallup, then east on Interstate 66?"

I reckoned that to be about a hundred miles on flat, wide, straight and empty roads across the Navajo reservation to Gallup, and then another hundred to Albuquerque.

"Ner. This is the best way." He replied confidently.

It suited me fine, anything for a nice view. I assumed he must know what he was doing. So, back east through Mancos and Durango again, following the southern flank of the San Juan's until we turned to climb in the direction of Wolf Creek Pass.

Huge, soft flakes of snow began to fall gently to earth. Dave began to get excited.

"Hey! What the fuck's *this?* It *can't* be snow!"

"I think it is, Dave."

"Oh, Jesus *Christ!* Oh *God!*"

"Maybe it won't do much."

"Jesus! What if it gets worse? I haven't got my snow chains with

me. Oh *God!*"

The miles crept slowly by. The hills began to rise more steeply into the mountains; the snow began to look like real Christmas card stuff. The expletives got more panicky, the voice rose still higher.

"Oh *shit!* Why didn't I pack my snow chains? Oh God, what the *fuck* am I going to do? Ask somebody! You've gotta ask somebody what it's like. Get out and ask somebody what it's like further up! Ask if the snow ploughs are out on the pass!"

He stopped at a roadside café and almost pushed me out the cab in search of coffee and information. I passed on what I was told.

"They don't know for sure. They said the workmen were in earlier and were talking about sending ploughs out, but they don't know if they've gone."

I wasn't sure if Dave *wanted* the snowploughs to be out so that the road would be clear for him, or whether the fact that they were out would be an indication that it was too bad to go further up the mountain.

"Oh, *Jesus!* What shall I do? What d'ya reckon? Heh? What d'ya think?"

He was nearly apoplectic. I resisted the temptation to tell him that he was a total dickhead for coming this way in the first place, and why ask me for Christ's sake – he was the bloody driver – what the hell did I know about articulated trucks, snow chains and mountain passes in the Rockies in November. But the poor guy was nearly freaking out with worry and indecision and I felt sorry for him.

"If I was driving I'd go back," I answered. "You've got to deliver your stuff, you've no chains, you don't know how bad it is up there. It's not worth the time or the risk."

Half a mile further on we came to a local authority yard.

"Go and find someone. Ask what's happening on the pass."

I jumped out and went in search of a workman. I gave Dave the news.

"The ploughs are out clearing Wolf Creek Pass now."

"*That's* it! *That's* it! We're going back! *We're going back!* I'm not going up there, *no way! No way!*" he shouted.

And so we went all the way back. Twelve hours after leaving Cortez we passed back through it again.

"We'll go down to Gallup," Dave said, "and then east on the 66. I reckon that's the best, don't you?"

"Er... yes, Dave... I guess it is."

Sometimes it is hard to resist saying 'I *told* you so.'

Everything was calm until we got to Shiprock, on the Navajo Reservation.

"Which way do we go now?"

"Just straight on."

"There's another turning," said Dave, his voice starting to rise.

"It's *OK*. We just head straight through on the same road."

"No. We have to turn somewhere," insisted Dave.

"No!" I answered. "We just go straight ahead. There's only one road, for Christ's sake!"

The road took us down the eastern side of the Navajo Reservation – a vast, flat expanse of sagebrush desert with only an occasional bluff interrupting the skyline. Straight as a die it ran, on and on. There were no turn-offs, so at least that was one less worry for Dave, but the snow had made an impression that was slow to fade. We passed some scattered white powdery deposits by the side of the road.

"What's that?" he asked.

"What?" I answered innocently, knowing full well what was going through his mind.

"That *white* stuff!"

"It's just salt."

"My God; it's fuckin' *snow* again!" he yelled.

"Of course it's not. It's just salt."

"*Salt!*" his voice was going off the radar again. "*What do you mean – salt?* 'Course it's not salt! How could it be *salt*, for Christ's sake? It's fuckin' *snow.*"

"Of course it's not snow," I yelled back at him. "How could it be *snow*, for Christ's sake?"

This could have gone on forever.

"All right then. Stop the truck. Let's go and see!"

Dave jammed the brakes on and we did as quick an emergency stop as a yorkie truck is capable of. We jumped out and sprinted back to the 'white stuff'. I put my finger in it and tasted. Salt! This time I really *was* going to say 'I told you so.'

But I didn't get the chance. My disgusting roadside habits had driven everything else from his brain. Our diverging views were forgotten. His attention was now on my personal habits.

"*Ugh!* You *licked* it! Eurghh! You licked *dirt!*"

He was nearly freaking out over this sign of my complete degeneracy.

"Of *course* it's not dirt! It's *salt!* And how *else* could we know what it was if somebody didn't lick it?" I defended myself.

"*Eurghh!* It's *dirt*. You licked *dirt!* That's *disgusting!*"

Dave really was a total and absolute dickhead, but it was impossible not to like him. He made no attempt to fake a cool, truckie image.

"You don't seem to like your job very much." I tentatively suggested.

"I *hate* it!" he said with emotion. "I really hate it! That's why I'm outa here next week. Ten more days and I'm finally outta this shit. I just want a job in a factory so I can go home every night. I want a girlfriend – I'll never get one while I'm in this job. I hate being away so much on my own. If I get a job at home, then I can get a proper girlfriend and settle down."

My heart warmed to him. I sincerely hope that he has found a really lovely, homely girl who can manage to keep him calm, content and secure.

Eventually, sometime in the middle of the night, we finally got to Albuquerque. Dave tried to get me a lift but no one was heading my way. He went to his cab to sleep and I sat around watching television. After a while, two men approached me.

"Where're ya'll heading?" they asked.

"Washington State."

"Well, we can drop you off in Salt Lake City."

"Perfect!" I said.

"Then let's go."

I rushed out to say goodbye to Dave but he was asleep, so I left him to his hopefully peaceful and homely dreams and climbed into Al and Ed's truck.

They were Texans. Al was young, blond, innocent and not too bright, but even though I had real problems understanding his slow

Texan drawl, he seemed a nice enough bloke. Ed was a different kettle of fish; in his forties, tight-lipped and mean-eyed, he had a Gene Hackman look about him.

In getting into the truck with two strange men, some would say that I was not merely reckless, I was just plain downright stupid, and the thought of any daughter of mine doing such a thing would fill me with horror. After all, if you want to raise your chances of dying in your own bed, there are certain guidelines which it is wise to follow. These include:

1. Don't hitchhike.
2. Don't hitchhike if you're female.
3. Don't hitchhike if you're alone.
4. Don't hitchhike in the USA.
5. Don't get in with a man (if you're female, alone or in the USA).
6. Don't get in with two men (if you're of either sex, alone and anywhere).

So, as a lone female hitching a lift with two guys in the USA, I suppose it's amazing that I am not now floating around on some cloud reserved for the brain dead.

Generally it is by far safer to stick to large trucks with enormous letters of the driver's employer emblazoned on the side. This is not to say that drivers will not try it on, but hopefully they will also be glad of a bit of company and not get too pushy because they could be so easily identified.

Al and Ed took a right turn at Gallup, so for the *third time in twenty-four hours*, I found myself passing once more through Cortez. *Déjà vu* can get a bit tiresome after a while. I began to feel I was strapped onto a carousel which was taking me on endless Albuquerque/Cortez re-runs, through never ending horizons of sagebrush plains.

With hindsight I think it was fate giving me a chance to change my mind – perhaps it knew more about what lay ahead than I did. I always believe that if you are held back from doing something three times then you shouldn't do it; something invariably goes wrong.

As dawn broke we were passing through the stark desert country of Moab, lying between the maze of Canyonlands and Arches National

Park, where Edward Abbey had spent his early summers as a ranger. This is the desert at its most ruthless, where – on a blistering July day – a lost track, a forgotten water bottle or a sprained ankle can mean the end to more than just a summer holiday.

While the early morning light rose over those unforgiving rocks, Ed managed to move his talk round to Sex and the American Woman. After each of his driving breaks he warmed ever more to his theme and I found his reduction of the whole of American womanhood to lustful, craving, sex-obsessed nymphomaniacs increasingly offensive. I think it was wishful thinking on his part! Unfortunately I knew where all this was heading and I could quite see that Ed was not a man to take rejection lightly. At least if I was ejected onto the side of the road it was still early morning.

Luckily for me, Fate decided to be easy on me; at a roadside café Ed returned from a phone call to his boss bad-tempered and cursing.

"*Fuck!* We've got to pick up another load in Salt Lake and head straight out."

As his plans had now been thwarted so his mood changed and thankfully he stopped talking to me. I was deposited in unceremonious silence in the parking lot of a large Salt Lake truck stop. Thanks Ed!

The drivers I found in the lot were a sullen, unfriendly bunch, so I went out to the nearby interstate and waited; and waited. Only a smarmy local schoolteacher kept stopping to ask repeatedly if I wanted to go along the road a few miles.

So I waited some more. These southern drivers were clearly not in need of company. Besides, a rather large proportion of them looked like some of the old grey matter had dribbled out; I was waiting for the kindly gentlemen of the highways, not the blobs.

It was getting late and cold, and I began to worry about where I could spend the night without freezing to death. Suddenly, a giant, shiny, brand new truck applied its brakes with great gasps of air and glided to a halt a hundred yards ahead of me. Its chrome gleamed and its paint work shone. I was so desperate for a lift that I couldn't afford to be too choosy – I just had to get in with anyone but an obvious axe murderer. I climbed in. I shut the door. When I looked up my heart sank; 'Oh god. What have I done?'

Alan was a brutish-looking, ugly devil; a prematurely lined and aged man in his late thirties. He was an all-over ash grey from his life behind glass – dull, ash-blond hair, drab white-grey skin, pale eyes. He didn't say a word to me, but picked up his radio and started bellowing into it.

"Sidewinder, Sidewinder. Are you there, Sidewinder? I got me a ride, I got me a ride. Are you hearing me, Sidewinder?"

No one answered.

This went on for thirty minutes, during which time he gave me neither word nor glance; I really thought I had got myself a lift with Neanderthal man. At last, contact was made with Sidewinder, from when on the topic was sex. It was time to start thinking and planning for the night ahead. I made sure my door was unlocked, my pepper spray was in my hand and my knife in my belt. I checked that essentials such as money and passport were with me in case I had to make a quick exit, and I planned my escape strategy in the event of things getting tough. I then felt more confident in my ability to extricate myself from a difficult situation and relaxed a little.

After one and a half hours Alan turned to me and spoke; he asked me my name and what I was doing. Then we stopped at a truck stop and met up with Sidewinder who, to my relief, turned out to be as straight as they come – the sort of man who would stop his kid's pocket money for kicking the cat. What was more, he was driving as a team with his new bride, Julie, who was a huge obese woman in her early thirties. She was also huge in personality – outgoing, generous, friendly – and I liked her tremendously. I knew now that I had nothing to fear from Alan when he had such a nice convoy, and felt a little guilty for labelling him a brute when really he was a good guy. He did not even look so ugly now that I knew he was okay – I even decided that he could have been quite dishy before his premature ageing. He changed my piece of pie for a dinner of chicken and hash browns, saying; "I think you need it." And when, later, I declined to share his bunk, he simply said, "Shit!" and climbed into his bed with a "Goodnight. Sleep well."

I enjoyed the two days I spent travelling in Alan's cab. I enjoyed his cabbie stories and listening to him talk about the woman he always went to see when he was in Seattle. I even enjoyed listening to the terrible CB conversations between himself, Julie and Sidewinder. These were all based on the theme of 'My truck's better than yours,' and seemed to provide endless entertainment. I suppose you're hardly likely to practise for Mastermind as you eat up the miles, but I think that after a few weeks of CB speak I would be doubting my position at the top of the evolutionary tree.

I loved sitting secure in my cab, knowing I was safe for a while and getting on my way, watching the great, rolling, grassy folds of Oregon's hills open themselves up to me. Long slow hauls up to the top of seductively rounded summits, and then infinitely slow rides down into the valleys; as the loaded truck shifted into low gear the great rasps of air brakes thrilled me in some unidentifiable, elemental way that I chose not to analyze.

Alan took me all the ways to Ellensburg, Washington. He said he would ring me in ten days to see if I wanted a return lift. Sadly I got out my cab, once more at the mercy of the road. It was getting late and from now on I would be on small back road. Soon, an old Indian woman picked me up and drove me a few miles, dropping me in the dark at the quiet junction which led to her home. A young Mexican migrant boy of nineteen, without a word of English but with the profile of Montezuma took me to the rabbit box provided to migrant workers and let me sleep on a mattress on the floor. The next day a man in a pickup enlightened me on the attitude of many whites towards the migrants:

"Mexicans work hard, they're friendly and honest. But to most whites, they're shit."

Finally, a very flash Mexican – all in black, silver studs and shades, took me to the junction which led into Okanogan. I had arrived. Three and a half days and I was knackered, but very pleased with myself. I felt as though I had achieved great things!

If the visit to my friends in Okanogan had gone well, I might have considered spending a longer time there, but it was a total and unmitigated disaster which sent me scuttling back to the highway after eight days screaming; 'Let me out of here.'

Quite simply, both Stan and Sue had some kind of dark obsessions that I couldn't, and didn't want to, fathom. Sue was a real Jekyll and Hyde, whose girly friendliness was simply the veneer to her bossy, domineering, ranting and ruthless personality. Her grown son made the understatement of the year when he said, 'Yes, she is a bit extreme sometimes.'

Stan's charm meanwhile, lasted only as long as the beer in his veins, and I soon learnt that when this had gone down the toilet he was a very unpleasant person who took himself and his delusions very seriously.

Deciding that my sanity and a healthy attitude to life were dependent on getting out of town, I picked up my bag and headed back to the highway.

With friends like those, who needs enemies?

While I had been experiencing the subtle joys of Okanogan the clocks had gone back an hour, snow had fallen and the nights were icy cold. It was even more imperative to get lifts that would carry me through the night or I would be in serious trouble. Finally, after two days and several lifts I was deposited at midnight on the doorstep of the du Beau hostel in Flagstaff, Arizona, by Roger, a water engineer who had driven a hundred miles out of his way to get me there.

Flagstaff. I liked its name and thought I would stay a little so I asked about the possibility of work at the hostel.

"Three hours work a day. Free bed and breakfast. Start immediately." I did.

It was November, and one day the snow descended on Arizona in a fantastic snow blizzard which transformed the whole of southern Arizona into a primordial wasteland, (I know because I got stuck in it whilst hiring a car for a day); the streets became muffled and silent. I cursed myself for leaving my return to Cortez so late, and worried about having to cross the state in this weather.

Luckily I found a shop selling thick fleece on the roll and gortexy stuff, which would ease my entry back into Arctic conditions. Only one problem – money.

Then I discovered that by claiming to be resident (with the help of the hostel manager) I could sell my blood at a private clinic in town. Twenty-five dollars for the first two sessions, less for subsequent ones; blood could be donated every four days. I earned eighty dollars and made myself some wonderful warm goodies for the next leg of my trip.

I enjoyed my time in Flagstaff, especially under its snowy winter coat, and felt at home there. I had enjoyed wandering the slushy streets, visiting the thrift shop, the bars and Navajo jewellery shops. I had hung around the hostel, overdosed on videos, made good friends with longer term hostel residents, and enjoyed talking to passing travellers – saddened that, even though Flagstaff was an ideal base for exploring the southwest, few took the opportunity and would return home ignorant of the wonders they had missed.

The snow finally cleared and it was time to leave. From my two trips to the phenomenal Grand Canyon (go before you die!!) I had a bit of sandstone from which I had carved a figure, and some juniper, whose faded smell still evokes memories of those sandy south-west canyons.

Going to stand by Route 66, I once more stuck my thumb out, excited about the coming reunion with my bike. At midnight I was dropped right outside Janie and April's front door. Boy, it was good to be back!

BACK TO THE SADDLE

At last, under the glory of the blue, blue sky of a cold December day, I climbed astride my neglected faithful Dawes, waved goodbye to Janie and April, and set off once more. Ahead of me, I had the exciting challenge of a winter crossing of the huge red-blue-grey beauty of the Navajo and Hopi Reservations.

I entered the Ute Mountain Indian Reservation just south of Cortez and immediately plunged into a world so different to that just north of the town that they could have been a thousand miles apart. North is rolling green hills, leading to snow covered peaks; south is a desert leading to the middle of forever. Ahead lay millions of acres of almost empty land; a land which, except for the one-time visit of the curious tourist, whites shun. (In one month of crossing it on my bike, I only saw two whites, young Mormon men.)

After five weeks of sharing cabs, caravans, cabins and cars, my aloneness embraced me like an old friend. I felt ecstatic. I sang loudly as I rode along the deserted road, once again in my element and free to follow my own inclinations.

Where everything lay so open and exposed, a secret camping spot was not easy to find and I knew that camping on Navajo lands was forbidden. I wasn't keen to blatantly break tribal rules. Just as I was about to cross the reservation border, the San Juan River peered up and invited me to sleep by its willow-covered banks. At nine o'clock, a full moon rose to greet me, as though it had been saving its fullness just for my homecoming. I welcomed it, breathed in the freshness of the crisp, sharp night air, and listened to the glowing starry night – no voices, no traffic – only Mother Earth letting me know that she was close by.

But although the heavens above were blue and beguiling, the

reservation proved a harsh mistress. The nights were the coldest yet, and as there was nothing to break the wind for hundreds of miles, it blew continuously day after day. More infuriatingly, whichever direction I turned in, it stayed head on. Where the roads were long, straight and flat, the miles dragged by, every pedal an effort, my speedometer frequently stuck on ten miles an hour.

The reservation had another trick up its sleeve – hidden dips, which rapidly became the bane of my life. You can't see them until you are already on their rim, they just lurk, and in your innocence you look across what you assume to be fifty miles of tabletop flatness. Oh, easy cycling, you smugly sigh. What you soon find out is that between here and there are ten thousand symmetrical descents and ascents. Down and up, down and up. They are not even proper hills that you can whinge or whine about, and anyone who has driven across this part of Arizona will now be saying, 'Hills? What hills?'

In spite of all my moaning, I was captivated by this bluff-studded land of sage and sheep. The Rockies may be staggering in their beauty, and the grandeur of their scale; the contrasting of colours and shapes may leave you gaping. But in Arizona it is the vast openness and long horizons – a feeling that nothing has changed here in thousands of years.

Traditionally, the Navajo lived isolated lives. While the Hopi lived communally, as their Anazasi ancestors had before them, the Navajo lived separated from each other in their cosy, single-roomed, five-sided log hogans. This way still continues, and though concrete has largely replaced logs, the hogans are still five-sided, their doorways still face the sun rising in the east, and they are still scattered in single isolation around the reservation. Sadly, but inevitably, the modern villages, and what I took to be boarding schools, do not maintain the round tradition. They were ugly blots on the land, looking like nothing less than army barracks, or detention centres. It is ironic that accumulations of people can produce feelings of loneliness far greater than any place devoid of humanity. With the brutal intrusion of such alien ugliness, the desert then drops its soft veneer and takes on a more depressing and unforgiving aspect.

But I have no doubt that to the young Navajo, the villages were places of excitement where they could act out the television fantasies of the culture around them. There really was no need for the genocide of the last centuries – the cultural imperialism of television and Coca Cola is now achieving all that the gun and the Bible spent five hundred years struggling, and failing, to do. Young Native Americans everywhere are clamouring to be part of twentieth-century America.

Camping was a problem. I was shocked and disappointed to find barbed wire stretched unendingly along the road. I was forced to camp on the wide verges, trying to hide behind junipers – not a brilliant spot but made up for by a spectacular night sky. In these dry southern states the low humidity causes the stars to glimmer and glitter like a billion packs of sparklers.

The temperatures were getting more severe. At six o'clock one evening I knocked my bottle of water over. The red hot cooker was blazing twelve inches away, and a candle six inches away, but the water did not even run – it just froze instantly. My radio told me that night time temperatures had fallen to 15 degrees F (minus 10 C).

The next day, coming down a slope, I came upon a place so atmospheric that I had to stop. The remarkable vibes of sites like this have little to do with outstanding beauty, and much to do with the coincidental harmonious interaction of physical features combined, I believe, with whatever has gone before in that place. It was as though the experiences that had taken place there had been absorbed into the very rocks and earth.

If one subscribes to a belief in what can loosely be described as earth spirits, then places like this have them whizzing around in such numbers that you cannot avoid being bashed around by them. After all, what did this insignificant nook have that was outstanding? Rounded mesas of bright red surrounding lawn-flat areas of sage, and that was it. I also believe that travelling alone has the potential to sensitize us to whatever is around, and enable us to hear the silence which is normally drowned out by modern conveniences or the chatter of voices.

Even the tumbleweed seemed possessed. On this breezeless day I watched as one danced back and forth to its own rhythm, five seconds one way, pause, five the other. When I was ten metres away it stopped motionless, only resuming again when I had passed by.

I absorbed whatever it was that was going on there, feeling absolutely that this was, or had been, an important place for the Navajo. Before I left, a pick-up stopped and a man stepped out. In the cab sat an old wrinkled couple.

"I thought you might like a lift," he said with lowered eyes.

I always feel ungracious refusing lifts from sympathetic souls.

"Thanks, but I'm okay at the moment."

"Only I think it might snow soon," he said, still, disconcertingly, avoiding my eyes.

I looked up at the clear blue sky, trying not to show scepticism on my face. As I did, I remembered that traditionally Navajo do not make eye contact. It is considered rude and invasive, although many people do not follow this custom so much now. I did not know the rules about who you could, and who you could not, look directly at, but clearly I was included in the 'not looks'.

It is funny how the same customs can develop for opposite reasons. In the white west, it is rude *not* to make eye contact – only the shifty and untrustworthy avoid looking directly at you. (I remembered my Maori friend telling me of his experiences teaching English in the Philippines. The children were taught by their parents that it was rude to look an adult in the eye, so naturally, wanting to be polite to their white teachers, they would stand before them with lowered eyes. Teachers ignorant of local customs would then berate the children, 'Look at me when I'm talking to you.')

The lack of forceful exchange is continued in the gentle handshake. I doubted whether this was part of Navajo culture anyway, but they had certainly not adopted the white custom of the firm handshake, which to us denotes trustworthiness. The Navajo shake is just the barest touch of the fingers. With great difficulty, I now kept my own eyes averted. I tried not to seem ungrateful.

"If it snows, I'm going to wish I'd taken a lift with you."

"I live over by Kayenta. You could cycle over to Monument Valley from there. It's really nice."

"I know, I've already been there. It's beautiful."

"Well you take care now," he said, and drove off.

So far, I had found the people on the reservation very friendly. Twice more that day I was offered lifts whilst resting, on the chance that I had a problem. Pick-up trucks were usually full of children and they passed me by with waving hands and smiling faces. In villages, people would often come and talk to me. I was convinced this was because I was alone, (and maybe being female helped) and therefore more approachable. Even *I* found tourists in pairs or groups intimidating and often too involved with each other to be interested in communicating with those around them.

I was excited to find that Navajo, not English, is still the first, and the everyday, language on the reservation. (Among northern tribes, it is often only the old who still know their own language, although some tribes now teach it as a second language in schools, or as a vocation course in college.) It was thrilling to sit in a cafe in the heart of America and hear the sound of this ancient language being spoken, knowing that a thousand years ago the same words may have been used. I was told that during the Second World War Navajo was used as a code as it was the only language which was indecipherable to the Japanese.

The Navajo and Hopi have been on these lands (with hiccups caused by you-know-who) for hundreds of years. In fact, the thousand-year-old, mesa-top Hopi village of Oraibi is supposedly the longest continuously inhabited town in America. The whole of northern Arizona is soaked with their history, and it is the light presence of the native people which softens the desert's harsh edges and gives it a more benign feel. I tried to imagine the reservation as white ranch land with a thin scattering of huge ranches sitting in the place of the hogans. I felt sure that under white control the desert would lose much of its powerful and unique beauty, though I was not sure that my reasoning was founded on any rational base. How can I say that the soul would seep out of it and expect to be taken seriously?

It was a pity that the elements did not look upon me as kindly as the people or the spirits. The last sixteen miles into Round Rock nearly finished me. As the sun sank behind the rocks, I fought against the buffeting wind, cursing as only a cyclist with a head wind can curse. Only a personal feud with my bike left me with enough pride to keep me pedalling instead of walking; usually we worked in harmony, but at times like this I thought she could make a bit more effort to help me along, especially as it would very soon be dark. Eventually, after an infinity, I came to the village and nearly fell on my knees before two women in the village store. The village had a bridge with a trickle of water running under it which I thought looked a good spot to pitch camp.

"Oh, no," said the women. "It's too dangerous there. The local kids go down there at night. But there's another place further along the wash in the bushes where you should be safe."

I was to come across this spectre of murderous local youth many times on my journey, usually in villages and small towns. As with the image of the supposedly drink and drug sodden youth of small-town America, I had no way of knowing whether it was true. Out of politeness, and because I had no wish to have gangs of teenagers, harmless or otherwise, watching my every movement and keeping me awake with their noise, I hauled my bike through the darkness and the bushes and found a cosy spot, where I could sleep instead to the sound of horses munching.

Since leaving Cortez, the sub zero nights had forced me to develop an efficient cold-weather strategy. This was vital, as once the sun slipped over the horizon the temperatures plummeted rapidly. There was no longer any of the leisurely unpacking and cups of coffee before getting everything organised. Darkness came early, so by four o'clock everything had to be in order. Step one was a rapid five minute tent erection. Step two was a quick, methodical and thorough collection of sufficient dead wood to last me for several hours. This was arranged in four piles according to size. Then came the most important part of the routine. I rapidly removed my trousers and replaced them by the marvellous polar-plus trousers and socks which I had made with my Flagstaff blood money. Polar-plus vest went on top of existing vest, long-sleeved thermal and T-shirt, and underneath a down waistcoat, Shetland wool jumper, fleece jumper, windproof cycling jacket and sympatex waterproof jacket. Balaclava and scarf were added.

By this time I could hardly move, but once the fire was lit at least I was warm. Due to my inadequate sleeping bag I had to sleep with most of this gear on, and as I also had a sleeping-bag liner and a home-made waterproof liner, the struggle to get in was mammoth, and was certainly my least favourite chore. Having a down bag didn't help either, as in the cold conditions my body heat condensed onto its surface which then penetrated inside and dampened the feathers, thereby reducing their effectiveness.

I was unable to do any serious washing or clothes changes during this icy month; washes were brief, soapless, utility affairs, and underwear, T-shirt and thermals never left my body – day or night. In spite of this, I was odourless (I think) for as soon as any hopeful, nasty bacteria decided to turn me into a dung heap, they were zapped to oblivion by the cold. (Years ago, I read about how clean and odourless Eskimos were in their igloo days, and presumably it's for the same reason. Maybe they are as smelly as the rest of us now that they too have their square boxes and central heating.)

As soon as my Arctic layers were on, I immediately set about lighting my fire.With everything so dry, this was an easy job, and there was usually plenty burnable material around. Sage burnt well but too quickly, so it was good starting material. Juniper burnt hot and long and gave out a lovely aroma; the only problem being that it would spit everywhere, so that everything quickly became covered in burn holes.

Only when the fire was well on the go did I relax. I would then sit in my sleeping bag, prepare my food, and have a coffee. After eating, I would write my diary, before spending the remainder of the evening gazing hypnotically into the fire and watching shadows leaping around me in the surrounding vegetation. In order to see the night sky more clearly, I would make several excursions into the blackness around me. As the fire died, I would retreat into my tent, light my candle, and read a lightweight book; finished pages would be used to light the next day's fire.

In contrast to my tiny tent, chosen solely for its lightness, Justin used a much larger igloo tent in which he could stand up. I thought it was crazy lugging such a weighty thing around until I spent a couple of days with him in Death Valley when we met up for the New Year. Whilst my nights revolved totally around avoiding freezing to death, Justin simply retreated into his tent, lit his cooker and enjoyed a cosy evening indoors. Similarly in the mornings, he just switched his cooker on and stayed toasty inside.

I told myself that at least I was more in contact with my environment. I saw the skies, and had wonderful fires, and long hours of quiet meditation looking into the flames. But at times I seriously wondered whether sometimes it was worth sacrificing light gear for comfort, and, although my routine quickly became second-nature, the effort of keeping warm did use a great deal of mental and physical energy.

The camp at Round Rock was good. I always enjoy camping by washes when there is no flash-flood danger. At seven o'clock I wrote in my diary:

'The moon will be up late tonight. Trees illuminated by my fire. Already my water bottle is frozen solid but I am warm, warm, warm with my fire blazing. If the fire would stay in all night, perfection would be achieved.'

And it did! And it was! And I can think of no other time in my life, living in a house, when such a small simple thing could make life perfect.

CANYON DE CHELLEY

The ride to Chinle was easy. For once there was no headwind and no unending procession of dips and rises. Most of the day was spent circling a large red mesa which was probably how Round Rock got its name, not from its shape, but because you had to go round it to get anywhere. But it was mostly memorable for the roadside carnage of dead dogs, killed by reckless drivers. One day, on my side of the road alone, I counted four, the saddest sight being that of a lovely, large, beige dog which lay motionless under a bush a few feet from the road. Its dead mate lay nearby. As I passed by, it gazed at me so mournfully that it was hard to resist the temptation to go and comfort it.

I had no fear of these good-natured reservation dogs, but I knew it could be disastrous to make contact with them. Dogs in the Third World – in which I include the Indian Reservations of America – are not like their English counterparts. For one thing, they are often hungrier, and because of this, they have become experts in the art of survival, pragmatists able to identify the potential in a situation and exploiting it according to their needs – this necessitates a good understanding of the human mind. Incredibly they know that a tourist is a soft touch and can pick one out at a glance; you only have to cast a sympathetic look on a hopeful hound and you will have a loyal and steadfast servant, one which will follow you to the ends of the earth in the belief that one day you may toss it a morsel. I have had many experiences with these sad mutts around the world, and have learnt my lesson well. Some of them still come back to haunt me.

So I arrived in Chinle. There may be something nice about this town, but I couldn't tell you what it was. Several men in various stages of inebriation were lolling outside the supermarket. I was approached by one as I entered the shop. He told me his life story before asking for money. As I left, another tried to sell me a knife. I could only imagine the level of mental and cultural disintegration which causes the shopping mall to become the centre of your life. Pity may be patronising, but I felt pity. Plenty of it!

On the upside, two miles down the road lies the beautiful Canyon de Chelly, (pronounced Shay) which makes up for any shortcomings Chinle may have.

There is another reason to praise Chinle. Next to the Canyon's Visitor Centre is a lovely campsite which nestles in a cosy dip beneath tall trees. Better still, it was deserted and it was free. I decided to crash out there for three days. Even though everything was shut down and switched off I could hardly have chosen a better place to make my temporary home.

There were others who were excited about my presence there. Dogs again! As soon as I arrived, a motley gang of five large and very boisterous dogs bounded over to welcome me.

These dogs were great. They were fun. They did not beg, or look pathetic or hard done by, and although I never saw anyone around they looked well fed. They checked all my gear out and watched me put my tent up with a knowing eye; these were old hands and knew that they were not allowed to touch anything.

I woke in the morning to find my food had been raided and even my candles had been eaten. I put the blame for this on raiding racoons; no way would my dogs have done such a thing. I paid a visit to the Visitors Centre where I met a young Navajo man selling dream catchers. I like dream catchers, I like the idea of the web catching the bad dreams and letting the good ones through. I explained that I was cycling and that feathers would be in the way.

"I'll make you one without feathers," he said. "Four dollars. I'll meet you here at 8.30 a.m. tomorrow." I thought four dollars was a good deal and agreed.

That night I slept the sleep of the dead, with three dogs guarding my door. In the morning I acquired my dream catcher which I hung up religiously every night, until I lost it on a beach in Mexico.

My purchase threw any idea of a day at the Canyon out the

window for, as I took a short cut down a steep bank from the Centre, a thousand barbed seedpods leapt out the sand and implanted themselves in my front and back tyres. My unpunctured record was well and truly shattered, so instead I spent the time with my hounds and had a major repair session. In the early stages of my trip I checked my bike every day but lately I had become a bit lax; the days were too short and I was focussed solely on surviving the long cold nights and the strong head winds. So the occasions when I *had* to stay put was a great chance to catch up with mending holes, repairing panniers, sealing the tent and sleep mat, servicing the bike, cleaning the cooker. It's incredibly satisfying, and removes the feeling that everything is slowly disintegrating into a shambles.

The next day was Canyon Day. The Canyon de Chelley is a long, deep and very beautiful gash in the dune-bedded sandstone and it is a sacred place to the Navajo. For hundreds of years they have lived and farmed in its depths, and before that the Anasazi made it their home. In winter it provides a milder environment to the cold, flat lands which surround it.

Millions of years have weathered it into a soft, rounded, and mellow place. The rain, and the river meandering idly in the bottom, have washed the rocks into exquisite curves and caves, all smooth tactile shapes and gentle bends. Soothing hues of orange, yellow-orange, red-orange, cream-orange bathe the eye. Where minerals have been washed down from above, more extravagant colours sweep down the massive smooth, vertical rock faces in great swathes of streaks and stripes – lilacs, reds, purples, burgundies – getting darker and darker until sooty black. The atmosphere of these sandstone gorges is subtly evocative, reminiscent of Mesa Verde, and I felt similar emotions.

Nothing remained of those sad days long ago when, instead of a warbler's melancholic notes, the rocks had resonated to the sound of gunfire and screams. The days when, early in the nineteenth century, a Mexican general had marched his men through the Canyon's translucent reflections and made a sport of ricocheting bullets from a cave roof into the bodies of the men, women, and children hiding there. Neither did the cold winter of 1864 linger in the air, when so-called 'Friend of the Indian', Kit Carson, routed the Navajo living in the Canyon, killing some, capturing others, and destroying the animals and crops – including one thousand precious old peach trees on which they depended for their lives.

The Navajo were then marched, together with other remnants of the Navajo nation, three hundred miles to Fort Sumner, their new 'home'. Many died. This walk is still known as the Long March and though they were allowed to return four years later many more died. Now, in this winter time one hundred and thirty years later, it was quiet, not even a tourist (except me) to disturb the solitude.

Although these formations are not particularly old on a geological time scale, the past comes unbidden to mind. For me, the ghosts which sighed on the breeze came not only from last century's brutalities, but also from the time of the Anasazi, when they slept in the ruins which now watch over the green river; and long before that, when the only visitors to these hushed cathedrals were the deer, the coyote, the mountain lion, the bear, who came down in the dusk to drink. Lastly, to that time so unimaginably far off that we can barely conceive of it – days of true and absolute stillness, when the sand was being laid down by gently swishing waters, in shallow blue seas.

The silence which speaks so loud in these canyons is a listening silence. It is that of an old monastery, a Buddhist retreat, and it quickly dissolves any negative emotional baggage you may have dragged along with you. These welcoming depths do not have the dark colours or rough jaggedness which characterise many gorges, though it is true that you would end up as a jam sandwich at the bottom of the cliffs of the Canyon de Chelley, just as you would if you jumped off anywhere else. But if I should choose to end my days by jumping off a cliff, I certainly prefer the idea of bouncing off these golden rocks, and being nibbled by coyotes in the softness of the Canyon de Chelley, than being smashed against the jagged dark rocks and washed away by the swirling grey waters, in the grim darkness of the Black Canyon of the Gunnison.

The Navajo still live and farm in the Canyon. Sheep and cattle were grazing in small fields, and young men on horseback rode through the shallow water. Being a sacred place, visitors are not allowed to wander willy nilly and are permitted only to take the narrow track to White House Ruins – Anasazi cave dwellings which were also abandoned in the thirteenth century. These ruins sit across the river in a natural cave at the base of an absolutely sheer and smooth rock face, several hundred feet high. Juniper grows on the slopes down to the river; along the sandy valley, the soft grey-green of flickering tamarix and willow complement the surrounding yellows and oranges. An old log hogan still stands in the sandy soil, and lots of little grey birds fluttered around – warm little jewels of energy, like the sequins twinkling on a golden dress, giving a refreshing sparkle of life and light to this holy shrine.

I walked down to the ruins, and sat among the tamarix; I lay my hands on the warm rocks. I did not ride the whole road around the rim of the Canyon. I did not go to look at Spider Rock – a single rock projecting dramatically from the floor of the gorge. What I saw and felt was enough for a lifetime. Long ago, I found there is far more pleasure and satisfaction to be found exploring and experiencing a single place, than by whizzing around trying to 'cover everything'.

I envy the Navajo their Canyon de Chelley, but I am very happy that they have still managed to keep us lot out (they should also chuck us out from access to the ruins, there are plenty others to see). It is a place of magic and wonder – a place which has no care for us newcomers. Thank God there is one place on this earth that we tourists are not allowed to invade with our noisy voices and flashing cameras!

I think I could have actually walked more miles in a day than I was cycling. I was getting up late because it was so cold and dark, and the cold slowed the morning routine down. Then, because it got dark so early, I could not ride into the evening. The long gradual slopes nearly ground me to a stop, and I even had to cycle *down*hill as the head-winds were so strong. My speed reached ridiculous lows and I found it increasingly difficult to put the wind aside, to accept it as part of the day, rather than visualise it as my personal enemy to be fought and beaten. Also, due to the restriction on my camping places, I had to stop as soon as I got to a convenient spot which sometimes entailed stopping as early as three o'clock. Even then, by the time I was organised it was getting dark.

There is little to say about the ride to Ganado. It was only forty miles, but it could just as well have been a thousand as I was bashed around. If I could have camped anywhere I would just have stopped when I had had enough. As it was, I only made it by working in blocks of five miles, then having a few minutes rest before continuing. This may not be the most efficient way to cope physically, but it was the only way to survive the distance mentally.

I thought of the story a friend told me about the time he was cycling through Syria and Jordan. For weeks he had had a strong head-wind and he promised himself that when he reached his destination in Israel, he was going to crash out on a beach and relax for a couple of weeks before setting off for Egypt. He arrived at his beach, but instead of slackening, the wind blew with a new vengeance, all day and every day. The only way he could escape its vindictiveness was to jump on a boat to Egypt. He really believed it affected his sanity.

I could only laugh when he told me, and pretend that I understood, but of course I couldn't. But now I saw how quickly it was affecting me, and I began to understand.

I was aiming for Hubbell's Trading Post, a couple of miles outside Ganado. I arrived there at five minutes after five and it had just closed. But these were nice people. I tracked down the woman from the Visitor's Centre and she told me I could camp down by the wash. She then took me to the Trading Post and persuaded the brusque manager to open up again for me to buy some of his very expensive food. (Even away from Hubbell's the food prices on the reservation were very high. Unless the residents went many miles, they had to shop at the Thriftway mini-supermarkets where some of the prices were more than double those of large off-reservation supermarkets, although the difference was reduced somewhat as tax wasn't added at the till as it is off-reservation. It is ironic that some of the country's poorest citizens have to pay the highest prices.)

Hubbell's has a long history. Set up to trade with the Indians in the 19th century, it has never stopped doing business with them, and now combines business with its role as a tourist attraction. It still trades Indian goods for food, and no tribal art which I had seen so far could remotely compare to the exquisite artefacts which were on show there. I only hope the craftsmen and women got a good percentage of the high selling prices.

I was paid a visit by Lawrence who worked at the Post and lived in a caravan on the workers' site nearby. He felt sorry for me outside and invited me to spend the night in his caravan. As my tent was already up, I declined. Anyway, I knew that sleep would have been impossible in such a shut-in environment, better a cold night than one of lying awake for hours. Instead, I invited myself over for a coffee.

Lawrence told me of his life on the reservation, and of how his parents still live in the old way, without modern conveniences. He said that he could never go back to that way, even though he was brought up to it. He liked his television, and he liked to have people around him, not be isolated for days or weeks on end in the back of beyond.

I could sympathise with his attitude. To maintain the past culture necessitates a way of life that very few could tolerate today – certainly not the young ones. But rather than assuming that this is the end of the line and all roads lead to a cultural hiatus, maybe a compromise is the only thing to aim for. After all, the Navajo had stopped being a warrior nation well before Sitting Bull and Geronimo gave the army a hard time, and the Hopi never were bellicose, so their customs are not so dependent on the glories to be attained on the warpath. Maybe they can be successfully combined with a more modern way of life. Electricity, television and a more communal life may not make it easier to believe in the great mysteries of the universe, but they do not necessarily rule it out. At least the Navajo would be starting off from a higher cultural plane than the rest of us.

Another thing Lawrence told me was that he knew nothing about camping being forbidden on the reservation. He was quite sure no one would give a damn anyway.

Without a fire to warm me, the night was long and hardly bearable. I added waterproof trousers and an extra scarf to my clothing, but failed to warm up. As I cycled back to the cross-roads the following morning a tribal policeman pulled up beside me.

"Is everything okay? Any problems?" he asked.

"Everything's fine, thanks. But can you tell me about camping round here? I'm not allowed, am I?"

"Why not?"

"Well, I read in a tourist leaflet that camping is not allowed on the reservation. Only sometimes it's really difficult for me to get to the next place before dark, because of the wind."

"I don't know anything about you not being able to camp. I don't see why you can't. Anyway, if you can't get to the next place you *have* to stop, don't you?"

Of course! I hadn't thought of that. This man must have had a bit of Irish nationality and rationality in his blood. (A friend of mine got on a country bus in Ireland. As she did so, she said to the driver,

"I'm sorry but I haven't got the money to pay."

"Well," he said, "If you haven't got the money, you *can't* pay can you, so you'd better get on.")

I thought of the effort I had made to avoid causing offence, to respect tribal rules, when even a tribal policeman didn't know what they were. At least it would take some pressure off me.

That night I managed to hide away in some junipers by the roadside – my hiding skills were honed to a fine art by now. The only problem with being so close to the road was that I could not have a fire, and without it the nights were reduced to something to struggle through, rather than actively enjoy; I felt it gradually draining me. But a fire would have drawn too much unwanted attention. I stood in the warmth of nearby launderette, stripped off as far as was decent, and threw my clothes in the washer and drier. Finally I felt things were a bit more under control once more.

In the morning, I was packing up when suddenly I heard shouting. At first I ignored it, but then I heard a horse whinnying. I looked over my bank, and running along the road were three mirages covered in feathers and with masks on their faces. Even though I had no idea what it meant, I was excited to see what I took to be a bit of authentic Navajo ritual. They ran off down the road, followed by the untethered horse.

The village of Keam's Canyon was just a short ride, and the countryside had become softened by the gentle fragrance of junipers. The village lay just inside the Hopi Reservation, and it was truly a desert oasis, lying hidden and sheltered in a wooded valley. On the edge of the village, under the riverside cottonwoods, was an overgrown area available for picnics, camping, courting, or just playing hide and seek. It was empty. Across the road was a café and a large store.

Everything was perfect. I loved everything about Keam's Canyon and was very happy, so I settled down for a couple of days. There was enough dead wood to have enormous fires which lit up the skies, my site was lovely, and I had everything I needed.

It was still early, so I thought that a query about camping on the Hopi Reservation would be a good excuse to visit the Tribal Headquarters. I was in an office looking at maps, when a man invited me into his room. He had just come back from a holiday in Scotland, where he had been astonished and frightened by the narrow lanes. He gave me coffee, told me about his holiday, told me about the Reservation, and told me that I had his permission to camp on it. As I left I asked him what his job was.

"I'm the Superintendent," he replied.

NAVAJO DAYS

The following morning I walked across to the cafe. Two cars had driven onto my site and five young men had been dashing around frantically. Now, as I sat by the cafe window, five monsters emerged from my campsite entrance, and I realised what was going on. The men had been transformed into the surreal spectres of the day before. I had to do a reality check. Okay, so five hundred years ago these guys would not have been hassling people in the car park of the reservation store, but apart from that it was probably not so much different.

The gruesome fivesome were chasing any unfortunate customers trying to escape from the store next door, and everyone ran away from them laughing and screaming in excitement. I determined to stay where I was until the coast was clear. Besides, I didn't know what the expected response was. Then they spied me watching them, and came banging on the window, talking some kind of gibberish that did not sound like any real language. I turned to a woman nearby.

"Who are they?" I asked, "What do they want?"

"Oh, it's the Yay Bee Chay (Navajo) ceremony," she said, "It lasts for one week in December every year. They want you to give them something. A dollar is enough. No more."

I went out and gave a dollar to one guy, and another to another. They were still jabbering to me and gesturing me to follow them, but I was too shy to do so. I went back into the cafe. The woman working in the cassette store next door came and asked me, "You didn't give them anything did you?"

"Just a couple of dollars," I answered.

"You shouldn't have given them anything. I don't know what they're doing. They are just a nuisance pestering everyone. Try and keep away from them and then you won't have to give them anything."

Well, so much for inter-tribal harmony. We may think that it is great when native people keep their old rituals and customs, and may fondly believe that they are all fighting to do so. In reality some aboriginal people may be embarrassed by them, and find them anachronisms irrelevant in the modern age. Of course, the complaining woman was Hopi, and the men were Navajo, so she could not necessarily be expected to be overly sympathetic to their customs, although I found it incredible that she professed not to know what it was all about.

I tried to dredge my memory for things I had read about Hopi/Navajo relations. I remembered that there was friction within the Hopi tribe between the progressives and the traditionals. The terms speak for themselves, but as an example, the progressives were in favour of the devastating open-cast coal-mining on the reservation in order to get royalties from the Peabody company, whilst the traditionals regarded it as the butchery of Mother Earth.

I also recalled watching a television documentary outlining government landholding policy on the two reservations. Navajo outnumber Hopi hugely and they have the largest reservation in the USA (which completely surrounds the Hopi), but many have lived on Hopi land for generations. Even though the Hopi supposedly have no problem with this, US government policy is to remove Navajo from Hopi land – uprooting old and young alike from their homes – and replanting them onto the Navajo Reservation.

This has obviously caused a lot of distress. From this documentary it was made clear that there is no antagonism between the two tribes. Indeed, after living as such close and intermingling neighbours for so long, it hardly seems viable that they cannot tolerate each other. But nothing is simple, and the irritation this woman showed against a harmless Navajo custom may have indicated that harmonious relations aren't universal. I was also to find that some Hopi regard the Navajo as interlopers who have no culture of their own, only those stolen from the Hopi and the Spanish – weaving, sheep, pottery, silverwork.

Again I sat and watched the apparitions at work, thinking that I would now be left in peace. But no, a tourist was a good target for fun. They had seen my bike propped against the wall. They started leaping around in pretended glee, and made as if to take it away. I matched them with pretended horror, waving my hands, and shouting, "No, no, not my bike, not my bike."

It was all good fun, and I felt that my visit to Keam's Canyon was worth it just for that bit of surreal experience. I watched the children being chased around, as, terrified and screaming in real fear, they ran for their lives. Later when I met some on the road, I asked them, "Who were those monsters? What were they doing? Were you really frightened of them?"

"They're cannibals," I was told by these wide-eyed, brown-skinned tots. "If they catch you, they take you away and eat you."

Uh oh!

I returned to my camp and spent the afternoon trying to repair my wheel which was now far from round after crashing into a pothole in Chinle. That night my camp was again one of superb organisation and I felt energetic, rejuvenated and very at home in Keam's Canyon. Again the night sky was bright with the flames from my fire.

The next morning I went for my customary coffee in the cafe, and was approached by Eddie. He was forty, a Navajo, and he lived a couple of miles away. We spoke awhile, and he invited me to his hogan.

"If you've never been in one then you should come." I thought the same. "If you don't like it then I'll bring you back to your camp. If you do like it, you can stay. I have to go to a peyote ceremony tonight which goes on all night. I'm the Fire Chief and have to make sure the fire stays in."

I weighed the pros and cons and decided the experience would probably be worth the risk. I am prepared to take quite large risks for a potentially high reward.

We drove up to his hogan so that I could check it out. It was the usual five-sided type, built of concrete and surrounded by sand. In such a sandy, dry environment gardens are not possible, so instead most people rake their patch of sand into a nice pattern every day. A sweat lodge stood about ten metres away. On the other side of the hogan was a pen with Eddie's three horses in, one of which was his old rodeo horse.

I fancied a night in the hogan, feeding and watering the horses,

129

sitting in the sweat lodge, and looking over the sagebrush and juniper from a perspective other than the road. It was only about a mile off the road through the juniper, but it felt like the end of the world. It was wonderful. We went back to the village in his car where he went up to some people sitting in their pick-up. "I need some alfalfa for my horses," he instructed them. "Can you go and get it and then come and take some other gear to my place?"

We went to my camp-site, dismantled everything and piled it into the pick-up. I watched with apprehension as all my things were driven away. I was not used to trusting total strangers with all my possessions.

"It's okay. They're relations of mine. My aunt, uncle and nephew."

Inside, the hogan consisted of a single room with a wood-burner in the centre. A bed took up one wall, horse saddles and bridles took up another; three punctured bikes took up the third, television and music centre the fourth.

The remainder of the interior was Eddie's silversmith work area. He made the most exquisitely designed traditional silver and turquoise jewellery, which he sold to outlets all over Arizona and beyond. Being of a very high quality, he charged correspondingly high prices for it.

Squeezed in between all this orderly chaos was a small sink and cooker. Around his walls were photos of Eddie riding bucking horses and bulls, and posing with a variety of blondes. There was an interesting photo of him dancing with hoops around his body. I asked him what it was all about.

"I was the over-forty hoop dancing champion in Phoenix last year" he said. "I'll show you the video."

I had never heard about hoop dancing, but apparently it is a native tradition. I watched the video in which he managed to conjure a wide configuration of different patterns and arrangements with twelve hoops as he danced. It must have taken years to learn.

Clearly this was a man of many talents. And yet he was also an enigma. He was certainly an expert in traditional Navajo skills such as horse-riding, jewellery-making, hoop-dancing, and he was closely involved in old customs such as peyote ceremonies, the Yay Bee Chay, the sweat lodge. As he lived on a small island of Navajo land within the Hopi Reservation, he also spent much of his time on the Hopi

Reservation, socialising with Hopi people.

And yet, and yet! I felt that he really did not know quite where he was at. He boasted about the beautiful famous white women he had met and claimed that Clint Eastwood, country singer Tanya Tucker and others had visited him in his hogan. Clint had ridden his horses and left him his watch. I did not disbelieve him, as he was clearly the sort of man who would promote himself. But what was most confusing was his attitude to the Hopi.

"They're crazy," he said vehemently. "You can't do anything on their reservation. You can't do this and you can't do that. They don't let you take photos, you can't camp anywhere. And the Hopi boys are all crazy. They are always drunk and violent. If you camp on their reservation, they'll beat you up and rape you. Why do they all think they're so special? And what's so special about Polacco; you're not even allowed drive round it."

He mentioned Polacco because I had shown an interest in visiting it. It is an ancient mesa-top village and it was true that you were not allowed to drive in one part of the village, where some of the houses had *kivas* under their houses. *Kivas* are underground rooms reserved for the secret religious ceremonies which I had seen in the ruins of Mesa Verde. It was thrilling to know they were still part of Hopi life.

That night Eddie went to his peyote ceremony and I spent the hours pootling around happily. I fed and watered the horses, lit the wood-burner and swept alfalfa straw out the Hogan. I raked pretty patterns in the sand, sat in the sweat lodge, and tried to mend Eddie's bike punctures. If this was housework the Navajo way then it suited me.

Eddie returned at noon the next day, by which time the wind was swirling wildly around the hogan and snow covered the patterned sand. Cycling was out of the question.

"Let's go to Polacca if you want to see it, then you'll know what to expect on the road when you leave." Eddie said.

The road to Polacca climbed up onto the mesa top, a car lay smashed at the bottom of the cliffs. However interesting the village may have been from a historical, archaeological or anthropological perspective, it was not picturesque. Except at the end of the village where the *kivas* were, the houses were single storey stone, with some breeze block constructions – the dull colours blending in with the landscape around. It was light years away from America, and apart from the breezeblock I doubt whether the Spaniards would have found it much different.

It was very quiet; only an old woman, a teenage boy and a few children appeared in the streets. They put their hand up to Eddie, a fellow American Indian, but I thought I would have been uncomfortable coming alone as a tourist – I would have felt like an intruder, a voyeur, which indeed I was. I tried hard to imagine life in this tiny isolated mesa-top community, but, as an outsider, could only feel the isolation and the loneliness. Though the splendid vantage point brought a whole fantastical world within sight, tempting the viewer to visualise its mysteries, in reality it was a world of unbearable distance. And as there were no fences on the Hopi land to break up the horizons, the space seemed to go on for ever.

"So now you've seen it!" said Eddie accusingly. "Now you know there's nothing here."

I was irritated by his dismissal of all things Hopi. I could think of nothing to say.

That night I decided it was time to move on. Eddie was trying to persuade me to stay longer saying he would take me to the Yay Bee Chay ceremony that night, following the invitation with: "It's not interesting though – just a lot of singing and dancing." I suspect that he thought that only by putting down native customs could he present himself as a sophisticated modern guy.

The next day I stated firmly that if I didn't leave that day I could be caught in even worse weather than at present. Though yesterday's snow had mostly blown away, I had now seen how bad December weather could be. And at Hubbell's Lawrence had told me that it could get much worse – much colder and wetter – not the blue skies I had experienced so far.

"Stay a few more days, then I can take you where you want to go in my car. At least let me take you to Tuba City."

"No thanks, I want to cycle across the Hopi lands."

"What do you want to do that for? It's boring, there's nothing there, just a whole load of space. I can help you get across quicker."

Why do some people think that all a touring cyclist wants to do is get in a car?

"Why don't you let me help you? Why don't you let me take you there?"

He was starting to shout.

"Because cycling is what I'm *doing!* That's what it's all *about.* If I wanted to be travelling by car then I wouldn't be on a *bike.*"

It was clear that if Eddie were to be pacified I would have to let him take me some of the way. I didn't want to leave on bad terms.

"Okay, then. But not to Tuba City, that's too far. You could take me to Oraibi." This was about twenty miles away, and was still on the Hopi reservation. (Orabi is reputed to be the longest continuing inhabited town in the USA – maybe for a thousand years.)

All went well until we were approaching Oraibi, when Eddie started getting agitated.

"This isn't far. It's not worth taking you this far. And you can't camp anywhere. You can't camp on this reservation. They won't let you."

"There's a place to camp at Oraibi. I've got permission from the Hopi Superintendent, and he said it's okay to stop at Oraibi."

"Those crazy Hopi boys will get you. They'll kill you. They're always drunk and they go crazy. You don't know what they're like."

"I'll hide away from the road where they can't find me."

"They'll know where you are. They'll find you."

I was getting depressed by all this aggro. The fact is, the wind was so awful by now that I really was unhappy about going out into it at all and I really could do without him yelling at me. I found a place to stop, and when he finally realised I was leaving, Eddie mellowed. He gave me detailed instructions of when he would be at home, and when not, so that I could come back. I sent him a card from Mexico!

When Eddie went off in his car, it was cold enough to freeze the balls off absolutely *anything,* it was nearly dark, and the wind was so bad that I had to stand horizontally. I hid behind a rock in order to get my embattled head into order. The first thing it had to accept was that it had no choice but to get my body moving. The next thing was to mentally break every action into smaller manageable parts. For example, I could break putting the tent up into about ten actions; take it off bike, open bag, remove tent, remove pegs, remove poles, stake floor, put poles together, insert in tent, insert front pole, stake guy ropes; and so on. This way the five-minute task of putting it up did not seem such a mammoth job, and every small action seemed an achievement, a bit like breaking the ride into five mile sections on a bad day. Once I had my shelter, the worst was over, and I felt only relief at being on my own again.

The next day, thank God, the wind had dropped.

Hopi Horizons

Much as I have enthused about the Navajo Reservation, I actually preferred the Hopi land. You would think there could only be so much variation in basically flat, sagebrush country; but there were often changes which were sometimes so subtle that it took a while to identify them – it would just *feel* different. Hopi land is largely flat, but rather than the mesas being isolated rock projections, they form semi-continuous distant stretches of hills. This meant that you could not see forever across an endless plain because your horizon was limited by a lumpy, bumpy border. This made me feel a little less exposed and vulnerable. It also made for more interesting cycling.

But best of all, there were no fences. Everywhere was open – whether due to philosophy or lack of sheep, I don't know. I had the illusion that I could step off the road and walk for ever, always with my eyes on the horizon.

Continuous fencing depresses me after a while. However necessary it may be I start to see it as a form of violent social control which has been imposed on us so gradually, and over such a long period of time, that we no longer notice how shut in (or out) we are; how much our movements and freedoms are restricted. It is like the whole natural world is closed to us and concrete and tarmac are the only experiences left. I tried to imagine a world without fences and the concept was astounding. It was not only the world which would be more beautiful, our minds would have the chance to roam the infinitesimal linking and encircling lines of the earth. I wondered if the lack of fences on the Hopi Reservation had allowed their thoughts and ideas to flow freer; certainly their approach to life and the earth is unique and compelling.

There were tiny plots of corn dotted about the reservation and when I arrived at the tiny village of Hotevilla, I went into the corn store-room where beautiful red and blue corn sat around in buckets. The arresting young woman working there explained that it has to be stored for at least two years before it is suitable for grinding. I went next door and bought a couple of Christmas cards made by handicapped Hopi children. The boy working there was keen to know about my trip and we talked for a while.

I liked the Hopi individuals I had met so far. They struck me as a thoughtful and intelligent people who would be unlikely to succumb easily to the short-lived thrills of modern America. I stopped looking for the murderous youth of Eddie's imagination, hiding round every corner waiting to bring me to my doom.

Perhaps, ironically, one of the reasons Hopi culture has survived relatively intact for so long is because, rather than fighting to the end, they superficially 'took on' Christianity and whatever else was pushed at them by the early missionaries. But, whilst pretending to adopt the religion of the missionaries, they continued to practise their own customs secretly. They had seen the brutality which the sword and Bible of early Spanish gold seekers could wreak and reasoned that passive resistance was the only way to avoid a tough crack-down and thereby survive both physically and culturally.

But, as I passed near to Coal Mine Mesa, I had another lesson in the value of keeping people off pedestals if we do not want them to *fall* off. The Hopi are famous for the close relation which they have to the earth, and all words about them revolve around this very special and harmonious bond. And yet here, in a lovely nook of limestone rocks, a little hidden corner in an exposed land, rubbish had been dumped and scattered far around.

This was not the first time I had noticed there was an uncaring element on the roads of the Hopi Reservation. Neither was it so different on Navajo land, where the roadside had been littered with lager cans, Tokay bottles and engine oil containers.

Maybe we have too high an expectation of native cultures; maybe they are just as destructive of their environment as we are of ours; maybe slobbishness is innate in humans, so that the tendency to litter our own nests is always within us. But even a one-hour-old fledgling has the intuition to hang its bum over the edge of its nest before it shits.

By ascribing such high spiritual values to traditional cultures such as the Hopi, we assume they have some innate characteristic which makes them closer to the earth, and thus we make no allowance for the ordinary variations in human behaviour, refusing them what we allow ourselves – a few unruly members who are not representative of the whole society.

There is another perspective. I had already been confused by that aspect of American Indian life which was able to separate spiritual beliefs connected with nature from the *real* physical world. Thus, for example, you may talk about the 'wings' protecting and guarding you; you may believe that the feathers which you place on the altar before a sweat lodge have religious significance; but this does not necessarily mean that you know the difference between a golden eagle or a sparrow, or know anything about its habits or ecology. The bird of the spirit world is *not* the bird of the real world, and the welfare of the real bird may be of little concern or interest.

Similarly, it is possible to go to a ceremony where Mother Earth is praised and glorified, and on the way home throw the empty drink cans and dirty baby diapers out the window. I do not understand it, but it clearly is possible. Of course, it was so much easier to be environmentally correct before they invented all these horrid indestructible nasties; it was so much harder to be a hypocrite when all you had to throw into the grass was a bit of beef jerky.

I re-entered the Navajo Reservation and arrived at Tuba City, the largest town on the reservation. It had a large supermarket, which I remember as being the place where a shabby middle-aged woman stared in apparent disgust at my state; it was a strange sensation being a second-class citizen to a second-class citizen.

In this small, non-descript town, I approached a tribal policeman to ask if there was anywhere to camp nearby.

"You mustn't camp around town. There are some *really* weird guys around who would give you a hard time if they found you," he told me. "And on the other side of town is an extremely dangerous gang. I don't want you to be raped or anything."

Actually, neither did I. It looked as though the myth of the murderous 'Yoof' had risen again.

"Is there nowhere I can hide out?" I asked.

"Well, you could go down to the reservoir, but the drunks go down there so that's too dangerous. I'll get on the radio and see if my colleagues can help. Maybe you could stay at the station."

That was the very last thing I wanted, but he was trying so hard to help me that I prayed he did not come up with the option of a police cell, which I would feel obliged to accept. I did not doubt what he said about the dangers, but found it incredible that vicious gang warfare and violence was such a serious problem in this small town.

The policeman came back with an excellent idea. If I cycled out of town a few miles I could camp along the Dinosaur Tracks, where a young man gave guided summer tours around the ancient petroglyphs.

The guide told me that I could camp down the track, but said that there were two Navajo communities living by the cliffs and I mustn't go too close to them. A permanent spring spouted from the rocks which enabled them to grow crops in this otherwise barren landscape.

As I cycled down the rough track closer to the cliffs, I could see a green line of trees which marked the course of the spring. I found a lovely spot under the shelter of old willows and cottonwoods, and watched as the new moon shyly showed its face once more. I slept to the glow of my dying fire, and awoke to the sound of snowflakes gently sizzling on its remaining warmth.

I thought I had seen most of the colours possible in these southern lands, but as I left the Dinosaur Tracks I saw strata of the most astounding metallic electric midnight blue. Across the road, nature contrasted this with every shade of green imaginable. The back-drop was a long high cliff of bright red sandstone.

This part of the country was giving out very different vibes. The landscape had changed greatly, gone were the long flat reaches of land. I was now coming close to the great Colorado and the Grand Canyon was not far away. Tributaries had cut their way through these rocks and created many dry gorges. Though the urban unpleasantness of Tuba City lay so close, nevertheless the Indian presence felt more traditional. For the first time I passed windowless hogans built with mud, not logs.

Before entering Page, I stopped and looked at Lake Powell below me. A lake with nakedness all around, not a tree or shrub graced its shores, only a jumble of cliffs and rocks, beige under the blue sky. Beyond, the panorama of hazy mesas continued to the far horizon. A timeless wilderness! This was also a place of optical illusions, where I would have staked my life that the stepped hills going into Page went uphill, not downhill. I groaned until I found that once I started on the first slope that unbelievably it went down. How was it possible to be so deceived?

Dinosaurs could still be hidden in those pale vaults; God could still be deciding what to add to his basic plan – a bit of colour maybe! It was a prehistoric scene of such drama that words to describe it were reduced to cliches. But America has not always been modern, it has not always been the 'New World' and with a kick and a little mental readjusting it is possible to remember that it used to be two million BC here, just as it did everywhere else.

Recollections of Edward Abbey's words to describe this part of the world came to mind – words like 'holy' and 'sacred'.

Yet I am sure that Abbey would have been horrified that I put his words, and this surreal scene, together in one moment of thought and vision. This is because the town of Page, and the reason for its existence, were a cause of great distress to him, for Lake Powell is not a lake, but a reservoir made by the damning of the Colorado River. A greater beauty had been destroyed to make it, and Page was the town built to house all those involved in its construction.

Before the Canyon went under, Abbey spent ten bitter-sweet days drifting down the Colorado and savouring its last days, seeking out the secret chasms and dripping dells which now and forever lie hidden beneath the azure waters.

I only intended to get a short way out of town because I wanted to camp on the lakeshore. As I left town I called into the Visitor Centre at the dam where three rangers stood behind a desk; we got chatting. They were very interested in my trip. One of them asked me:

"Are you very rich or what, that you can spend your time doing this?"

"No! That's why I'm on a budget of $5 a day, live on porridge and eggs and camp wild. I've been saving up for a long time."

I wandered round the exhibition. Suddenly the ranger appeared next to me.

"I hope you won't be embarrassed," he said, "but we've been talking and we really admire what you're doing, so we had a little collection for you for Christmas. It's not much but we hope it will help you a little."

He handed me twenty dollars. I was so touched by this gesture that I was speechless. In that small gift those three rangers wiped out the sins of their Mesa Verde brothers!

I found a track to the lake and camped at a lonely spot where I thought I might spend a couple of days, it was so quiet. The moon shrouded the cliffs in an unearthly silver glow which was reflected sharply in the still water.

A landscape devoid of trees can be a bleak, depressing place. But some places in the world just look better without them, and Lake Powell is one of them. The resulting simplicity confers a satisfying pureness of line, form and colour which vegetation would disturb.

My plans to stay longer vanished when the air suddenly transformed from absolute stillness to a whirling tornado. I ate sand in my food and crunched it in my coffee, it rasped me in bed, and drove me crazy in my hair and clothes. I stuck it until noon the next day and then gave up.

So finally I arrived at Zion National Park. A ranger hauled my bike onto her truck to carry me through the park tunnel and I cycled down into the valley bottom.

I was in for a surprise. In this country where I had only seen one other small-tent camper, and where everyone hibernated after September, the Zion site was not only half full, but it was also half full of young car campers. Not an RV to be seen. Okay; there were no cyclists, but then few people are so stupid. Better still, unlike the bike-unfriendly Mesa Verde Park, this one was welcoming, with a lovely laid back ranger. Although I couldn't have a fire, I had noticed a definite warming in the temperature since coming down from the high plateau. Others commented on the cold and the snow and if I had not become used to sub-zero cold I would have agreed. I felt myself relax, as though a pressure had been lifted.

I had to make an effort to get off my ass so I rode along the valley and took one of the walks up the cliffs. As with national parks everywhere, there is a price to be paid for giving visitors such easy access. That price is pollution. I don't know how many tens of thousands of cars come to Zion each year, but I do know that almost every one of them will take that single road through the gorge and leave its fumes hovering and trapped in the narrow confines. Visitors will park at the point nearest to the track which they want to walk, park next to the restaurant where they want to eat, and by the museum they want to visit. If I had a car, I am sure I would do the same. I was just fortunate that I had no other option and could ride the road with an easy conscience.

I took off up to Angel's Landing. Once beyond the point which few took, everything changed. The path narrowed and became covered with ice and snow and a look over the sides revealed heart-stopping sheer drops of thousands of feet – absolutely vertical plummets which would have dispatched me to the valley floor without a scratch (until I reached the bottom). Though they reminded you that this was no longer true wilderness, I was thankful for the chains which lined the path and up which I could use to haul myself over the more treacherous icy parts.

On reaching the top of Angel's Landing in such hazardous conditions I felt as though I had conquered Everest.

I'd arranged to spend New Year with Justin and family in Pahrump, Nevada, and we were to meet at the town of St. George the next day.

My final night saw me camped in the garden of Selina, an ancient and very sick looking woman who smoked sixty cigarettes a day and said her lungs were as healthy as a teenager. Her hilarious tales of her drunken, licentious and long-dead husband kept me smiling all the way to St. George.

BORDER COUNTRY

As you progress southward you may be forgiven for thinking you have crossed over the Mexican border as Spanish increasingly becomes the tongue you will hear. But it wasn't a Mexican who bestowed on me the unfriendly treatment I got in Havisu City (actually a small town) and which made me childishly happy about the cock-up they made over their London scenario. I will explain! The site of this desert town is about as far removed from a River Thames ambience as it is possible to get, nevertheless the dignitaries-that-be have selected this place to be the second London – a London look-a-like. So at great expense, and to make it so realistic that no one would notice, they bought Tower Bridge.

Well, they *thought* they had bought Tower Bridge! But it turned out to be the far less lucrative London Bridge! Thus they were robbed of the chance of flaunting images of torture racks, gruesome executions and the whole associated paraphernalia of that ancient monument. As if we would sell Tower Bridge indeed!

So, London Bridge spans this bit of the Colorado, upon which ducks swim in the homely shadow of one red London bus, one English telephone box and one red letterbox. It was all rather ridiculous! I would have been more forgiving if this display of apparent love for English traditions made *me*, as a genuine English specimen, worthy of some degree of politeness.

This is also the winter home of the white-haired 'snow-birds'. When the chill bites further north they soothe their chilblains in this balmier climate. Entire retirement complexes for the not-so-young are sprouting up in this scorching desert – alien and depressing settlements where the occupants are cut off from the rest of America. If residents dare to hint that since they reached eighty they like to have a nap after lunch, then they are liable to be dragged off to the baseball pitch and made to whoop and holler with all the other good sports!

Okay, that's a bit over the top, but if you wish to slow down a bit in your later years, then this is not the place for you.

I am not suggesting that the elderly should sit alone by the window all day, thinking about dying – but there is a middle way, which I think lots of American towns have found, where it is possible to age in a mature way, accepting the realities of ageing but also living a full community life, not one based on hyperactivity in a strange place, with strange people and in a desperate pretence that nirvana means being over seventy.

In spite of the shimmering heat, the mountains are dark and sombre along the south-eastern California border area; mountains isolated by seas of sage and desert which spread up their sides leaving their peaks pushing through into the skies, like summits through the clouds, and inspiring awe and intimidation. These 'Sky Islands' are natural wilderness areas antipathetic to human beings. Only the Apache had the skills to make them home and knew them well enough to hide out in them during their flight from the US army. Perhaps some corners of the earth are just not meant to be poked about and pried in and should be left alone forever – not only because they cannot easily support human life, but also because they erect an invisible but very tangible barrier which we should respect. To enter would be to go into a place without sympathy, one which will not offer anything towards our sustenance.

Before entering the flat agricultural land of the Mexican border region, I stopped and spent my final night of camping in the USA on salt-encrusted soils by a canal. Wanting to get off early in the morning, and with night time temperatures raised to a tolerable degree, I decided against erecting my tent.

That night the coyotes moved in! Now I have never heard of coyotes attacking a person and I am sure they wouldn't. But at two o'clock in the morning, when you lie alone and exposed to the stars, it is very unnerving to find yourself completely surrounded at close

Arriving at the place of Chief Joseph's exile and burial: Colville Reservation, Washington.

Big Hole, Montana. The site of the tragic dawn slaying of the Nez Perce by the army. Tipi frames mark the site of the massacre.

San Juan mountains, Colorado. The long, slow, thirteen mile haul up to the 11,018 ft Red Mountain Pass – all soft green and brown.

Cliff Palace, Mesa Verde, Colorado. The biggest cliff dwelling in the USA, abandoned in the thirteenth century.

Janie and April outside their home in Cortez, Colorado.

Navajo Reservation, Arizona. Mellow and magical, the sacred Canon de Chelley.

Cloud descending on Monument Valley, Navajo Reservation.

An archway of elk antlers at Jackson, Wyoming.

Gwen just before crossing the Mexican border.

The Tarahumara family in Copper Canyon, Mexico.

The exquisite town of Taxco, Mexico.

A beautiful waterfall at Agua Azul.

Maya ruins in Palenque, Mexico.

Armin and Maria who Gwen stayed with in Santa Tecla, El Salvador.

Catching fish in Castilla, Honduras.

Woman cooking on the beach in Garifuna, Honduras.

quarters by a yipping yapping gang of them. I heard them moving in, closer and closer, and when they were about four metres away I began to have visions of ripped throats and intestines hanging from creosote bushes. What *did* I know about coyotes, after all? Absolutely zilch! But I did know that in theory, a group of them would have no trouble dispensing with me – unprotected as I was.

I remembered Justin telling me of a strange experience he had had up in Wyoming as he was cycling along a road which ran by some low rocks. Cars passing him flashed their lights, tooted their horns and pointed behind him. He turned, and running at shoulder height immediately next to him was a coyote. Normally coyotes are very shy of humans, so he put this strange behaviour down to the fact that it had never seen someone on a bike before and was simply curious; it probably didn't know whether he was animal or human. I told myself that my coyotes were similarly curious and just wanted to check me out before going off for the rest of the night. Of course, the morning found me still in one piece, and I cursed my night nerves and a fertile imagination for a sleepless night.

At El Centro, my last stop before crossing the border, I found it was Sunday again and there were no campsites and nowhere else to camp. I was directed to a Salvation Army hostel. This was closed until six, but as it lay across from an open park I thought I could put my tent up there.

(Throughout America church charities offer temporary accommodation to the desperate. The rules are often Draconian and residents treated as wayward children, but nevertheless as their meals, showers, beds and full facilities are free the service must be praised.)

As I sat and waited, several of the hostel residents came over to talk to me. These were Jack, who had come over from Tucson to sort some financial problem out; Pete, who had just come out of jail and was on some trip of his own; and Stu, who was handing a cream cake around and trying to sell me a toothbrush and tin-opener.

Maggie, a young Navajo woman, was living outside the hostel doors (so she could use its facilities) in a ten foot caravan which she shared with her Mexican boyfriend, her son and two bikes. She was from Yuma and wanted to go back but, predictably, had a complicated emotional and family life back there which she was escaping. (Jerry

Springer's guests really are not actors! Americans must have the most out-of-control emotional lives of anyone in the world.)

Everyone assured me that it was not safe to camp in the park; it was a weirdo hang-out and the police always made night-time patrols and would move me on. Even at that early hour there were some pretty unsavoury characters hanging around who were not from the hostel. My new friends were also rather weird but at least they were friendly and likeable and I felt very protected by them.

The hostel was free and was run like a military camp. I was accepted as a resident and ordered by the unsmiling manager to hand over my knife and take my cap off. I handed over the knife but vanity made me pretend that I hadn't heard the other bit. My hair was like a flattened haystack.

"I told you to take your cap *off!* I will *not* tell you a second time! If you want to stay here, you obey the rules!"

Whoops!

Actually, compared to a rescue mission I stayed in when I ran out of money on my return journey (at the Juarez/El Paso border) the rules here were pretty gentle. There may have been a long list about noise, drugs, drink, intermingling of sexes, curfews, compulsory Bible study and so on, but the only two I remember are that a daily shower was compulsory, and that you had to vacate the premises for the day at around eight in the morning. This was a pain, but at least in that milder climate it was not downright sadistic as it would have been in the freezing winters of the north.

Apart from Jack, who was a kind and sensible man, there was only one other person who I felt was relatively normal. Almost everyone was a bit wacky and two of them had completely lost the plot. I had a long conversation with a friendly and very good-looking blonde boy in his twenties. He seemed normal, but I sensed that he wasn't.

I became friends with three other women who were very bright and friendly. Again, they seemed normal, but again, I sensed that they weren't. Another woman trapped me in a corner and preached at me about God. Each night another apparently normal woman got into bed wearing thick black woollen tights, a calf-length black woollen skirt, a long-sleeved black woollen jumper and a long black woollen cardigan. On the third night I got up at four o'clock to go to the bathroom. She was in there, still dressed.

"I think there's something wrong with me. I think I have a fever, I'm so hot!"

It took me a few seconds to realise she was serious.

"Oh... well... Do you think you might feel better if you didn't wear so many clothes in bed?" I suggested tentatively.

"Do you think I would?" she asked.

I really liked most of the residents there, and yet there was something they reminded me of; something I could not quite put my finger on. Then it came to me. Remember those old films where the aliens came to town and tried to pass off as humans? Remember how there were little things which sometimes gave them away, and you studied every character for a clue which gave them away and identified them as the bad-guy alien?

"Hey. *He's* one!"

"Ner! He's *definitely* a human."

"No way. Look, you can tell. He looks sort of fishy."

"If he was one, he would have killed someone by now."

"I bet he is. He's got a funny smile."

These old unsophisticated aliens hadn't quite perfected what it was that makes a person human. It is not enough to copy the physical form; not enough to laugh and smile and to put sentences together. There are also those thousands of little social nuances, subtle responses, body language.

And that was it! I felt as though some of the people at the hostel hadn't quite perfected *their* earthly art. There were differences which my senses detected but which were so subtle that I could not consciously identify them. (Yes, alright, going to bed in black wool in a Mexican border town *was* a bit of a give-away I suppose.) Their social interaction was slightly off-beam. Maybe they were a little too friendly a little too soon; maybe they laughed a bit too much at not quite the right places; maybe they tried a bit too hard; maybe I saw the sadness on their faces when there was no one to talk to. They seemed to have a vulnerability about them.

Maybe this was why I liked them so much and why I doubted their ability to function 'properly' in 'normal' society. We are conditioned to erect barriers between ourselves and others. When you meet strangers you may be friendly and polite, but that barrier remains very firmly in place. These people did not have this boundary; they put nothing up. They were just who they were and did not have the skills to hide it. Somewhere along the way, they had missed out on the conditioning.

As I passed my last three days in America with my new-found friends, I decided that there can be no country in the world so fantastic and so variable as the United States. It has it all – searing deserts, soaring mountains, endless plains and prairies, gaping gorges, rushing rivers, huge forests. It has winter temperatures of minus 60 C and, at Death Valley, one of the hottest places on earth.

It also has some of the most friendly, kind and generous people in the world alongside some of the rudest and most disenchanted; it is the icon of modernity encompassing some of the most fascinating ancient cultures; it is the richest country in the world, housing some of the poorest. Within its boundaries it encompasses everything!

The next day I crossed the Mexican border.

South of the Border

Mexico to Costa Rica

Map: Mexico to Costa Rica

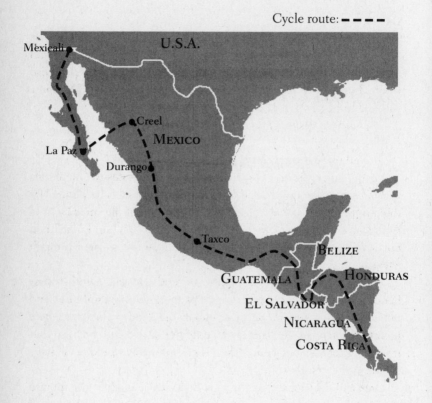

Cycle route: - - - -

Mexicali

U.S.A.

Creel

La Paz

Durango

MEXICO

Taxco

BELIZE

GUATEMALA

HONDURAS

EL SALVADOR

NICARAGUA

COSTA RICA

SOUTH OF THE BORDER

The first thing you should do when deciding on a cycle trip is to look very carefully at a map of the areas you wish to travel through. In my case it was a bit like the part in Thelma and Louise where Louise said she wanted to get to Mexico from Oklahoma without going through Texas.

"You want to get to Mexico without going through Texas?!"

"Yes!"

"But all there is between here and Mexico is Texas!!"

My dilemma was how to get from the United States to Guatemala without going through Mexico. Of course, it couldn't be done. The thing is, I had long been interested in the politics of the small Central American republics and wanted to see them at first hand, but I had not actually absorbed the fact that I would have to pass through Mexico.

This may sound ridiculous, and with hindsight it is. On the other hand, if I had sat down with a map for more than five minutes and noticed the inescapable fact that not only did Mexico block my whole path to Guatemala, and therefore could not be avoided, but also that it was absolutely bloody enormous, then I probably would never have set off in the first place.

Even my decision to go through Baja was a sudden last minute change of mind. This long peninsula of desert is an extension of California except that it changes its name from the United States to Mexico.

It is only since the 1970s that Baja has been accessible to motorised travel; even the conquistadors were conquered by its harsh conditions. It took over 150 years of abortive expeditions before the Jesuits finally managed to gain a precarious foothold there in

1697. Sadly, the remaining stretch of rough track down the eastern seaboard was being surveyed as I cycled along it prior to the laying of hard pavement. This will open this last piece of beautiful and wild coastline up to those blasted RVs. At present, the invasion there has been relatively gentle, and generally by loners who have a real love for the remaining wildness and quiet of Baja.

To cross the border from the United States into Mexico is to be thrown immediately into a turmoil of chaos, excitement and confusion. It is to go from a state of control and calm, from a world where you know what the basic ground rules are, into one where you know nothing; the contrast which takes place within a few short metres is scarcely credible.

Cast into the sudden noise and bustle of Mexicali, I felt uneasy enough to stop only briefly to buy water, not because I was in Mexico but because I was in a border town which harboured higher than the usual proportion of dodgy to non-dodgy folk as well as, in this case, being a centre of the huge drug business which operates between Mexico and the USA. There was an air of tension, and the bustle was not that of a healthy city which had developed and matured organically and cohesively, but of one which had suddenly had throngs of humanity thrust upon it, much of it desperate.

For twenty miles south of Mexicali I could scarcely get a view of what lay beyond the roadside fence as the rubbish of the city was piled up against it. The mess continued south for as far as the wind could blow it. (It was in the Baja that I realised the real evil of the plastic bag; later I was to add disposable nappies to my list of hates. In twenty years the peninsula will surely be buried under a metre of plastic and shit.)

Eventually the rubbish thinned out and I started to enter the sombre darkness of the northern desert. A sullen ridge of mountains runs the length of the peninsula, coming ever closer as the land closes in. Though the sun shone unhindered in an empty blue sky, there was little light reflecting from this brown moonscape. The day had been tiring, so when I felt as though I had left the border far behind I found myself a secret spot, hidden in the tamarix and reeds by one of the Colorado River's many tentacles, and put my tent up on the banks of what I thought was a quiet backwater.

That first night under Mexican stars, it was a rumbustuous presence that made itself felt. One which for me was what made the Baja truly bewitching: its wildlife. Because it has been left relatively undisturbed, it is there in abundance and it makes itself very evident. Stand on the beach and watch the dolphins leap across the bay, or the whales in the nursery with their young. Turkey vultures follow you hopefully, and pelicans watch you accusingly with their long prehistoric faces. Among the cacti humming birds will 'thrum' and the shimmering metallic luminescence of their colours will hold you spellbound. At night the coyotes will haunt your dreams.

As I sat silently looking across the calm water, reflections gradually dimming in the fading light, the escalating noise of the resident birds burst upon my senses. The racket was deafening – hooting, squawking, twittering, cackling, squealing, crying. They swam and dived, reeled and squabbled, crash-landed with great splashes and flapped frantically, feet paddling, to take off. That was one of the noisiest nights I had ever known. As a lover of birds, I was in paradise. How could anyone feel nervous or alone with such energetic company? I revelled in every note that came to me that night – a fairytale night of rippling water, silver moonlight and life. Raccoons moved silently and furtively by the water's edge; shapes moved in the reeds; across the water something large fell into the water from the darkness of the bushes. All around was a moving thing of rustling shadows and invisible life.

I was in the San Felipe Pemex garage, trying to find out if the tap water was okay for drinking, when a bus full of American tourists drove in. Attached to the front of the bus was the head of what appeared to be a stuffed bison. After a few minutes, a man detached himself from the other passengers and approached me.

"Where're ya'll heading?" he asked.

"Panama."

His eyes rolled skyward. "She's heading to Panama", he called back to his group.

"Where've ya'll come from?" he asked.

"Seattle," I answered.

His mouth dropped open; he started to look disheartened. "She's come from Seattle," he called back.

"Ya go down the coast?"

"No; via the Rocky Mountains."

With that he raised his arms up to the heavens, and walked away shaking his head and muttering:

"She came through the Rocky Mountains; she came through the Rocky Mountains! Jesus Christ!"

Without another word to me he returned to his group.

The road from San Felipe to the shabby divided town of Puetecitos (a gated community in Baja, how ridiculous is that!) became more interesting as it slipped around bends, and assumed a gentle hilly character with scattered saguaro cacti the size of small trees. Colour was added by the thousands of flowers which grew along the roadside – white, yellow, purple, salmon. Though the days were sunny and bright, the wind made it too cold to stop for long without the shelter of rocks or hills.

I had now reached the 'tarmac gap' and had ninety miles of rough track to tackle. I had asked the opinion of the Tourist Office back in San Felipe;

"It's bad; you won't be able to make it," I was told. "You'd be better heading back over onto the west coast road."

As I left Puetecitos I met two friendly strapping Americans.

"You're not heading out there are you?" they asked. "We haven't been all the way along – only about twenty miles but it was bad even in our four-wheel-drive. You'll never make it. We're heading up to San Diego, you could put your gear in our truck and we could drop you at Highway 1."

They were friendly guys but this eastern route was quiet and the unpaved road would now reduce traffic to virtually nil. It was no contest to choose between a few days alone in the desert, and the swoosh-swoosh-swoosh of RV's with hair-brained drivers trying to shave my legs.

"No, thanks all the same, but I'd rather see for myself what the road is like."

"Well, it sure as hell will be an adventure. Good luck."

I had read a book by a Scottish man who walked around the peninsula, although not in one go. It was an interesting book, but it had made me nervous about that most problematic of Baja characteristics – water. The lack of drinkable water had been the lament of the earliest Jesuit settlers and had totally controlled and limited the number and locations of their missions. The Jesuit Baegert had complained that:

"Where there is water there is often no soil, but merely sand and stone; and where there is soil there is usually no water..."

So on the premise that it's better to be safe than sorry, I went completely over the top and set off with five gallons of water hanging off the back of my carriers. This effectively turned my bike into a tank. I could not even lift my back wheel off the ground, let alone cycle it over rocky inclines.

Those ninety miles took me more than three cycling days. The first day I managed seventeen miles and regarded that as an achievement of major proportions. I lost count of how many times I came crashing to the ground trying to struggle up hills and over rocks. Every time, the luggage slipped and the water crashed down. In the end I gave up the fight and walked. At least it all took my mind off the unrelenting pain of my bum which, as I lost weight, meant I was increasingly sitting on my bones.

I had christened my bike Sylvia, Sylvia Dawes (it was a Dawes Mean Street), but during those hours she was re-christened many times. Of course, a fully-fledged mountain bike would have given more grip on the unstable and steep surfaces, but I soon discovered that even where the going was better she would aim for every rock she could find. If there was one stone, or one pothole in an otherwise perfect road, she would aim for it, as though it had some kind of magnetic draw for her, and I would crash into it in a cloud of adjectives.

It was the same when she decided to fall over. I would spend careful minutes propping her up with Charlie before making coffee or going for a pee. There she would stand quite happily until, for no apparent reason, she would suddenly decide to topple upside down into a ditch, creating mayhem with the luggage and giving me a hell of a job to haul her out.

One of the most frustrating things about riding on rough tracks is that you cannot take your eyes off the road for a second and, as such roads frequently go through the most beautiful places, the only way you can fully appreciate them is to keep stopping, except that it was better to stop vertically rather than horizontally.

But the effort of that first day was worth it. The road was so peaceful – only three local pickup trucks passing me the whole day – and the scenery was stupendous. The high bank of mountains in the west had been replaced by grassy hills which rolled and tumbled their way right to the water's edge. The track wiggled its way round, over, and in and out of these hills, each bend revealing yet another fantastic view of those old 'blue receding headlands', all hiding wild deserted coves whose charms in any other part of the world would quickly have been usurped by hotels and beach umbrellas.

As the sun slithered down, the pelicans were out in droves and long-tailed frigate birds swooped gracefully above me. Suddenly the sea gave a loud crack and I looked up to see the distant shapes of whales swimming slowly across the bay. This was one of the most exhilarating moments of my life, and when, shortly after, a shoal of dolphins leapt their way in pursuit, I knew life was pretty good.

I also knew that the paving of this road would be a disaster for this section of the coast – somebody once said that Baja was a good example of what bad roads can do for a country. This is true, for though civilisation may not have been too far away, everything felt very primitive and wild, and the wildlife took its rightful place of prominence in the environment.

The terrific concentration needed to stay upright on my bike, and the effort of dragging it up steep rocky gradients, left me so drained that by seven o'clock on that first day out from Puetecitos I was falling asleep. As I did so, I heard little scampering and scratching noises around me. I opened my eyes to find I was sharing my tent with a beautiful and fearless little mouse with the biggest, shiniest eyes in the world. After five minutes, it ran across my fingers and out into the night.

Floating on the Old Wharf

The road tried a different tactic, one well remembered from earlier days – corrugations. The advantage of knowing beforehand that a road is going to be tough is that you are mentally prepared and your patience is likely to be greater than if you had come upon it unexpectedly. Anticipating a continuation of terrible I set myself the pathetic target of fifteen miles for the day; this way they wouldn't freak me out too much. Mostly I could only bump along at three miles an hour and even then I fell off three times.

The rolling hills had become red jagged mountains and thousands of rooks circled the cliffs in noisy congregations, their cries echoing around me. There were lots of footprints of small ponies or donkeys. A man told me there were wild horses in the hills but the only ones I did see were sad old things with projecting ribs and spreading hooves which had been kicked out in their unproductive old age. I felt desperately sorry for them, as anything that was green was also prickly and unsuitable for the delicate mouth of a horse. They stood around with their heads down awaiting their slow deaths with resignation.

My way continued in an anonymous blur of swirling wind and dust, my eyes focused solely on the route of my front wheel as I was thrown around like an old rag. It threw me into rocks, slithered me around in loose gravel and ground me to a sudden halt in sandy ruts. I no longer counted miles, just celebrated every tenth of a mile that I stuttered past.

I was aiming for the beach community of Alfonsina. In the past it was an isolated fishing camp and whilst it was still that, it was now also the hangout of a few hardy Americans who arrived in their small private planes in order to seek a lonesome experience. The whole coast of Baja is scattered with tiny fishing camps, most of them accessible only with difficulty down long sandy tracks or by boat, where for ten months of the year a handful of fishermen and their families live only with the basics necessary for survival.

When I was within sight of the bleak beachside row of buildings which was Alfonsina, I stopped. All I wanted was to lie down and go to sleep for a while, just a little while, somewhere calm, somewhere – anywhere – out of the wind. I leaned by a rock and closed my eyes. At that moment the third vehicle of the day stopped by me. It was Michael, a photographer from the mainland. I asked about Alfonsina and if I'd be able to get gas there.

"Alfonsina is the name of the woman that owns the land, just like Papa Fernandez owns Papa Fernandez camp, but you can camp down there. There's a cafe and you should be able to get gas from the Americans. I'm going there to eat when I've finished – perhaps we could meet?"

These words were bliss to my ears. Normally I am at one with solo camper Steve Gill, who believes that if each day is separated by a retreat to a hotel or to the company of others unconnected with the day's journey then the adventure becomes a 'disjointed, staccato thing, lived only in fits and starts'. By camping the journey becomes a cohesive, uninterrupted totally absorbing and immeasurably heightened experience.

But that day I said 'Sod it!' I had absorbed enough heightened experiences for one day and was ready for a bit of disjointed, staccato travelling. I didn't want to camp among the cacti; I wanted beer and burritos. I wanted to feel that I was not the only person in the world, I wanted to talk with someone.

Besides, Alfonsina was not exactly the height of civilisation. In fact, it felt like the end of the world; a row of lonely, empty, wooden houses straddled along the strip of beach on this desperately beautiful bay. Behind were empty marshes and a small runway, and in front the rocks spread their arms to shelter the shacks from the sea. Fulmars, pelicans and other sea birds flew in convoys across the water, and dolphins billowed in the waves. It was a magical oasis and I loved it; it really was a place to recover from the rat race, to remember where you had come from, and to regain a clear perspective on life.

But how the wind shook that place; there was nowhere to hide from it. I searched behind rocks and under chalets but every nook was immediately invaded; eventually I put my tent in the lee of an empty shack and went into the cosy wooden cafe. This soon filled up with Mexican road workers, Baja fishermen, two Californians (Steve and Dale) down to do some fishing, Michael the Mexican photographer, the cafe owners, and last but not least, their ten-year-old daughter, Maria.

Maria was lovely and I felt a little sorry for her. In this isolated corner of the world there were no schools, and no other children of any age for her to talk to or play with; she must have been lonely. This was evident by the fact that, although I was older than her own mother, she adopted me at first sight.

I stayed at Alfonsina for three days and whenever she did not have to help out in the kitchen, Maria was by my side. My Spanish was still abysmal and her English was non-existent, and yet for those days I was her friend and she was mine. We collected firewood together and sat by the fire, we collected shells and walked along the beach, we laughed at the pelicans and watched the fish being brought in.

Dale had a farm in California and came regularly to Alfonsina. He asked me:

"But don't you ever get days when you think, 'Oh, to hell with it!' When you just want to pack up and go home?"

"Not really. I have shitty days like today when I can't go any further, and when every mile is an endurance test, but I've never for a moment thought of actually packing up."

"Yes, but you've already gone a hell of a long way. It's not as though you only managed to get down the road."

I thought about this later and questioned myself. It was true, I had had so many days which were a struggle, there was always something to test my physical or mental endurance; wind, bad roads, painful bum, hills, mountains, and later on, the awful heat. I did not doubt my mental stamina, it was my physical limitations which were usually the cause of my difficulties. I wondered if someone of much greater physical strength and stamina would have found it significantly easier than I did. It wasn't simply that I was female and lacking muscle and lung capacity, after all Dervla Murphy and Bettina Selby seemed to float through their one-hundred-plus miles per day with no trouble, and some super-human cyclists supposedly achieve two hundred. I could only balk at the thought of that.

So why then did I never give a thought to packing the whole thing up? Why, even on days when I was almost reduced to tears, did I not entertain the idea of stopping? It was hard to know why not. Part of it of course, was that I was determined to finish what I had started; to paraphrase Bill Bryson 'Cycling is what I did'.

But I think it was also due to what I can only call the 'completeness' of my journey. It was not merely a bike ride, it was a whole, rounded thing and because I was camp-oriented rather than mileage-oriented, my camp at the end of the day was a constant pleasure to me. The hours organising my campsite and enjoying in utter silence the new sights around me, gave me considerable satisfaction. Thus my nights and days were not separate items, they flowed into one another, each as valuable to me as the other, the evenings restoring me to calm after the difficulties of the day. In addition, the total sense of freedom I was experiencing, travelling alone with all my possessions, fulfilled some deep-seated need.

Eventually I had to tear myself away from this haven, so after having a shower (four dollars for a bucket of tepid water) I prepared myself for more of the washboard road. Flash floods of the previous year had washed parts of it away and reduced it to impassable sandy ditches. In this land of blistering deserts and sterile soil, where the rain may not fall for several years, it was a great exercise of the imagination to visualise great torrents of water raging down the hills wiping out all in its path. But in the dry river beds piles of bleached rubbish was stranded three metres up into the trees, proving that the incredible was indeed possible.

Finally, – after another day of corrugations, hill hauling and headwinds – I reached the highway. I was sorry to leave the silence of the track, but I was very glad to reach tarmac. I soared along, not stopping for breath until I passed Punta Prieta.

I camped on a ledge overlooking a crowded cactus valley, lively with the calls of birds and the thrum of humming birds; such massive energy in such tiny bodies. There were horses around; one trying lethargically to browse from the bushes, another standing head down, a white one lay dead beneath a large spreading cardon cactus.

The road was busier now it was paved, and I was coming into contact with more people. I began to notice that whilst Mexicans of Baja were usually friendly and would often approach me for a chat, middle-class Mexican tourists from the mainland clearly disapproved of me. (Many American RV owners weren't impressed either!)

Rightly or wrongly, I blamed American cultural imperialism for this snobbery. Mexico and Central America are swamped with north American values – soaps, films, music and advertisements, all of which show a vision of life which is given and received as the standard everyone should all be aiming for. The message is clear: 'Buy this and you too can be just like us!'

I found it very depressing when school signboards were adorned with the Coca-Cola slogan and when people who could not afford a decent meal would drink Coca-Cola to quench their thirst; when young men would buy Marlboro instead of the cheap national brands because it was 'cool'; when the aim of so, so many was to go to the States.

And I found it infuriating when these snobby people looked down their noses at me because I wasn't peroxided, pastelled, or travelling in a nice car. And, of course, because I wasn't accompanied by a man!

By no stretch of the imagination can the small town of Guerroro Negro be called attractive, quite the opposite in fact, but once I got into it I liked its scruffiness – and it had a great cake shop. To raise its status further it had ospreys nesting on the telegraph poles and lovely friendly people. I gave it a tick of approval.

What made Guerroro Negro worth a visit for me was its Old Wharf – Puerto Viejo – about seven miles out of town along a dirt track of potholes which takes you by salt evaporation ponds (it's the world's biggest exporter of salt), past marshes full of herons, through sand-dunes, and on to the abandoned buildings that are the Old Wharf.

At the wharf a whole translucent and iridescent space opens up, where it's hard to believe that the ground is still solid and that the world is not about to float away into the clouds. The sky merged with the sea, not a ripple disturbed the mirrored surface. All was white and cream, blue and grey; edges merged, smoothed and blurred whilst remaining sharp and clear; everything was pure and clean. It was as though the whole world had been simplified to its bare essentials, rather like afterlife images of golden light and silence. Across the bay was a fantasy world of isolated beaches with sand as white as snow.

The only thing which moved through this dreamy mirage was the wildlife, hundreds of seabirds, herons, waders, – just a few of the 150 species of birds which live along this coast. Fish leapt out the water and, to complete the illusion of Eden, whales moseyed around out in the bay.

This part of the west coast is famous for its grey whales, and just over the silvery dunes lay Scammon's Lagoon, one of Baja's whale nurseries. In January each year hundreds of them arrive after a long, four-month swim from the Bering Straits – some females come to mate, others to give birth to the young conceived here the previous year (safe from the predatory killer whales of the north). A couple of months after the young are born, the return journey begins.

To see the whales at the Old Wharf, and to know that a lagoon of hundreds more lay peacefully nearby, made me ridiculously happy, partly because I knew that if I had been sitting there a hundred years earlier the sea would not have mirrored the blue sky but would have been a scarlet arena of carnage wrought by the whaling frenzy begun in 1857 by Charles Scammon.

When the secret of his lucrative discovery was out, the coast around Guerroro Negro became a slaughtering ground for the hundreds of whaling ships which descended each year. From an estimated population of 25,000 the grey whale was down to 250 by the 1930s, and it was not until 1972 that full protection was achieved.

For once we have a story that does not end in the usual doom and gloom, for from the brink of extinction the grey whale is now breeding itself back to survival. Looking over the whale-studded waters from my shabby wharf I felt some optimism about the world, some hope that awareness and regret will be enough to reverse our terrible history of ecological destruction before it is too late.

A final irony is that after leading the rest of the world's whalers to these calm lagoons to kill the grey whale, Scammon later became a marine naturalist and expert!

While I was sitting in rapture on the wharf I was besieged by several small children in various stages of filth and decrepitude. They were accompanied by a few fluffy six-week-old puppies of assorted colours. Some of the children were brothers and sisters and they lived with their parents, and others, in the abandoned wharf buildings. They were inquisitive kids and asked me worrying questions like:

"Are you a man?" (Blimey, did I look that rough?)

"Do I look like a man?"

"No, but you don't look like a lady?"

"I've got long hair, look."

"You could still be a man."

"Well... yes."

"What are you?"

"What do you think I am?"

"A lady."

And then:

"Why are you on a bike?"

"Because I like it."

"Why aren't you in a car?"

"Because I like a bike best."

"Have you got a car?"

"No."

"Why haven't you got one?"

"Because I don't want one."

"You can go faster."

"I don't want to go fast."

"Why not?"

"Because then I can't see anything."

"What do you want to see?" (It was time to end this.)

"I don't want a car because they're too expensive."

"Oohh, si, muy caro!"

Something they understood!

A couple of smart middle-aged American women were wandering around watching people fishing from the walls. They spotted the puppies and children and dashed over to them gushing:

"Oh, look! Aren't they just the cutest kids you ever saw? And just look at those cute little puppies!" I noticed they didn't go too near.

They popped out their cameras and snapped away; no doubt their photos would prove once again just how photogenic poverty is. They continued to 'ooo' and 'coo' until their husbands appeared and quickly whisked them away to the safety of their Mitsubishi.

I wanted to camp at the wharf, but there were too many men hanging around. After all my sanctimonious ramblings, I thought maybe my unacknowledged prejudices were coming home to roost. Just because a load of people, including several men, lived in an abandoned wharf did not mean they weren't honest, decent people. I knew that, I really did.

But I was also realistic, and knew that a female all alone – beyond reach of any help and presumably with money on her – would be a temptation to many a man not on a winning streak. I also knew from experience that this was the sort of place where men came at night, to drink, do drugs, or whatever. I did not want to be woken by strange masculine voices muttering around my tent in the middle of the night – harmless or not, they would keep me awake waiting to find out.

I cycled back a little way towards the sand-dunes and managed to haul myself out of sight onto a small low dune, just big enough for my tent and gear. The water in the bay was far out, but it was obvious that the sea would rise in my direction so I had to make sure that my little 'island' was above high tide. I checked the vegetation, how deep down the dry sand went, any signs of a tide mark; I was sure it was okay.

At two in the morning I was woken by a strange noise and it took me a few seconds to register what was going on; it was a gentle 'lap, lap, lap' mingled with a 'spatter, spatter'. To my horror, I translated the sounds. With a sinking heart I realised it was the too-close lapping of the Pacific Ocean around my island, under the patter of a hard, steady downpour of rain.

I had cursed the rain when it had started at nine o'clock, because I had had to trek out and gather everything into the shelter of my tent; usually it was just scattered around. But as I shone my torch out into the darkness, my horrified gaze falling on the shiny blackness of the ocean only a metre away and surrounding me on all sides, I was thankful for that rain – otherwise everything would now be on its way to Asia.

I was also thankful that the water was in such a gentle mood, at least no waves were threatening to crash down on me and carry me off to join the whales. Only one handlebar of my horizontal bike projected through the waters which, so tranquil in daylight, had now transformed into black, murky depths holding only death and terror in their grip.

Trying to keep calm, I thought of the options available if the waters continued to rise. As I could swim to dry land, the worst thing that could happen was that I would lose something, or everything. I tried to work out the time I had arrived at the Wharf, where the tide was then, and whether it had been going in or out, but my mind refused to function.

I decided to wait it out. For two hours I lay there, praying to any god who was prepared to listen, and willing, willing, willing the sea not to come further. I promised I would be good for ever and never say another nasty thing about RV owners; and finally, after an infinity, that huge, all-powerful ocean did just as I asked and stayed right where it was. When I got up it was safely back in its bay. Sometimes you've just gotta be lucky!

Since August I had not really experienced proper rain, but here in the middle of the desert, in the company of birds, it poured relentlessly down. I sat cold and miserable in my tent, the inside of which was rapidly getting as wet as the outside. As I was nearly out of water and my cooker fuel was finished, I had to move. At midday, after fifteen hours of continuous hard rain, I cycled back to town against a fierce head wind where, cold and soaking, I took refuge in a cosy cafe.

I think I had hit Sod's Law. I was now on the edge of the Vizcaino Desert and had read that it was nothing unusual for six years to pass without rain, and here I was wetter than I had been in the past six months. But at two o'clock it finally stopped, and I set off into the southern half of the peninsula – Baja Sur.

BEACH BUMS

The road which crosses the Vizcaino Desert stretches flat, straight, windy and oh, so monotonously out of Guerroro Negro. Named after the Spanish explorer Vizcaino in 1602, it was part of the nomadic territory of the Cochima Indians who, after thousands of years, had got survival in this most brutal of regions down to a fine art.

With almost no drinkable water, saline soils and constant year round winds, little can survive in this flat featureless land, and the imagination and adaptability needed for humans to live here, or anywhere in central Baja, were qualities which labelled them as primitive rather than finely honed for their environmental conditions.

One survival technique widely reported by the Jesuits was the custom of 'second harvest'. When the patahaya fruit was available this sudden abundance of food meant that the Cochima could come together in larger groups and could stay in one place for a while, a communal place being used as the toilet. When the sun and wind had dried the 'deposits' they were sifted for excreted seeds which were roasted and eaten again – hence 'second harvest'.

Another imaginative practice unpalatable to our times was the custom of attaching a string to a piece of meat, lightly chewing it, swallowing it, and pulling it out the stomach again to be re-eaten. This was repeated until it had disintegrated. Sometimes it was passed around the group and children supposedly cried if they were given a piece of meat without a string.

Alas, the Cochima are no more, and – though their encounters with the Spanish were less directly barbaric than on the mainland – the diseases introduced by the Europeans, exacerbated by the missionary system, still succeeded in wiping out every last one of them.

I soon found myself in another rural dustbin even worse than those miles south of Mexicali, at least there the rubbish had been concentrated along the roadside – here it dispersed in the wild winds from dumps; every village had its circle of rubbish and every cacti its plastic bag. In addition, there was a constant stream of disposable nappies along the verges, with periodic heavy dumping hot-spots. What do these women do with their babies for heaven's sake? The world is starting to stink of discarded disposable nappies.

'Hey the baby's nappy needs changing. Let's go for a drive.'

San Ignacio is a hidden green gem sheltering in a valley of this unforgiving land. Even in the moderate temperatures of February it was a joy to reach, and in the blistering heat of summer visitors must think they have reached Nirvana. The local Indians had called it Kadakaaman , which means 'reed covered arroyo' and as I rode under the cool of its palm trees and passed between its two reed-lined lakes, I thought I had been transported to a semi-tropical wonderland; it was a true desert oasis.

The early Jesuits of San Ignacio had easy soul-picking for a while, but by 1840 the customary presumptions, cruelties and western diseases sent the aboriginal populations to their usual extinctions. The presence of the abandoned missions still lies heavy in the quiet of the shady colonial zocalo (plaza) and in the grandeur of the magnificent church. The date palms which make the air so deliciously cool are the naturalised descendants of those planted by the Jesuits over 200 years ago.

The downside to the town is that, with notable exceptions, the shopkeepers are not very friendly. I left a shop of desirable camping goodies when the owner, for some reason that only he can know, got himself into a near-apoplectic state when I asked if he had a box suitable for attaching to the front of my bike. The next grumpy shopkeeper overcharged me by four hundred percent.

Then I went to the post office. This was run by a most peculiar man who had clearly been watching too many Donald Duck re-runs.

"Good afternoon. Three stamps please."

"Three stamps?"

"Yes please." He started flying maniacally around the room – lifting papers, books, leaflets; putting things down, picking them up, putting them down.

"Was that three stamps?"

"Yes. Three. Three stamps." I put three fingers up so he could count them himself.

"Three stamps?"

"Yes. I would like three stamps" I re-erected three fingers and left them there.

He continued to flap around frantically, desperately trying to be helpful, but the really curious thing was that all the time he was zapping around his office he kept up a constant stream of squeaks and squawks and weeeeee's and wooooo's. He didn't seem at all embarrassed by this and in the end I did what we all do in awkward and unusual circumstances, I treated it as a perfectly normal everyday event. In all, he asked me six times if I wanted three stamps, and six times I said yes. It was a fascinating experience.

I arrived in my favourite town in Baja – Santa Rosalia. This is an old copper company town established by the French in the 1880s and its main claim to fame (and the only thing guidebooks mention) is the imported iron church designed by Eiffel. As I came into town I was met with a dreary scene. My diary records: 'Beach horrible. Load of garbage on way into town. Factories, old smelt works, ugly, depressing, grubby, bad feel. Getting dark, asked restaurant if could put tent in their yard.'

I was up at five-thirty, packed up and wandered into town. I was astonished, this little town was wonderful; its French origins and influence have given it a very un-Mexican feel and a charming and unique individuality all of its own.

The narrow streets were laid out in a grid pattern, and lined with faded, yet colourful little wooden houses with little wooden fences. Tiny gardens were filled with plants and trees, and climbing plants with large purple, red, pink and white flowers rambled riotously around doors and windows, and up and over the quaint wooden balconies and verandas which adorned every house. Small, old-time shops, where you could buy one of absolutely anything (even sugar came by the ounce) completed the picture. Everything was on a healthy human scale; the crowning touch was its friendly people, even the shop assistants were smiling and cheerful, and twice payment for small items was adamantly refused.

I wondered if the differences between the two towns of San Ignacio and Santa Rosalia could be due to the numbers of tourists they each received, but as I didn't see a single foreigner in either I couldn't judge. Unfortunately, whatever the case, the economics of this poor land meant that those without tourists wanted them, and those who lived by the unpaved section of the east coast road couldn't wait for the tarmac to be laid and the gringos to come flooding in – they wanted pennies, not peace; people, not pelicans.

Mulege is set in a hidden coastal valley where the river meets the sea and, like San Ignacio, it was established as a mission town in the early eighteenth century. Also like San Ignacio, it is another semi-tropical wonder, lush with palm trees and water. However, it differs from San Ignacio in that – for some reason I couldn't quite fathom – it has a strong Caribbean atmosphere. I could imagine the beat of drums, reggae and calypso throbbing on sweaty summer nights. Once again the Baja had amazed me; to describe it briefly is to say it is a poor desert peninsula with beautiful beaches, but in three days I had seen three towns of strongly differing characters and atmospheres – Spanish, French and now Caribbean

Searching for the beach I met an American boy who gave me directions. It was deserted except for a penniless young German boy hitching down from San Francisco; an 'alternative' Swedish couple who had been cycling for two years but who were now living on the beach in an old van and a brusque, aged Alaskan with a long, shaggy beard who was also a permanent beach van resident.

Finally, in complete contrast, there was an immaculate up-market Californian couple who were cycling the length of Baja during their holidays, and who, after only two weeks in the saddle to my seven months, tried to tell me how to ride my bike – I should pull over for buses and lorries, I should watch out for lorry drivers, I shouldn't camp near the road, I should look out for this and look out for that. The arrogance of know-alls is sometimes amazing.

The next morning, a local man came round selling banana cake which he had made himself. He was a victim of one of the hundreds of road accidents of which I had seen evidence, and he was legless. His daughter had been killed in the crash. In England he would have claimed his disability pension and any compensation due, but the Baja offered no such luxuries, so he had built himself a low tricycle, adapted from a normal bike, which he could drive with his arms. It was so efficient that he competed successfully against regular cyclists in the annual bike race. Selling his cake was another of his survival strategies.

The Swedish couple also had to use a fair bit of resourcefulness to get by. They were living at rock bottom, not having the money to get back home. One of their schemes to put bread on the table was the collecting of empty cola cans. I had seen them scattered along the roadside and assumed it was just another example of a litter mentality, until I discovered that the kindest thing you can do with your cans is throw them out the window as they can be exchanged for money.

Everyone who is travelling long-term thinks they are doing something special. But no matter what you do, you inevitably hear about someone who is doing something even more incredible. At Mulege I heard the first of two such stories. The Swedish couple had met a Japanese couple who had been cycling for nineteen months, from Canada to Mexico (or the other way round). Okay, nothing there to make the mouth drop open, until they showed me a photo. There was the couple; but with them were their three children. The man had towed the two youngest in a bike trailer for the nineteen months, and the oldest one, a boy around ten or eleven, had cycled under his own steam. Nearly as amazing, the whole family was kitted out in glimmering white T-shirts.

The road from Mulege follows the western side of the Bahia de Concepcion for about fifty miles. This is a deep, sheltered bay with beaches to die for (needless to say, all the best ones were taken over by the Recreational Vehicle contingent). Although the late afternoon winds grew cold by the sea I was reluctant to leave such lovely coastal vistas, so I let them blow me to the El Coyote campsite where I stopped for possibly my last beach camp.

One half of the beach was an RV ghetto, but the 'primitive' end was quiet and only consisted of a handful of downbeat travellers in a beat-up Volkswagen. For two dollars a night I had the privilege of gazing on a scene worth a million dollars. Calm, crystal clear water of turquoise blue, its tranquil surface broken by rocky islands, pelicans, seabirds and the occasional small boat. As the sun nestled, waves lapped the shore, and the nearby islands reflected a burnished copper, I thought about what one of those old Jesuits had said a long time ago:

"Everything is of such little importance that it is hardly worth the trouble to write about it. Of poor shrubs, useless thorn bushes and bare rocks, of miles of sand without water or woods, of a handful of people who, beside their physical shape and ability to think, have nothing to distinguish them from animals, what shall I or what can I report?"

Of such things are wildernesses made! Thankfully in these late days we are finally able to recognise that it is not only the economically exploitable that has value.

It was at El Coyote that I encountered my next heroes – a young couple cycling from Washington State to Guatemala – with their eight-month-old baby. Even more impressive, they had a thoroughly laudable aim and were not just bumming around like me: he was a doctor hoping to get work when they arrived at their destination.

To avoid crumpling into a heap beneath their awesomeness, I told myself that maybe they did not have my mischievous little friend Motivation tweaking their ears in their weakest moments:

'What the hell do you think you're doing here, stupid? Why don't you just pack up and go home? What are you trying to prove, hey? Nobody cares whether you finish or not.'

'I care.'

'And who are you, Little Miss Dot On The Earth? Excuse me while I find my magnifying glass!'

But sitting in the all pervading sunset on El Coyote beach, nothing could daunt me, I was invincible. I felt so positive and strong, so thoroughly content, so certain that I would achieve my goal and would not be harmed. I was convinced that I had finally found my vocation, my niche in life.

For the rest of my journey I often thought of that couple making their way steadily down the coast, parallel to me as I ventured inland. Just knowing they were out there, in the same country, having good days and bad days just like me, uplifted me and gave me comfort whenever I was feeling alone, jaded or just plain knackered. In fact, the thought of women travelling with courage in difficult circumstances always gave me strength – even if their journeys had taken place a year, a decade, or a century ago. Their achievements took away the loneliness and the fear. I imagined their voices coming to me over the centuries:

We did it and so can you.

And then there are the show-offs!

A Mexican came to the beach one morning. He took from his bag four of the most exquisite handmade papier-mâché dolls I had ever seen. Perfect down to the finest detail, and painted with great care in the subtlest of colours. Worth at least fifty dollars. We admired their craftsmanship and beauty. The dealing was conducted in Spanish.

Vendor: "Twelve dollars."

Up pops Show Off, bursting out of his expensive shirt: "I'll give you nine."

Vendor: "You must be joking. You can see how well-made they are."

Show Off: "They're only worth eight."

Vendor: "In Mexicali they sell for not less than thirty."

Show Off, smirking at his own cleverness: "Ha... but you're not in Mexicali now."

Vendor, voice heavy with sarcasm: "No, that's why I'm only asking twelve!"

"Well... it's nine or nothing."

Vendor, with sigh: "Okay, I'll let you have one for eleven. But it's a joke."

Show Off laughs nonchalantly: "Nine or nothing."

Vendor: "Ten. That's the bottom price. The absolute lowest. I can't take less than that. I have to make a living. The workers have to make a living."

Show Off, playing to his audience: "Nine. Another dollar off, you get my business!"

Clearly he had never heard that the aim of bartering was to meet somewhere in the middle. But the vendor had assessed the character of his client well; he knew a power trip when he saw one. For the benefit of all he converted to good English and answered:

"Yes sir, I know you speak Spanish very well. All your friends can hear how well you speak it, and I'm sure they are very impressed by you. But I have to make a living and I will not come down one more dollar for you. I will sell them to people who know their value."

Without another word he put his dolls calmly in his bag and left the beach. We all looked at Show Off in silence while he tried to bluff it out:

"They're all the same, these Mexicans. He obviously didn't need a sale very much else he'd have taken nine dollars. Anyway I've seen better dolls in Tijuana."

Nobody answered him. I looked at his expensive mobile home, his Mitsubishi, his sleek, plump, sun-tanned body, his immaculate clothes, and for the rest of the day I thought of that one single dollar that he refused to pay.

The next day my second lot of eggs vanished, but I didn't mind. A little dog with seven tiny pups was running around in a perpetual frantic hunt for food so I thought the sacrifice worthwhile.

The hills were getting bigger, the land grassier, the desert more interesting, and the air pulsated with the sound of humming birds. That night my private place was shared with a mule, and a donkey so white that the air around it almost shone. I sat by my fire in the squat shadow of my elephant trees and pondered their relative value, and whether it is true that a tree is a tree is a tree, and whether, as science and commerce unite to spread lollipop trees across our land, we will have to come to the Third World to remember that chestnuts used to twist and willows used to creak.

BAG LADY

I stopped in Loreto, stocked up with food and had a lunch-time feast on the beach. Loreto was the site of the first Jesuit mission and the first permanent settlement in Baja. It was also through the port that the diseases entered which ravaged the Indian communities – smallpox, dysentery, malaria, typhoid, measles. Things got progressively worse. The Jesuits were replaced by the Franciscans and Dominicans, and women were routinely debauched by muleteers, soldiers, sailors and padres. In the last years of the Indians' demise throughout Baja there was scarcely a baby born which did not have congenital syphilis.

In this poisonous environment the women died in much greater numbers than the men – in the later years there were twice the number of men to women – mainly because the padres inflicted their own European codes of behaviour onto the Indians, which included removing the women from their traditional role of food gathering, shutting them up day and night in locked unsanitary rooms where viruses spread like wildfire, and where the loss of both liberty and hope deprived them of any motivation to live.

My diet in the Baja was a vast improvement on earlier days but I still found that my energy was extremely erratic. Most days I would start off vigorously and quickly clock up good mileage. Still feeling good, I would be confident that I could easily continue for at least another thirty or forty miles. The first twenty would be okay, but then within minutes, I would come to a full stop. After sixty relatively easy miles I would suddenly be unable to do another two, and the sight of even the slightest of slopes ahead would fill me with despair.

It was still very windy, but as I left Loreto my luck was holding and it remained at my back. My rise in blood sugar should have had me raring to go, and so it did for ten miles. But again my energy level plummeted, so suddenly and dramatically that I had to stop there and then, at that very minute.

Luckily there was a stony beach near the road, wild and dense with mangroves, a rough fisherman's home nearby. I dragged my bike through the bushes and dropped it on the stones. I dropped with it.

The heavens could have opened then and God could have poured his wrath upon me, but I would not, could not, have moved. After all these days, so many days when I thought that I really knew what tiredness was, I had found a new level of exhaustion. This was total exhaustion. It was as though a giant suction had been applied to my feet and sucked my body of all its blood, its oxygen, its life-giving juices, leaving just a drained dried-out husk, all force spent, like a discarded snake skin.

For twenty minutes I lay as though dead, until my brain took in the fact that I was still earthbound. My body tingled and was hot so I walked to the water and waded to my knees. This produced a sensation of painful bliss; the cold water was icy to my overheated body and took my breath away. I don't know if the body can drink water through the skin, but that was how it felt. My body craved water and coolness – not merely through the mouth as I was not thirsty – and I felt my legs soaking that cold liquid up, up, up into every pore, cooling and thinning my blood, flowing into the dried out corners, pouring like a torrent through my brain, oiling my aching joints, nourishing my organs. I was revived. I put my tent up and collected firewood for the evening.

This lassitude was a precursor of days to come and though the trials of later days in the hot humid oven of Central America came to be blurred in my mind, that day on the stony grey beach near Loreto still stands out in sharp isolation.

Next day I got a puncture, and stopped overlooking a deep valley. My water was low and traffic infrequent so when I saw an RV coming up the hill towards me I stuck my thumb out.

Not being able to avoid me, the vehicle stopped. I approached it on the passenger side where an elderly blank eyed woman was sitting, her thick white makeup filled her wrinkles, bright dabs of rouge circled her cheeks, scarlet lipstick outlined thin, tight, ugly lips. Blue hair was complemented by thick mascara and sky-blue eye shadow fixed to last the decade. A Barbara Cartland lookalike!

I spoke to her politely but she ignored me and continued to stare out the window, trying to pretend this awful intrusion wasn't happening. I turned to the driver, an elderly, portly man:

"I'm sorry to bother you, but I have a puncture and I'm nearly out of water. I wondered if you could spare me some as I'm not going to make it to a town before dark?"

The driver didn't answer, but took my one litre bottle and vanished solemnly into the back of the vehicle.

"I suppose we can let you have a little," he muttered grudgingly.

The woman continued to ignore me and my bottle was returned to me. I handed the second one over.

"Could you manage a second one?"

"Oh! You want another one?"

"Well, if you could manage it please."

He filled it in silence and handed it to me on his way back to his seat, that was definitely my lot! Oh, how I disliked them – their meanness and small mindedness, their ugly personalities.

What was really beyond my comprehension though, was what the hell such people were doing there. At least the El Coyote clique contributed something to the local economy, lived a relatively simple life on local produce and enjoyed Baja. I doubted this pair would be receptive to any of its charms, or entranced by its people.

I went on my way musing the human condition and wondering why people go to a place and then avoid everything that makes it what it is.

My bike tyre was splitting, my cooker wasn't working, I was filthy from making wood fires and I felt disorganised. Then, the last night before the final leg to La Paz, a wonderful camping place appeared at the side of the road; my favourite, a large wash full of shrubbery by a cliff face – unfortunately the river was dry, as they all had been so far. I settled in, replaced my tyre, dismantled my cooker for the thousandth time, and then I looked in my mirror. Suddenly I knew why everyone had been so unfriendly that day – staring, uncommunicative, no waves or smiles around there. I was a mess!

My clothes were dirty, my cap could not hide the greasy strands of hair which fell around my ears, my eyes were puffy, my hands and nails were ingrained with soot, and I saw to my shame that I had rings of black sweat lines around my neck. I looked more like a bum than a dollar-rich tourist. The most I was able to do was wipe the tidemark off my neck several times a day, make an effort to keep my hair out of sight till it could be washed, and try to get my hands a bit cleaner.

It was not only me of course. I had now been on the road about seven months, and my luggage and bike were no longer the posh tidy affair of earlier days. A small plastic laundry basket was now sitting on my front rack beneath my faded handlebar bag. My light-grey front pannier bags were no longer light-grey; they were carrying cooker, pans, fuel, oil and food basics, and had become black with soot, grease and petrol. I had sewn netting onto them to carry spare tyres and other projecting knick-knacks. There was usually a bag of eggs hanging from my handlebars (the avoidance of broken eggs was my life's mission), and still the bald eagle feather given to me by the Nez Perce Indian back on the Colville Reservation was still there.

My black rear Carradice panniers were covered in dust and dirt and were faded by the sun. They also had an assortment of patches and netting sewn on to increase their carrying capacity, more projecting items detracting from a neat appearance. My tent sat on the back rack. Hanging from, and draped over, everything was an assortment of plastic bags containing food, bottles containing water, drying clothes, towels and various other miscellaneous items. Finally, my bike itself was covered with a layer of dirt, paint was coming off, the mudguards were smashed; it looked just as a mature, working bike should look.

There wasn't much I could do about these things where water was so lacking, and though I wasn't prepared to attempt an impossibly high level of cleanliness just to impress others, nevertheless I did feel a bit embarrassed about my personal appearance.

This was really brought home to me the following day. I had stopped at El Cien for fuel and drink when, coming out of the café, I saw a mirage, a cyclist mirage, positively glowing with cleanliness and orderliness. I stared at him; I couldn't resist asking;

"My god! How do you manage to stay like that?"

He was spotless, his T-shirt gleamed white, he was even wearing

white socks. (I had dyed everything black so it wouldn't show the dirt.)
He was clean shaven, his hair was groomed. Even more astonishing
was his baggage; he had two neat little panniers on the front and two
on the rear – all four were immaculate and zipped up. (My zips were
either broken or the bags too full to zip.) Nothing hung off or stuck
out from anywhere, there was not a plastic bag to be seen. He had
just stepped out of a camping magazine advert.

My misgivings of the previous night, when I became aware of
my decline from relative respectability to near bag lady status, were
exacerbated. Now I could see clearly how far I had fallen; this was
the model to which I should aspire. He laughed at my question and
told me that he had only been on the road for two weeks and although
I felt somewhat mollified I knew that however long this man was on
the road, he would never degenerate to my standard. Some people
just aren't like that, they're like those self-cleaning ovens which never
get really dirty. I had been messier than him when I stepped off the
plane at Seattle.

By coincidence, a second cyclist then turned up. This one was
also 'Doing Baja' but unlike the first one was kitted out in all the
latest trendy cycling gear, including a skintight pair of very revealing
cycling shorts.

It may sound very petty to lose respect for someone because you
do not approve of their shorts, but sometimes little things reflect a
whole attitude. In America you can wear what you like on the cycling
circuit and his getup was the norm for there. In rural Mexico, if you
have any degree of sensitivity to the conservative nature of its society,
you do not. With his personal attitude, and in his skin tight shorts
he strutted around with his 'shopping' bulging out like a dozen eggs,
apparently unaware of the stares and titters of all who passed. I was
embarrassed and left his company as quickly as possible to return
to the cafe. I sat with the Mexican to whom I had been chatting
earlier.

"Why does he come here wearing those things?" he asked.

"Because he's stupid!"

I wish all questions were so easy to answer.

Fifty miles later I reached La Paz, to find, of course, that the shops
were shut because it was Sunday. Luckily for me this was more than

compensated for when I came across a public baths and was able to upgrade my appearance to a degree that surprised even me. Then I found that the numbers on my traveller's cheques (which I had been carrying in a plastic bag in my shoes for safety) had rubbed off and every last one of them was unacceptable to the banks.

The ferry to the mainland was a few miles out of town. I spent my last night watching the pelicans who still crash-dived like novices; maybe they will have got the knack by the time I return.

I thought of the dreamy uniqueness of Baja, the feeling that it is a land from an earlier wilder time, and how thrilling it would be if it could avoid further development and commercialization. Sadly, I doubt whether the pressure from the American leisure industry can be resisted in the long term – especially if it is allowed unfettered building access to the coast – and I am sure the peninsula's destiny is to be tidied up, spruced up, with more gated communities, more holiday homes, more private beaches, more luxury hotels. The real tragedy of Baja is that the poverty of its people means that they desperately want and need the roads which will bring the tourists to their door, the foreign businesses for jobs – they cannot afford to be 'romantic' about their land. Perhaps the best we can hope for is that, away from the coast, the baking heat of Baja's mountains, its pathless hills of thorns, its lack of roads, the fear of breakdown and the alien barrenness of its windy deserts will at least keep all but the truly dedicated from entering its heart.

COPPER CANYON

At the ferry station I met the boy who had directed me to the beach back in Mulege. He was saying goodbye to a departing friend of his, Pat from England, so Pat and I took the ferry to Los Mochis and then on to Creel together.

There is no road from Los Mochis to Creel – I suspect this is something to do with the rise in elevation from zero to two and a half thousand metres above sea level, and the fact that it necessitates traversing the somewhat lumpy Sierra Madre, and the spectacular Barranca del Cobre – the Copper Canyon, which is made up of around twenty canyons. These are not only deeper than the Grand Canyon of Arizona, they are also four times larger. When these dimensions are absorbed, the idea of a road is silly.

Where the road engineers have feared to tread, thank goodness, the rail engineers have conquered, their outstanding achievement being the Copper Canyon Railway which runs the six hundred and fifty-five miles from Los Mochis inland to Chihuahua; Creel lies about halfway.

Chihuahua to Creel was the first section to be completed in 1912, but it was 1962 before it eventually reached the coast, corkscrewing the track over thirty-nine bridges and through eighty-six tunnels between Los Mochis and Creel. Round and round until you can look into the guts of gorges beneath you and follow the switchbacks to where you have just come from.

The Canyon has been home to the Tarahumara Indians for hundreds of years, in the course of which they barely survived the sustained attentions of two of the world's most feared predators: first, from the Spanish, who wreaked death and destruction in the sixteenth century, and then from Apache raiders moving down from the north and who became the great terror of the desert realms of America and northern Mexico. They plundered and murdered at will, took livestock and slaves for use or sale, and then retreated into the inaccessible reaches of red canyon mazes and cottonwood washes.

Today there remain an estimated sixty thousand Tarahumara living in northwest Chihuahua, and it is the isolation and inaccessibility of the Copper Canyon which has enabled them to retain their old traditions and beliefs to a much greater degree than most other tribes. Sadly, threats have continued until recent times; lands have been opened up to settlement, gold and silver were discovered, lumbering became lucrative. Today the main dangers come from deforestation, and narcotics traffickers who have been intimidating Indians and forcing them to grow opium and marijuana on their hidden farms. This has resulted in the deaths of more than 150 Tarahumara Indians since 1988.

I had decided to cycle down into the very bottom of the Canyon, to an old silver village called Batopilas 140 kilometres away. As it meant a descent from 2400 metres down to a mere 500 metres I assumed it would be downhill all the way. If it was really bad I could get a lift out of the canyon on the bus which ran three times a week.

The road was a killer. After the first fifty kilometres it turned to gravel, sweeping me down to rivers and hauling me up the other side, throwing me onto the ground at will, until I gave up even trying to ride uphill. I passed through lovely pine woods, along trickling rivers where women and children were washing clothes, past staring donkeys and friendly dogs, through quiet villages with small clapboard or log houses, past small fields where men were ploughing with ponies.

I was impressed by the condition of all the animals, especially after the unhappy creatures I had seen in Baja. Without exception all the horses, cattle, donkeys, goats and sheep were sleek and plump with beautiful glossy coats (well, not the sheep). I put this down to the fact that they were mostly roaming free and could get their full calories and nutrition in this lush country. It was good to see, for how can you truly enjoy a country where the animals are half-starved or ill-treated?

The landscape became steeper, with stunning views of plunging gorges and I was beginning to wonder when the descent would begin, so far the ups had more than equalled the downs. The third day I found out! It occurred in one massive twelve mile plunge down an almost vertical cliff, the track snaking backwards and forwards in sharp switchbacks until it reached the river far, far below. From the top the swollen winter waters looked like a tiny trickle.

In my innocence I had imagined that downhill would be easier and faster than uphill. Of course anything was easier than the previous miles, but faster it was not. The steepness of the gradient and the roughness of the track meant that for the whole twelve miles I had to stand up to maintain my balance, and grip my handlebars tightly until my hands were red and blistered. There was no way that I was going to tackle this going the other way. I had difficulty imagining even a bus getting up such a steep hill.

Great rocks towered above me, some sheer and smooth, others more ragged where deciduous and evergreens trees clung tenuously to the steep slopes. The midnight-blue river surged through the valley, deep blue-green pools tempting the sweating passerby into their delicious coolness. Several plump, white-nosed black donkeys passed me by, laden with packs and accompanied by Taramuhara men in traditional clothes of baggy blouses in bright pinks or greens, and short, white skirts. They greeted me in Spanish with a polite smile. I couldn't help feeling excited meeting them; although reputedly they dislike and isolate themselves from both whites and Mexicans they always greeted me amiably; two even stopped to ask about my ride.

The lack of public transport and the poverty and isolated homes of the Tarahumara meant that walking was their usual method of getting around and their tribal name – Raramuri – translates as 'those who walk fast' or 'those with light feet'. History records their fantastic feats of endurance and their traditional hundred mile running races, not only contending with the gruelling ruggedness of their landscape but also simultaneously kicking a wooden ball. The Norwegian explorer Carl Lumholtz records a man running six hundred miles in five days.

One man I met was going in my direction, so I was able to get some idea of his stamina. On the descents, I overtook him; on the ascents he overtook me. It soon became a matter of pride that I show the superiority of the bike over the foot – everyone knows it's quicker and more efficient to cycle, don't they? But sweat and struggle as I did, he gradually gained on me until I finally gave up the chase. Never changing his pace, he kept up a fast but steady walk, uphill or down, always maintaining the same rhythm.

I was loathe to leave this cosy rural serenity just yet, so I camped beneath shady riverside willows, eking out my pleasure as long as possible before entering Batopilas ten miles away. In this secluded spot I bathed in the river and washed my grubby, sweat-soaked clothes. My weariness left me. The whole day had been glorious and the trials of the past two days were already worth it. It was this that kept me going – knowing that whatever depths of depravity my language reached in the daytime, at the end of the day I would feel that nowhere in the world could be as good as the place I was in.

I was realising something; as I looked back to Baja I realised it had been a sort of transition zone, a dreamland which separated the great differences of the American north from the Mexican south. Now I began to be conscious that it was not only language, culture and history which differed, it was something deeper.

North of the border lies a country which is its land in a way that Mexico is not. In Mexico the land felt like a passive stage on which the staggering human tragedies and exaggerated dramas had taken place and it does not retain, as America does, the quiet spirits of its ancestors – they do not come out to whisper bitter-sweet words in the misty valleys or linger to haunt in the forest pools.

In Mexico ghosts take another, more tangible, form. They exist in the evocativeness of some of the old colonial towns, in the clothes of the native people, their beliefs, their languages, their old temples and ruins, and what I can only call their 'otherness'. There is a heady mix of tradition and Catholicism, of old and new, which have merged into an exciting and indecipherable, inseparable mix, so that the outsider may never understand what goes on inside the heads and hearts of the native people, and always there is the feeling that their cultural carapace can never be penetrated.

The majority of the Mexican population is mixed-blood mestizo, formed by the merging of Spanish and Indian, and although this may distance them somewhat from the cultural 'depths' of the Indian, nevertheless it also takes you back to those brutal days of early conquest. Thus, every time you look into the face of a mestizo you are looking into the reality of a single moment in time, a moment of conception – maybe a vicious one – which took place ten, a hundred, five hundred years before, when the mixed-blood ancestor of that Mexican was conceived.

But whatever the origins of the new race, the fruit is sweet, for whether or not the mestizo honours the blood of one ancestor over the other it is clear that the two together produce a unique and beautiful blend. It is a cruel irony that the 'extinction' of such an ancient charismatic race should now live in such perfect genetic harmony with its slayer.

Batopilas is a quaint and pretty nineteenth century town with a resident population of about six hundred. It is almost the end of the road from which, unless you intend continuing by foot, you turn round and go back. Unfortunately I soon discovered that it was a town in which I was reluctant to stay because of its unfriendliness. Shopkeepers were unhelpful and pretended to misunderstand my Spanish – I mean you can't go far wrong with 'tomates' can you? Even when I wrote it down they professed ignorance; after similar treatment in several shops I gave up.

Evening vibes were no better. Teenagers sneered as I passed; men and women gave me angry stares. This was in such contrast to the friendly Tarahumara I had met on the road that I put it down to tourist fatigue, that was easier than taking it personally. And if the Tarahumara receive the same treatment as me it is to be hoped that they believe, as they used to, that night is day in the land of the dead, that the moon is the sun and that heaven is full of flowered gardens where good souls and the heavenly throng live happily together, then they have a good reason to smile, in spite of their earthly difficulties.

Doom Mongers

The bus was due to leave the next morning at the unearthly hour of four o'clock. If I missed it I would have to stay another three days, unless I wanted to drag my heavy bike up the impossible hill. It turned up in the dark on schedule, and the ways of the town continued as the driver and his helper refused to help me haul my bike or luggage onto the roof. They just stood and watched as I struggled to climb the ladder with one hand while hanging onto the bike with the other.

I got out at the Creel/Parral junction. The road was gravel as far as Balleza, but at least it was relatively flat and the ride followed rolling, chalky, pine-covered hills which covered everything in a dusting of white.

Though everyone knows that misery and poverty can be hidden behind a rich facade, we usually choose to shut out such thoughts; and why shouldn't we when the realities are not obvious? So although I was aware that Mexico was a poor country nevertheless its beauty, the immaculate turnout of many of residents and its supremely healthy animals, all combined to create an easy illusion of the wealth and comfort of its citizens.

So as I pootled along, enjoying the scenery, it was with shock and dismay that in the midst of this rural charm I came face to face with the spectre of utter destitution and hopelessness. A girl of about seven, carrying an adult-sized spade and accompanied by two toddlers of about two or three, stood by the road. A car passed and the girl held out her hand; pathetically the tiny ones aped her.

It was not only the fact that such tiny children were begging, or their obvious awful poverty, nor even the dangers of abuse to which they were exposed, that was so shocking – though these were disturbing enough. It was not even the rags they were dressed in or the filthiness of their bodies and clothes. What stayed with me was the sheer blank despair of their faces. To see expressions, which should have been bright with the excitement, anticipation and curiosity of childhood, blank of anything but utter misery and incomprehension. Their dirty little faces appeared stunned by a life which had known no joy – only hunger, hard work and who knows what other abuses.

They did not hold out their hands to me, just stood and stared like I was a ghost from the grave – and, rightly or wrongly, I left a few pesos on the road for them.

The area was ideal hiking territory, and the thought of striking out into those green and golden hills was tempting; but cattle were the kings here which meant that the road was now lined endlessly with infernal barbed-wire. In hundreds of miles there was not one gap, not a single unlocked gate, not a lane to wander down, nor a wood to hide in.

The wire ensured that the whole of northern Mexico is, in effect, off-limits to its own people. They are firmly excluded from their own countryside; the only limited access they may have to the land is if they work on one of the massive ranches which cover thousands of acres of their heritage. Only one small, dirty, miserable lake was available to the public, and half of that had a fence across.

Just before Balleza I went into a roadside cafe which looked welcoming and homely. This was run by Martha, who decided after ten minutes that she wanted me to share the day with her:

"You can have a shower and wash your things, then you can eat with me and my husband and stay the night."

"But I've only just set off today; I should keep going."

"No, you stay here, I want you to stay."

"Why do you want me to stay?"

"Because you are my friend."

It's hard to resist such easily conferred affection, but I have learnt the superficiality of the term 'friend', often cast with some intensity at casual acquaintances, and received in the early naive days of travel as a flattering sign of our likeability. Now I realise that our novelty value quickly palls. Once we have been exhibited to friends and family, and the laughter caused by our language gaffes fades, then we are left alone with our inadequate communications and our polite smiles, and it is time to move on. But Martha was different. She seemed to take a genuine pleasure in my company, and her husband was a kind, gentle man happy to indulge his wife's pleasures.

"You have to be really careful in Mexico," Martha told me. "Mexican men are very bad and you're a woman alone. They'll think you must be a bad woman because you're not with a man and they may attack you and rape you."

"Surely they won't think that. I'm on a bike. They can see I'm just a gringa travelling through your country."

"It doesn't make any difference. You're a lone woman and that's all they care about. They don't think beyond that. These men are stupid and bad. Mexican women never travel alone or go to discos or bars alone."

I had heard so much about Latin machismo and sexual harassment but I rarely met it. Only the fantasies of some car and truck drivers became tiresome. Their little trick was boringly predictable; they would overtake me and stop ahead, when I had nearly caught up they would decide they needed a pee and then, surprise, surprise, they would have the sudden urge to turn round and look at the scenery across the road as I passed. After a while, whenever a vehicle stopped ahead of me I would turn round and cycle the opposite way until out of view. I never felt physically threatened by these morons, but there was no way I was going to add fuel to their fantasies.

Martha was relatively well-to-do, her cafe was clean, cosy and well-frequented. But it was a rural house and the shower turned out to be a cold water tap outside by the road, the toilet was the field behind the house, and my bedroom a bench in the corner of Martha and her husband's own bedroom. In common with many of the better-off she employed Mexican Indians to do housework, hers being a silent woman with two dirty, snotty-nosed children; the three of them sat on the porch in a solemn group. I wondered what five hundred years of colonisation had done for them.

At teatime I was taken with Martha and her husband to the nearby town of Balleza where I was taken to visit Mother. This ancient but very alert lady lived in a grand old Spanish house and employed a smiling Indian girl. Black lace covered her head and a shawl hung over her shoulders. Her face wore that tragic expression so familiar on the faces of older Mediterranean and eastern women – one intended to convey a life of suffering and hardship borne with weary stoicism. In reality these women are usually as tough as old boots.

Martha's mum was a sweetie though. When she heard of my 'tragic' circumstances – that I was travelling alone – she held my hand in hers, stroked my hair and gripped my arm, gazing up into my eyes with an expression of overwhelming sympathy.

"Oh, you poor, poor thing. Alone! Alone! You are all alone. It is terrible to be alone. And so dangerous."

I could not bring myself to spoil her obvious enjoyment of the melodrama. She would be in her element telling the story to her coffee pals and would gain vital street cred for her central role. So I lowered my eyes in brave sorrow and tried to bear my pain heroically.

I should have introduced here my later ploy of Husband Tragically Killed In Car Crash – very useful when you get fed up of being bombarded with questions about your solitary state. But I had to admit the reality that I was in a country where a woman was respectable with a man, and to be pitied or despised if she was not – especially if she had no children. A country where the first six questions asked of a traveller are:

"Where are you going?"

"Where have you come from?"

"What religion are you?"

"How old are you?"

"Are you married?"

"Do you have children?"

So later I started proudly proclaiming that I was a Mother with three Sons; and unashamedly gave my ex-husband new status in my life. If he was not dead, then he was a couple of miles behind, or waiting for me ahead, or he had become ill, insisting that I carry on alone. I never knew that lying could be so much fun. I could be as inventive as I wanted, knowing that it was actually for a good cause – to avoid causing offence or discomfort, as well as gaining more respect and security.

I set off for Hidalgo de Parral. This town is renowned for being a site of Pancho Villa's garrison (he of numerous westerns where Mexicans were involved) and the place of his murder in 1923. Villa was the quick tempered Robin Hood of the Great Mexican Revolution of 1910. In true revolutionary style he mixed freely with his men, nurtured his injured, fed the starving and unemployed, loved children, and happily slaughtered his enemies with ruthless abandon, sometimes shooting three men with one bullet – each victim behind the other – to save ammunition.

The odd thing is that this was a revolution in which a million people died, a terrible civil war in which the poor rose up in their hundreds of thousands to fight against centuries of injustice. And yet in films it is always presented as a jolly chaotic romp in which prodigious amounts of alcohol are consumed and lovely lusty wenches sit on uniformed knees in the broiling godforsaken lands of northern Mexico. Always those same old Hollywood images of Mexicans as figures of fun, with sing-song voices, who laugh hysterically as they rape, kill, plunder and cheat their way through life.

Since day one I had been bombarded by doom mongers who assured me that destruction was awaiting round every corner, ready to pounce in some unspecified way, but I rarely took such warnings seriously as, unless I gave up the ride altogether there was nothing I could do that I wasn't already doing. I would just listen politely and move on. On the road to Durango however my temper finally frayed as yet another sought me out to inflict his prophecy of my early demise upon me. The catalyst for my irritation was the wind and my diary suggests that I was in no mood for idiots:

'Reduced to tears by the wind. Only thirty-three miles.'

Before retreating to my roadside juniper hideaway waiting for the wind to push off, I had taken a break in an isolated cafe where a group of five middle-class Mexicans were drinking beer. One of them came to sit by me. He spoke English.

"Where are you heading?"

"Next place, Durango."

"You'll never make it!"

"Oh, really?"

"No. This road is really dangerous."

"Oh, I think I've heard all this before."

"Really! It is! This is one of the worst areas in Mexico. The mafia are always travelling on this road. You won't make it to Durango."

"I don't think they'll be interested in a scruffy middle-aged gringa on a bike somehow. I'm hardly rich pickings."

"They'll go for anything. They'll rape you – take everything you have just for fun. Even if they don't, bandidos will. You must get off this road."

"And just how do I get off it without cycling on it? I'd have to cycle to Durango even if I decided to get a train. Are you suggesting I give everything up?"

"No, of course not."

"Well, why are you trying to frighten me then? I'm tired of people telling me there are murderers waiting round every corner. You know I have to stay on the road until Durango so what is the point of telling me how dangerous it is?"

"I'm sorry. I wasn't trying to frighten you. I wanted to warn you, to help you. I mean, just be careful, that's all. You don't know Mexico."

"Well of course I'm careful. I don't cycle at night and I don't camp where I can be seen by passing traffic. That's all I can do! I've just cycled through Baja so I do have a bit of an idea."

"You've just cycled through Baja?"

"Yes."

"Right through?"

"Down to La Paz."

"Jesus Christ; you're crazy. Forget everything I said. You'll be OK! You'll get there okay. I wish you good luck."

Crazies are clearly immune from mafiosi or bandidos!

Thankfully the wind passed on its way in the course of a night interrupted by yelping coyotes, a sound which swept away the blues immediately. A huge dog the size of a bear crawled under the fence and kept me company until the dark settled. I read a few pages of Father Melancholy's Daughter and fell asleep.

IN THE STEPS OF
PANCHO VILLA

Country life in Mexico is very photogenic. As I passed through the villages of the river valley chubby animals were everywhere; ducks, chickens and pigs wandered in the streets or squawked and grunted from shady gardens, donkeys ran along the road ahead of me, too stupid to realise they merely had to go on the verge to let me pass; horses and cattle gazed at me from their fields.

A wave and a smile brought reciprocal greetings from the old men of the villages. Women smiled more shyly and with astonishment at this lone woman doing what they themselves neither could, nor would want, to do. Several times I received the compliment from older adults of both sexes: "Muy valiente – you're very brave," with no trace of resentment of my privileged, unworking state.

Poverty was not obvious in these relatively fertile valleys, but there were indicators that life was not easy – lots of men walking around with machetes for example; men do not get a healthy bank balance by labouring with a machete for their living. Another sign could be seen out of the valleys and up on the hilltops where fields with more stones than soil were being laboriously ploughed with horse-drawn, single-bladed, hand-held ploughs.

I did not take any photographs but I'm sure they would have looked good if I had; beautiful mountains, simple technology, nice horse, handsome peasant – everything except the reality of sweat and poverty.

I had suddenly developed a craving for Coca-Cola; water no longer satisfied my thirst and my whole motivation for moving was the thought that the next village may have a shop with Coca-Cola. Food was a secondary concern. In some desperate moments I thought I could even have killed for that first delicious sip of relief, the cold fizz swishing around my mouth and sliding down my parched throat to gasps of bliss and ecstasy.

That day a car overtook me, and instead of faking a pee the driver took my photo for a periodical he worked for, gave me a jar of honey and drove off. Shortly after, another did the same and gave me a can of coke and a bottle of mineral water. Clearly it was my day.

At Cerro Gordo, and after only thirty-five miles, I finally gave up my fight against the wind for the day. By the time I went to bed I heartily wished that I had carried on.

The village had prison-like veneer emphasised by a gate and high fence encircling the village. On balance I thought it more likely that residents would to want to break out, than that outsiders would want to break in.

I asked the local shopkeeper if there was somewhere, anywhere, in the village for me to put my tent. A long silence followed. I hoped it was not going to get complicated. Eventually he instructed me brusquely:

"Come with me."

Followed by a score of children he took me to a small house, where he sat me down and proceeded to talk for forty minutes to the woman, Maria, who lived there, as they determined my fate. Clearly I had created a problem. Eventually I was taken round the corner to a cold and windowless concrete cell. That did not bother me, except that the lack of a window necessitated opening the door, and that meant being besieged by hordes of children. This was okay until my novelty value wore off and their friendliness turned to cockiness as they dared each other to ever braver and more tiresome feats.

The final straw was a visit from the local harridan who had decided that I was to blame for the behaviour of the little monsters. Fed up with her ranting I found myself apologising for the sins of the world just to get rid of her; then I slammed the door shut and suffered the pitch darkness in peace.

Eventually I couldn't stand my claustrophobic cell, so I went to visit Maria and her husband. They turned out to be a lovely couple, and after a pleasant couple of hours they insisted on escorting me back in the dark to my door. Awaiting my return was a committee of twelve villagers who had taken a communal decision that I was not to be allowed to stay where I was.

"You can't stay here, it isn't safe."

Here we go again. Apart from the kids I had only seen three youths of about seventeen and there did not seem to be any places selling alcohol or dubious men hanging around. All my gear was scattered over the room and I was loathe to pack it all up again by torchlight. I just wanted to be left alone to go to sleep, I neither wanted all the fuss and bother nor wanted others to be put out by my presence.

"Your door doesn't lock and the men will come and break it down."

I played ignorant in the hope that they would give up and go away.

"Thank you. It's really good here. I'll sleep really well."

"She doesn't understand what we're saying. She can't stay here."

This went on for fifteen minutes followed by group discussion. They tried again.

"The men are really bad here, they attack women. They'll come and break your door down and attack you. You can stay with this lady in her house. Come, we'll show you the room."

Two of them took my arm and marched me off. They had made the decision for me.

The house belonged to an old woman and was huge, with a large enclosed courtyard typical of old Spanish homes. I was to have a room to myself. Well, okay, I thought, maybe it is worth the effort to move. Neither did I want to seem ungrateful; besides, there is only so long you can play dumb, and when you realise that people are starting to think you are just plain thick, then pride takes over. So forty-five minutes after being escorted to my room I knew it was time to get a brain. We returned to my cell.

"Oh, now I understand. It's dangerous here. Men will come in the night and attack me. You want me to stay at the other house, yes?"

The whole group visibly relaxed in the darkness, smiles and sighs went round.

"Aahh. Yes, yes. It's dangerous. She understands us now. You didn't understand us before, did you?"

"No. I'm sorry. I didn't understand, but now I do."

Laughs all round, the world was in order now.

"It's okay now, she understands. She didn't understand us before. She doesn't understand Spanish."

"No, she didn't understand us before."

I felt a right heel!

The following morning I paid a departing visit to Maria.

"What about these bad men?" I asked. "Who did they attack? Is it true? What happened? Why does everyone say the village men are so awful?"

"Yes, it's true. They are bad. They would have attacked you in the night. Two years ago they raped a girl."

"Oh, no. What happened? Was it a village girl? What happened to the men?"

I felt ashamed that I had doubted their word.

"No, it wasn't a girl from this village. She worked on a ranch ten miles away and a man raped her there."

"Oh, so it didn't happen in this village? Was the man from here?"

"No. He was from somewhere else. He was sent to prison."

So the bad village men waiting to break down my door and ravage me turned out to be a single man from another village who raped a girl ten miles away and who was now in prison. If that is not seeing bogeymen under the bed I don't know what is. Maybe they were frightened of the remotest possibility of anything happening to a gringa in their care and were not prepared to take the risk; they presumably knew only too well the unpleasant complications which would ensue; and surely they knew the hard time their own police would give them!

Being a prestigious town in the north, the cobbles of Zacatecas had also rung to the boots of Pancho Villa, who had stormed the town with guns and machetes, leaving the blood of ten thousand draining through the alleys.

But if tragic death sometimes leaves its traces in the stones and mortar of a place, in its air, then none of it was evident here, for this was a wonderfully lively town, made more so because, being so far north, it was not on the gringo route – in four days I didn't see a single white. Gringos head south to trendy places like Oaxaca, San Cristobal or the beach resorts, and sadly for them they miss this lovely, relaxed city where lovers kiss in the parks and are openly affectionate in a way I had not seen until now. Teenage girls sat on the grass chatting and giggling, men chatted to me, couples with children smiled, and a man in mini skirt, heels and heavy makeup invited me for a drink. (I chickened out). On the street I watched as a boy struggled to fell an old eucalyptus with a small hand axe. A man on a donkey laden with earthenware pots walked beneath.

By the time I neared Guanajuato, the heat had become intense, the traffic frantic, and the last couple of hills sent me to the tourist booth on the perimeter of town, where I paid ten pesos for the luxury of a lift to a camp site the other side of town. The almost vertical and intricate road system made it the best ten pesos ever spent. The small camp was situated on a steep hillside cut into a series of ledges to accommodate campers.

If I raved over Zacatecas, I was in ecstasy over Guanajuato, another sixteenth century silver town. This really was a place to live in, and invasion by legions of retired potbellied gringos had mercifully not yet taken place. I suspect it was not quite sedate or conventionally pretty enough for them. Guanajuato was an example of how town life should be; a place where you felt alive and 'connected'. There were no quiet suburbs and carefully manicured gardens, the streets were not empty after six o'clock. It was full of noise and energy – a glorious eccentric jumble of nooks and crannies, of steps, narrow roads disappearing into black tunnels, high walls and secret zocalos.

Sitting as it did in a steep valley, surrounded by dry rocky hills and ravines, the evening sounds of the town resonated back and forward across the valley. The echoes of dogs, children and music intermingled in the evening dusk in a comforting cacophony of noise; morning began with the crowing of cocks and bleating of goats. Even the magpies and crows which hopped clumsily around the trees had a long and noisy tale to tell. I felt I was part of a living organism. Mexico never ceases to be outrageously tragic, it never ceases to be complicated, and it never ceases to be intoxicating. I loved it!

Though some of the vibrancy of the city must come from the existence of the university, nevertheless everybody seemed happy and friendly. Every woman over sixteen seemed to have a baby or to be pregnant, and they all smiled when you caught their eye. I ate a banana, threw the peel in a bin, and a man came over and thanked me. Even the policeman was smiling. I had been wanting a good whistle, and when I saw that the policeman directing the congested traffic in the middle of town was blowing one that could have been heard in Mexico City I dashed out to him in the middle of the road.

"Excuse me. But I want a whistle like yours. Can you tell me where I can buy one," I asked.

He beamed with pride.

"This is a police whistle, but you can buy a football referee whistle at the market. They also are very loud."

As I sat in the dark on my grassy ledge overlooking the town, a middle-aged couple emerged from an adjacent house and introduced themselves as Roger and Emily. They were Americans who lived in Guanajuato for six months of each year and they were shortly to go off on a refugee feeding programme in Guatemala.

They were just about to return indoors when a taxi drew up and ejected an elderly and very drunk American. This person began shouting some gobbledygook, insisting that Roger and Emily extend their hospitality to him. As they had never seen him before, and as he was becoming increasingly offensive, they paid the taxi driver to take him away and deposit him outside the police station for a night in the cells.

By this time the guy was sprawled on the ground yelling that we were all a load of effing bastards and all Mexicans were effing mother fuckers. With difficulty but without sympathy we bundled him back into the car and left him to his fate. There really is nothing so disgusting or shameful as the sight of a drunken westerner staggering around in a third world country.

I was very happy in shabby lived-in Guanajuato. Final proof of the relaxed nature of its inhabitants came as I was leaving. A car jammed its brakes on too sharply, the one behind crashed into it with a loud thwack. Anywhere else there would have been an argument. Not in Guanajuato! The front driver calmly got out, looked at his smashed lights, then walked over and placed his hand on the other's shoulder in commiseration; he smiled meekly and shrugged his shoulders in acknowledgement of his fault.

It is Sod's Law in cycling that one type of obstacle will always be ready to take the place of another. If there are no mile-high mountains to clamber up there will be a thousand smaller hills to kill you, if it is flat there will be a head wind, if there is no head wind you will forced onto a busy main road, if the road is quiet there will be ten zillion potholes, and if everything is perfect you will get a puncture. Finally, in those very, very rare moments when all the gods are with you and you should be bowling along in ecstatic abandon, you can be absolutely certain that your bum will be killing you.

'Sod' was very energetic as I left Abasolo. Wanting an early start I was up at five thirty and off by seven, only to find my back tyre was flat. I unloaded everything. Neither my pump, nor that of the family in whose garden I was camping, would work. They told me the garage was only half a mile away. Three miles later I reached it. I reloaded and rode into town to find the turn-off sign for Zacapu, as I was instructed. I couldn't find it, so decided to have a snack in the market. The tortilla was disgusting and I gave it to a dog.

I decided to phone Justin, who was still in Nevada, but the phone office wasn't open. I tried another, but the operator wouldn't answer. I gave up. I then found that the turn-off was not in town after all but was out on the main road where I had come from. I turned onto quiet back roads, only to find myself on a patchwork of atrociously repaired potholes and big holes. This then turned into a gravel track.

In spite of all this I had a good day's ride. I was now in the fertile state of Michoacan and the greater wealth of the people was beginning to show in the pretty villages and flower covered houses. I camped hidden among riverside willows and bamboo, the sounds of rural life carrying to me on the warm evening breeze. I had saved a bottle of coke which I cooled in the river. The day had ended well after all.

THE HOUSE OF
ELEVEN PATIOS

The nice thing about travelling without a guide book is that you are often surprised, and in Mexico that is usually a pleasant surprise. I had entered the country as a throughway to Guatemala, not in a particular desire to see it so, lacking preconceptions or expectations, everything good was exceptionally good.

Oddly though, nobody had suggested that Patzcuaro might be worth a visit. I called in only because I noticed Lake Patzcuaro on my map and fancied a night by water; nothing prepared me for the work of art that the town is. So exceptional were the architecture and the old mellowed colours, that my normal camera reserve broke down and in a couple of hours I had used a whole role of film.

As soon as I entered the beautiful shaded zocalo, surrounded by lovely arched seventeenth century buildings, the Indianness of the town was immediately apparent. Places with a large Indian presence and strong Indian culture have an altogether different ambience from those with a predominantly mestizo population – the invasions of the conquistadors could have been a mere generation before; the air is somehow heavier, richer; the past is closer.

Patzcuaro was the centre of the powerful Tarascan Indian empire when the Spanish turned up in the 1520s. Being enemies of the Aztecs the new young king (cazonci) thought that the Spanish (being the enemy of their enemy) would be their friend, but as he was slowly tortured to death on the instructions of the brutal conquistador Bloody Guzman he soon learnt his mistake. As I read of his bewildered weeping under torture: 'Why are they treating me so badly?', and of the heart-wrenching report that 'the cazonci's colour was now bad...

and his face was almost black,' I could almost see him before me. The reality of his human responses brought the tragedy of those times alive in a way that the anonymous deaths of all those other hundred million could not. By the time the good guy Quiroga arrived, Guzman had done an efficient job in smashing Indian culture and scattering the frightened people into the surrounding hills.

I wandered the town in a trance. I longed to live in one of the little, windowless, single-storey white and red/brown houses that lined the streets, and sit in the cool courtyards in their rear. I wanted my corner shop to be that tiny store where you could buy one nail or a single egg. I ached to take a room over the arches in the central zocalo and watch the busy town go by from my wooden balcony. I wanted, in the heat of the afternoons, to be able to walk into the cool of the ancient churches and sit awhile. I wanted that old Indian woman selling tomatoes to say Hello to me each morning as I passed by.

I especially loved the small, domed churches hiding in quiet back streets. They wore their age like a beautiful shawl, faded by time to shades so soft and subtle; hundreds of years under the baking heat of the sun and the cool fall of rain had mottled the cracked and chipped walls into warm, mellow hues of sand and gold that made the larger, grander structures look characterless and bare.

Round every corner came another joy: crooked steps climbing a time-soaked stone wall, an old doorway, the staining of a wall beneath crooked eaves, a warped balcony, the glimpse of a walled garden or courtyard, cool with plants, fountains and tile mosaics.

There was so much to see, but I could only go to places and things which were free. I had finally plucked up courage to calculate my finances and it was worse than I had feared. When I thought about it I panicked, so I tried not to think, just avoided lots of nice things like art galleries, museums, treats. So I did not go to the Popular Arts Centre, even though it had a tantalising courtyard, because it was thirteen pesos entry. Instead I wallowed in the Casa de Los Once Patios – the House of Eleven Patios – which was free.

And if I were a millionaire and had the choice of any house in the world, I would buy the House of Eleven Patios, a jewel in the crown of Spanish colonial architecture!. Dreamily I chose my bedroom and my reading room, the place for my morning coffee, the dimmed corner for my siesta. I experimented sitting in different positions on the balconies under the stone arches, and seeing the wonderful and changing juxtapositions of angles and shadows, the way the heavy dark doors turned red in reflected light, the undulations in the red tiles. It was painful to drag myself away, knowing that this was probably leaving my life for ever.

I was camped about a mile from the centre on a brilliant camp site, where I had the use of kitchen facilities and a swimming pool, the owner was a real gent. I was astonished to meet an English couple I had met in Guanajuato. She said to me:

"I admire what you're doing but you must admit that you see much more by car. In the time you've taken to get from Guanajuato we've been to half a dozen places and seen lots more than you."

Er…

The next morning started badly. I thought I would clean my gear as it was looking a bit scruffy again so I scrubbed a pannier and left it to dry. When I turned round five minutes later it had gone. In panic I realised the odd job boy must have taken it and I rushed out to find the owner. He took me to the pit where they burned rubbish but all that remained of my indispensable (and expensive) pannier was a smouldering zip.

I needed that bag, and even if I could buy another in Patzcuaro (which I doubted) I certainly could not afford it. I asked the owner if, given that it was his employee who had destroyed it, he would contribute towards another one.

"Certainly not. I didn't destroy it. I'm not responsible."

"But he's employed by you and he was stupid. It was obvious that it wasn't rubbish. He should have asked."

"It's not my problem."

I looked in town for alternatives but there was nothing. Then I had a brainwave, my roadside debris collections were ready to bear fruit. In the Baja I had found the cover of some piece of water sports equipment which was a heavy-duty and waterproof nylon. I went into town and bought bolts, washers, cord, elastic, hooks, rings, and a piece of plywood. By the time it was dark I had made a pannier to be proud of.

All day while I was sewing the camp owner had been walking past – we didn't speak. The following morning I packed slowly and when I was nearly finished he came over to me.

"I see you're leaving. I've been thinking about what you were saying and you're right, I have a moral responsibility to you. There are times when things are more important than money and the main thing now is that I fulfil my obligation to you. I'd like you to have these two nights free."

What a lovely, lovely, man. I was very happy, not only because this meant I would, in effect, get back the money I had spent, but because I had really liked this man and had been upset by our disagreement.

"I knew you were a gentleman!"

"I think I am. I always try to live my life like a gentleman and be honourable and I am sorry when people think that I'm not. I'm glad we are friends again and you will always be welcome here."

I rode away from the camp thinking how wonderful the human race is.

Towards Morelia the road became busy and I was unable to escape off the road unseen. I always ensured that my choice of night-time camping place went unobserved. Eventually I came across a sloping field overlooking a lake. There was a little house nearby so I went over to ask if it was okay to camp there. Half a dozen children of all ages emerged, all of them were thin, dirty and in rags, and all were barefoot. I asked if their mother was there, but received only frightened and uncomprehending stares. A teenage girl came from the back, took one look at me, screamed and ran away (and this was one of my better days).

A few miles further on, I took a track to a young eucalyptus plantation hugging a soft, grassy slope, cosy and hidden, no houses or villages to be seen. It was dusk and I was pleased with myself and with Jung. I drifted to sleep.

Now anyone who has camped alone in the wild knows how easy it is to interpret night-time rustlings around the tent as something malevolent, with dark designs on your being. The ultimate terror, of course, is hearing the undeniable sound of human footsteps around the tent in the small hours. That night it finally happened.

At four o'clock I was woken in the darkness by the unmistakable sound of footsteps coming stealthily but determinedly towards me. The footsteps stopped by my tent and all was quiet for a couple of minutes. Then the silence was broken:

"Hallo? Hallo?"

I didn't answer. His voice became sharper.

"Hallo? Where are you? Answer me."

I quickly located my teargas spray (available from American supermarkets) and my knife. Feeling more confident I unzipped the door and peered out. I decided to reply as though it was the most normal thing in the world for a man to appear at my tent in the dark at four in the morning.

"Hallo. You're up early."

For the next two and a half hours I invoked all my powers of tact and diplomacy like never before. I had to remember that this was Mexico so I had to make him like a Real Man at the same time as you are rejecting their attentions. A hard tightrope to walk.

First I made a physical barrier by placing my burning cooker, food and pans between us. Then I set about creating a 'safe' relationship by treating him as a respected friend whom I had invited to dinner, making him coffee and talking to him about his family, his mother, wife and children. I spoke of Mexico's beauty and its honourable people.

After about an hour I could see he was beginning to relax. He smiled, offered me a cigarette and lounged back on the grass. But when he asked what I was doing on my own, I thought it wise to be cautious:

"I'm not actually on my own. I'm cycling with my husband but he's faster than me, and I was tired so I decided to stop here. He's in Morelia now and if I don't turn up he'll be really worried and call the police out."

It was obviously a lie and he clearly doubted me, but couldn't be sure. Finally, at six-thirty, he said he should have been at his job on the ranch at six and he must go. I gave thanks that his brains had not been between his legs.

I was now coming within the vicinity of Mexico City, hence busier roads. Luckily for me, a new road had been built to the capital (it was not even on my map) which left the old road almost empty of traffic. As I rode higher into the hills I realized that the haze which brought a romantic veneer to the landscape was really the smog of pollution from Mexico City, a massive sprawling blotch of 25 million people swarming around beneath the sludge from countless thousands of exhaust fumes.

Yet just a few months before the Tarascan cazonci was tortured to death the modern planning horror of Mexico City was the site of the most beautiful city in the world: the city of floating gardens – Tenochtitlan – the capital of the great and fearsome Aztec empire.

Post Columbus history tells us that when conquistador Cortes arrived on the shores of Mexico he was thought by the Aztecs to be the historical legend god/king Quetzalcoatl returning to reclaim his empire. For this reason he was welcomed. But the suspicion that the Spanish distorted the prophecies themselves becomes stronger when we read that the supposed Aztec myth also conveniently stated that all the treasures of the kingdom were to be given to Cortes, the so-called returning Quetzalcoatl.

This was all very neat for Cortes, too neat in fact, as it very conveniently explains away the genocide of a continent by simply passing it off as a prophesy of the victims themselves, and their acceptance of it as a retribution for their past sins. Thus did the conquistadors justify their rape of a continent!

Cortes and his Indian allies marched on to the magnificent city of Tenochtitlan. What met his eyes was scarcely believable:

"...and when we saw so many cities and villages built in the water and great towns on dry land... we were amazed and said that it was like the enchantments they tell of in the legend of Amadis ... And some of our soldiers even asked whether the things that we saw were not a dream?"

But these wondrous glories did not prevent the conquistadors participating in what must be one of the most evil acts in the history of humankind as they went through the streets, day after day for weeks, systematically levelling and burning the city to the ground, slaughtering the citizens, sparing none. In one day alone they killed 40,000 inhabitants. Up to a third of a million people were killed.

Afterwards an Aztec poet wrote: 'We are crushed to the ground; we lie in ruins. There is nothing but grief and suffering... where once we saw beauty and valour.'

And this was just the beginning of the trail of death and despair which the Spanish left behind them – north through Mexico into the American southwest, south into Central and South America. They were a cancer which wiped out between 95% and 100% of populations. In the central valley of Mexico alone, it is estimated that between the years of 1519 and 1590 the population was reduced from 25 million to 1.3 million.

The carnage goes on to the present day, albeit on a smaller scale. But the thing that amazes is not how few tribal people still live, but how many. How did any survive the most terrible holocaust the world has ever seen? The tragedy is not only what has been done, and continues to be done, to such cultures, it is also the loss of what **could have been**. What a magnificent future the Americas could have had if the European mind had possessed a broader humanity and a wider perspective.

Bad Decisions in
the Valle

As I came into the vicinity of the Monarch Butterfly Sanctuary, hundreds of these enormous creatures fluttered by me, magnificent in their stately black and yellow plumage. But if their flutterings brought heavenly thoughts to the fore, on the ground less calming influences were at work. It turned out to be Holy Week, I was getting near to the recommended holiday resort of the Valle de Bravo, everyone was on holiday and going somewhere either by car or bus, and consequently the roads were hell. And then, like a bolt from the blue, it suddenly came to mind that of all the warnings I had been bombarded by, not since Colorado had anyone mentioned the most obvious danger – traffic – and in this part of the world, that meant buses.

Of course, lorries could also be rather scary but at least their intentions weren't deliberately malevolent, and they did at least try to avoid me. Although, having said that, my closest shave of the whole trip was actually with an articulated lorry; I now know that it is possible to be faced with certain doom from one of these monsters without feeling any fear. I was climbing – head down – a long, two-lane hill with no hard shoulder. Gradually my traffic-dulled senses became aware of a horn blaring continually ahead of me. I looked up to see a huge truck speeding rapidly downhill towards me. It was overtaking another vehicle, was on my side of the road directly in my path and was unable to pull over. I only had a ditch in which to leap.

This I would, and should, have done but, rather than spurring me into action, the shock of my impending death sent me into a kind of trance, and I continued cycling, staring hypnotically at the front fender of the oncoming lorry. He missed me by inches and I struggled to keep control in the surge of turbulence which buffeted me. After he had passed I got off my bike and sat by the road, feet in the ditch, ignoring the shouts and horns of passing traffic, until my shaking had subsided.

But as I say, lorries were never deliberately evil. Buses, on the other hand, were! Their malicious intent was independent of any driver, and had a life of its own, so much so that between Zitacuaro and the turnoff to the Valle I lost eight of my nine lives. Every other vehicle was a bus, of which every one had two missions. The first was to get to Mexico City before the bus in front; the second was to shave the hairs off my legs as they sped by at breakneck speed. Their method was to wait until they caught me on a hairpin bend with a forty-five degree camber just as something was coming in the opposite direction and then they would overtake me in a burst of stinking black exhaust fumes and blaring horn. The horn was simply to inform me that I was in the damn way and if I did not want to become a bus sandwich then I had better leap into the ditch or cliff face. After several buses had actually scraped my panniers in passing I took to leaping off.

Then there were the dogs. Why does no one ever mention them? I could fill volumes on the pain and pleasure brought by these animals in my forays here and there. Dogs that have licked me, loathed me, followed me, bitten me, chased me, frightened me, even, in America, died for me (but I don't want to think about that). In Istanbul I even got an ovation for standing my ground as a murderous mongrel charged towards me with the intention of ripping my head off – I was simply frozen in hypnotic shock, as with the charging lorry.

But here, in the company of butterflies, I finally had to use Charlie with serious intent. Three times they were nipping at my heels before I managed to increase my speed and evade them. Twice I could not and was forced from my bike to face them with my weapon, but these were not animals used to cosseting and the threat of Charlie simply provoked them even more. Once I was saved by two men dragging the brute away, the other time I brought Charlie crashing down on the animal's back. It yelped and briefly backed off, only to return to face me instantly. Again I brought it down, this time catching it on the side of its head. It was kill or be killed, and it ran off with a great yelping. I spent the rest of the day feeling guilty as hell!

The decision to detour to the Valle de Bravo was probably one of the worst one I made. The attraction of the Valle was a large, undeniably picturesque, lake, which was a playground for middle and upper class Mexicans from Mexico City and nearby Toluca. Not exactly a prime destination for a scruffy, cash-strapped cyclist, especially as all accessible waterside sites had been eaten up by the lakeside properties of the rich.

I rode downhill for several miles until I came to the lakeside, where I soon realised that there was absolutely nowhere to camp. I asked a policeman for help, but clearly I was an Undesirable and he wanted me out of town.

"There is nowhere," he answered brusquely, and walked away.

I cycled down to the municipal wharf which was busy with visitors. I asked the girl on the refreshment kiosk if it was possible to camp at the wharf.

"No!"

I found a municipal worker and asked the same question.

"No!"

"Well, could you tell me if there is a campsite anywhere?"

"Across there." He pointed to the distant inaccessible shore and walked away.

I decided to have a coke at another stall. The boy almost threw it at me. Everywhere I walked staff and customers stared and laughed at me, looking away quickly when I looked at them. I think these people must have been some of the occupants of the hundreds of hooting tooting jeering cars that had passed me on the way, several times throwing items at me at they passed. I had never had this treatment before, but I recognised it – it was my old friend middle-class snobbery again.

I thought of the less advantaged people of Mexico and the prejudice which they must have to suffer from their fellow country people. At least their opinions had no influence over my life – other than to put me in a grumpy mood.

Riding out of town I eventually gave up my search and stopped at a cafe. A young woman smiled at me so I asked if she could help me. She told me her father would be along shortly and he could tell me where I could go; how good it was to find civilised people. Soon a bearded, grey-haired man arrived and told me to follow his car. Eventually he stopped at the top of a gravel slope.

"I can't go further by car, it's too steep, but if you follow this track down to the bottom you will be by the lake; there is a place to camp. It's not much but it's all there is."

I thanked him and looked down the dirt track. I could see the water through the trees far, far below down a precipitous drop. I knew that it would be one thing to get down, and another to get up. Skidding my way the two miles to the bottom, I found myself in a boat hire yard.

"You can't camp here," the girl told me, "but if you go on the other side of the fence it'll be okay."

So it was that, as the sun set over that beautiful lake, I sat crouched on weed-covered stones – the only spot not covered in rubbish, shit and toilet paper – and watched the rich at play. Behind me, an old Indian woman sat silently beneath a tree with a young boy, watching nobody.

Next morning I walked to the town where I bumped into Juan; he told me some pretty interesting things about the area. Apparently I was right about the place being unfriendly, and I was right about the bad vibes I had felt on the way as I passed groups of solemn teenage beggars. A village had been drowned to create the lake and the villagers forcibly relocated into the surrounding hills. Rich people then moved in, bought up all the prime areas and felled the trees. Consequently there was a lot of bad feeling towards tourists, residents and the moneyed classes. Juan said that many of the begging kids I had passed would be from families displaced to make room for the lake.

When I got back to my tent the old woman and her grandson were still sitting silently under a tree. I imagined the treatment they would have got at the wharf. I offered them a cup of tea, bought a few tomatoes from them and gave the boy a small knife which I did not need. How I preferred their silent, accepting company to that of the loud, brainless mob of yesterday. As it got dark they left and a little brown puppy ate my bread and discarded eggshells before curling up at the door for the night.

Your state of mind can influence a day, and the response of people towards you. After escaping the Valle de Bravo the positive state of my mind worked miracles. I saw a field of flowers so blue and vivid that I longed to have some, so I called the farmer in his field and asked if I could have a few for my bike. Refusing the money I offered and smiling broadly, he handed me a bunch.

Further on a flashing, hooting car with a laughing young couple stopped, offered me a coke and asked if I wanted a lift to the top of the hill.

The atmosphere continued in the town of Tenancingo. In the festivities of Holy Week the market and the zocalo were bustling with happy couples, smiling elders, playing children; large, long-tailed birds squabbled loudly in the trees overhead.

I could hardly believe the difference in atmosphere and my recent disillusionment with people quickly dissipated in the friendliness around me. Passing cars did the same as before, tooting, laughing and staring, but suddenly it had become good humoured and good fun. Everywhere youngsters were chasing each other around with buckets of water, and passing cars were throwing it over anyone too slow to move away, truck drivers reached out their windows to drench roadside pedestrians.

Entering the church in the small town of Talinica I laughed aloud as I saw once more what a wonderful country this was – engaging and enraging, conservative and wild, eccentric and thoroughly loveable. The church was fantastically over the top, swarming with angels and evil, ugly cherubs, with gold leaf slapped around in ornate, whirly squiggles, squirls and curls like it came free in fifty-litre buckets. It made me wonder whether Mexican Catholicism is even a Christian religion at all. Certainly in Talinica there were enough graven images and symbolism to satisfy the most deity-starved pagan. Outside, a man was peeing against the church wall.

TESTOSTERONE TAXCO

The countryside had become wild and rugged and cliff-faces even made a rare appearance; I realised just how much I had missed them. Mexico rarely reveals herself so openly, and I felt myself relax.

I had been told twenty kilometres back that it was only twenty-five kilometres to the old silver town of Taxco, so I imagined it was now literally just around the corner. I was looking forward to an easy and short day even though I knew enough to know that one should take mileage information with a large pinch of salt – everyone tells you the things they think you want to hear. After thirty kilometres continually uphill I was overtaken by four psychedelic cyclists.

"It's another thirty kilometres yet," they told me, "all uphill."

Bother! A stone's throw to a car driver, an easy ride to a healthy cyclist. For me, today, it could just as well have been Timbuktu. I found a roadside cafe and sat in its blessed shade, wanting nothing so much as to lie down and die and wake to a cool, cool breeze. As I sat there, my whole body tingling, I knew my gumption was at rock bottom, slithering around in a jellied mess. For the first time I seriously considered giving up; this was, after all, a voluntary journey. However, whatever decision I made I still had the problem of finding the willpower to get to bloody Taxco. I had no choice in that, but I do know that if that cafe had had a train service to the US border I would most certainly have been on it.

Oh, the perplexing, infuriating charms of Mexico! Like a temperamental Diva her tantrums and spiteful spells would throw me into the lowest depths, have me cursing and in despair, wanting only to seek revenge, and the very same day she would lift me to the heights of happiness and admiration when I could forgive her everything, forget even that she'd had a tantrum. But even I had to admit that on this Taxco day she was in one of her more trying moods, testing the bounds of my staying power, teasing me into submission.

By the time I got there I was stopping every mile. Then suddenly it was there – laid out on a hill with a steep climb into town. I should have made the effort and kept going but I didn't. Instead, I went into a bar and paid for an awful room; several seedy characters were hanging around. The shower was not working, so I went into the bar for a beer to recover. I had been back in my room for a few minutes when there was a knock at my door; opening it slightly I saw a young man from the bar.

"Yes, can I help you?"

"Can I come in?" he said, pushing at the door.

"Sorry, I'm busy and I want to go into town."

"You want sex? Yes? We have sex?" There's nothing like being direct.

"No! I don't want!"

"I'll pay you. Let me in." He started forcing the door open with his shoulder.

"No! Okay? Now get out!"

I was beginning to get a bit concerned. He was as determined to get into my room as I was to keep him out.

"Why won't you have sex with me? What is wrong with me? Are you a racist?"

I'd had this nonsense thrown at me before – the idea that if I did not have sex then I must be a racist was almost amusing in its preposterousness. At my age I was not about to fall for such stupid blackmail coercion tactics.

Finally, when my willpower had given me super physical strength against the door, my language had reached gutter level at high decibels, and my threats to get the police had become convincing, he finally shuffled away muttering indecipherable grumpy things.

I set off for the town centre. On the way I came across the tourist information office and went in to ask about accommodation in the town. A bald, middle-aged man welcomed me.

"You can stay here. You can camp in the garden or sleep indoors. We have a nice room you could sleep in, you wouldn't have to pay anything."

Immediately on my guard I asked to see it. He took me through and showed me a room that was obviously a part of the centre and was in no way a room for sleeping.

"Sit down," he said, indicating the couch.

I sat down. He joined me – too close for comfort – and within five minutes he too was propositioning me. My God; did the whole of Taxco have their dicks where their brains should be?! I was beginning to take this personally – did I have a big sign on me which yelled 'I WANT SEX'! I mean, I hardly looked like a symbol of unfettered passion. The saga continued. Further up the road was another tourist office so I tried again. A beefy man with wonky eyes and bad breath assumed outrage at my treatment in Taxco and gave me the address of an hospedaje. He then began talking about the town and invited me to see a mural in a town centre courtyard. As I looked at it he kept putting his hands on my shoulders in the pretence of positioning me for the best viewing. Time to quit! He said he would take me back to my room and tomorrow he would show me the town properly. We drove off.

"I don't want to go back to my room yet, and anyway I must get something to eat, I've had nothing all day. Can you drop me off in the zocalo."

"No; I will take you back to your room."

"Excuse me, but I want you to drop me off here. I must get something to eat."

"You can't eat here. You must go back to your room. You should not be here alone."

As the zocalo was packed full of men and women, boys and girls, just as in any Mexican town in the evening, he was clearly talking rubbish. Besides, the streets were safer than my room, especially with him in it, and it would not be as easy to push this big man out of my door as it had been my earlier assailant. Luckily the busy, twisting and hilly streets necessitated much stopping and slow driving so at an opportune moment I opened the door and jumped out.

The zocalo was buzzing with life, and I felt happy and recovered from my day's ordeal. As I walked back to my room a youth pinched my bum, and cars of youths yelled and jeered.

I don't know what problems the men in this town have, I never came across such male harassment anywhere else in Mexico. Tourism undoubtedly produces a less respectful sexuality in the male population, but why it should have been so much more evident in Taxco I have no idea but it was clear that any woman alone was considered fair game.

Next day I moved to the Jumil – a lovely old hospedaje tucked away in the centre of town. On the way, Wonky Eyes passed me in his car and shouted that I was to go to his office when I had unloaded. Like hell!

I was glad I decided to give Taxco another chance. Strolling around this thriving town in daylight I was able to see its real finery. And fine it is! In a country renowned for the beauty of its towns, nothing can surpass Taxco for pure picturesqueness. An indication of this is that the town has been declared a national monument, existing buildings to be preserved and new ones built in traditional style.

I spent the evening in the zocalo, admiring the beauty and style of the women; these were brought into greater relief by a school band from Wisconsin, USA, who were giving an open air concert. These children were around the age of eighteen, and a plainer, more miserable set of youngsters it would be hard to find. They ignored the clapping of their audience and sat sullenly throughout the entire proceedings. As I looked around at the laughing, happy and sociable Mexicans, I was ashamed at the lack of grace and grim countenances of their wealthy northern neighbours, and suddenly realised that I felt more attuned to the Mexicans around me than I did to this pasty podgy band.

Before leaving I sent a parcel of excess clothes back to England. Knowing that it was normal to tip the staff for wrapping parcels I pleaded my case to the two male counter staff;

"I'm really sorry but I can't give you a tip."

"Oh, you haven't got any money?"

"Well I've been cycling for months and I'm just about spent up."

"If you want some money I know where you can get some," a sideways smile at his colleague.

"Oh, where's that then?"

"I know a man who would give you some work. He'd like a gringa working for him, hey Juan?"

"Yes, she'd be able to earn some money there."

The penny finally dropped into my slow brain. But it was all good-natured and joking, and was certainly what I had come to expect from Taxco's male population; I laughed,

"Well, I'm not quite that desperate yet!"

I left Taxco in a good mood.

Although Oaxaca is firmly established on the gringo route there were few there. I was expecting letters and a bicycle tyre to be delivered, so had a few days to spend in the town. This meant serious pressure on my purse, but the manager of the hostel where I was staying said that for every three new customers I got each day I could have a free bed. This meant being at the bus and train stations, handing out leaflets and trying to charm people into checking the hostel out.

The evening is the time to hang out in the zocalos of Oaxaca, listening to musicians and theatre, watching the world go by. The zocalo is also the location for political protests and for several days of my stay it was crowded with Indians from the surrounding hills eating, sleeping and demonstrating. Although this pro-Zapatista protest was by desperate farmers facing severe land shortages and oppressive government policies, nevertheless bands played, silver, purple and red balloons floated over the heads of the crowds, and food stalls did rapid trade – the place vibrated and throbbed with the semblance of a festival.

In the smaller atmospheric squares, artists sold their work and musicians filled the trees with gentle evocative sounds. The sun flickered through the leaves – creating misty beams of light in the air and causing bright flecks of gold to dart around on the ground. Quiet voices and the strain of some melody in a minor key drifted unobtrusively through my mind. I felt the world slope away, rush and angst were anathema in these oases of tranquility; only in such places can the act of doing nothing seem so productive and so satisfying. I felt that nothing I had ever done had the value – the quality – of those moments.

One afternoon I went into a church. As I stood at the back a young Indian woman – a Lacandon – came in and stood silent and motionless in front of me. She was carrying a baby on her hip, and two small children stood at her side; her black, waist-length hair hung free down her back. With bare feet, and a tiny body covered by a loose, knee-length, white cotton shift, she could have been one of her own ancestors confronting conquistadors in the sixteenth century.

Back at the hostel a man who had recently spent six months in Guatemala told me that the country was highly dodgy at the moment, as many people believed that white women were kidnapping their children for body parts. In one town the police station had been burnt down in an attempt to get hold of a white woman whom the police were protecting.

The other story was more tragic. A Canadian woman was photographing some children during a festival, but unfortunately for her this coincided with the disappearance of a child. The people jumped to the conclusion that she must have kidnapped the child and she, too, was forced to flee to the police station. The police tried to protect her but were overcome by the crowd – the result being that she went back to Canada brain damaged. The child had been following the festival and later turned up. As a result of these incidents the American government was recommending that its citizens avoid Guatemala as a holiday destination.

My informant told me it would be foolhardy for a woman to cycle alone through the country, but if I did so, then I should make absolutely sure that I kept my camera (and presumably my knife and Tuppaware boxes!) in my bags, and did not talk to, or even look at, any children.

How bizarre it was (and what a turning of the tables) that in a country of mayhem and murder that it should be the likes of me who had been 'promoted' to Public Enemy Number One threat to the nation's children. A camera wielding gringa slaying the tots!

Undeterred by my new status as child snatcher I felt refreshed and was getting excited by my proximity to Guatemala. It had been a long journey but now it was finally within my sights – I only had the ride to San Cristobal de las Casas ahead of me, via the southern Sierra Madre mountains, along the coast and back into the mountains to the disturbed state of Chiapas.

Unlike Michoacan, the mountains here were wild and open, and it was a relief to have the problem of where to camp taken away. I ground my way up the long hills, breathing in rhythm with my pedalling, then flew down into the flat tropical valleys where the villages were concentrated. Up another mountain and down to the valley; it was exhilarating stuff, and here it was that I broke my mileage record and cycled ninety five miles.

But if the state of Oaxaca, attractive though it was, was not at its best under its winter mantle, nevertheless it offered me the greatest gift it could possibly have done: its birds. They re-entered my life with a vengeance, and every day became a thrill of sounds. These were no ordinary birds – they were large, they were bright and they were very noisy, rattling their way through an incredible repertoire in angry imitations of rusty saws, drills and chainsaws. One gave such a realistic sound of a car being crank-started that I actually turned to look for it.

It was a happy road too. In the villages people waved, smiled and cheered; children ran by my bike laughing. When I approached one village rapidly down a steep hill, I failed to see the speed ramp until it was too late. I was thrown into the air, and crashed heavily down onto the road surrounded by the food, panniers, pans and clothes which had been thrown from my bike. I was bruised and grazed, but the greatest damage was to my ego.

Three men had been working by the roadside, and they dashed over to help me, quickly dispelling my embarrassment as – once they had ascertained that I was not badly hurt – they laughed cheerfully at the humour of the accident, clapping me on the back as they retold the incident to each other.

I stopped in the dusty coastal town of Tehuantepec, not a pretty place but full of activity and with a great tale to tell. Apparently, the name Tehuantepec translates as 'jaguar hill' and refers to the hill around which the town is built. The story goes that it used to swarm with bloodthirsty jaguars which attacked the people. To solve this problem a sorcerer was called in and he caused a giant turtle to rise out of the sea and terrify the jaguars so much that they turned to stone. Of course, the locals were then frightened of the turtle so the sorcerer had to turn that into stone as well; its fossilised form still sits at the bottom of the hill.

As well as these more tangible terrors the isthmus of Tehuantepec is also a place full of spirits out to get you, fortunately these are not all evil. Tehuanos distinguish clearly between the regular day-to-day spirits that are just a pain in the butt – tricking people, and generally making a nuisance of themselves – and the really dangerous ones, which are human beings who can change into animals and suck the blood of people.

Luckily dogs are able to distinguish these bad spirit animals from ordinary ones and will start barking when they're around. Once identified, they can be got rid of by being urinated on or hit with a cloth soaked in urine.

I loved these stories and remembered an article I had read about Tehuano women, where one had said:

"We are big and fat and proud of it; and we are the boss."

Large they certainly were, with pigtailed hair and colourful long skirts and short blouses, shouting their wares in the market, and striding through the streets with a self-assurance I had not seen in other Mexican women. I had no problem visualising any of them emptying their bladders over an evil spirit.

I settled down to watch the street life – busy with open-backed cars taking schoolchildren to school, and four wheeled bicycles with cargo-carrying fronts used to ferry anything that needed ferrying – families, shopping, boxes, animals, everything that could be made to fit in, went in. A man gave me a mango for blowing up his tyre, another sold me a rock hard bread roll. Everywhere buzzed with the energetic pragmatism of a people who had things to do and found a way of doing them; a people who did not whine about their lot but got on with it instead.

In the nearby baking, sweaty, dusty town of Juchitan I knew I really had reached the humid tropics. As the town shimmered in the suffocating heat, I smelt my stinking, soaking body and thought only of finding the sea – I couldn't see it but I knew it was close.

After four miles of winding around rubbish strewn trails I was beginning to doubt its existence. Suddenly a group of youngsters appeared ahead of me – six boys and a girl in their late teens. When they saw me they blocked the way and the girl came towards me with an exaggerated swagger. As I stopped, my bike was grabbed and one boy tried to tug my necklace off; others opened my panniers and began taking things out. I acted as though nothing was out of the ordinary and addressed the intelligent looking boy who appeared to be their leader:

"I'm trying to find the way back into town. Could you tell me where it is?"

Meanwhile the girl had taken my knife. "What is this for?"

I tried a joke, "That's for when my husband becomes a problem."

She thought it was funny and repeated it to the others.

"Have you got money?"

"No, I only carry a small amount on me in case I'm robbed, and I've just spent that on food. I have to get some in the next town."

By this time most of my things were scattered around. It was not until someone started removing my spare tyre that I really protested;

"Don't take that, I need it. I can't get one anywhere in Mexico to fit my bike," I said, grabbing the tyre. "I'm not a rich tourist or I wouldn't be travelling by bike – I'd be in a car" I lied.

The leader looked at me, I looked at him. He turned to the others.

"Stop," he said, "put her things back."

Having discovered that in Mexico even the robbers were softies I forgot the idea of the sea and ploughed my way through the thick air along the flat coastal road until I found my dream camping spot – two small interlocking lakes fringed by trees and noisy with birdlife, where I discovered that lizards can walk on water. When it was dark a badger-like animal passed close by with a lizard in its mouth, unconcerned by the torch I was shining into its eyes. The morning revealed a food store devastated by huge red ants which had eaten through all my plastic bags and devoured everything that was not in a solid container.

BIKINI ANNA

The fifty miles from Tuxtla to the Chiapas town of San Cristobal de las Casas is basically one long hill which culminated in the blessed relief of a shower of rain at 2000 metres. This misty Maya town is named after Bartolomew de las Casas, a priest who travelled with the conquistadors and who recorded their dark passage through these lands. He was made the bishop of San Cristobal in 1545 and continually decried the Spanish treatment of the indigenous peoples.

Tragically, the past exploitations of the conquistadors are still continued in the lives of the present-day Indians of the region. Their Spanish descendants still deprive the poor of their rightful access to land, rights and power, and still bring about their brutal deaths. Two months before I arrived, between one hundred and fifty and four hundred Maya lost their lives at the hands of government soldiers when the rebels took over the town in protest. The Zapatista demonstrations which I had seen in Oaxaca had here been transformed into a full blown rebellion.

The response to this 1994 uprising was even more severe than the Zapatistas must have expected; fourteen thousand government troops descended onto the State of Chiapas and indulged in a campaign of bombing, torture, and execution which forced the withdrawal of the masked Mayan fighters into the forest.

Fascinating and interesting though this town undoubtedly is, there is sadness there too, for although it was a bit of an upmarket hippy hangout and abounded in all those things which normally do a brilliant 'cover-up-of-local-troubles' – bookshops, health stores, trendy boutiques, jewellery-selling hippies and resident gringos – nevertheless its atmosphere remained tense, and it lacked the relaxed, somewhat hedonistic, feel of Oaxaca.

Leaving my bike and gear at the hospedaje, I jumped on a bus to visit the Maya ruins at Palenque. The recent troubles were brought home by the three road blocks situated on the road out of the San Cristobal area. On each occasion all the men were taken from the bus and searched; women were allowed to remain on the bus which was odd, given that women were fighting side by side with the men in Chiapas, and had been fair game for soldiers to murder.

Palenque lies about two hundred kilometres north of San Cristobal, and the journey takes the traveller from the cool hills down into tierra caliente – hot, steamy, tropical rainforest. The very air sweats and clothes remain soaking from the moment of rising. It was thought to have been built around 1500 years ago, and the last date carved onto its stones is 799 AD after which it was abandoned – along with others throughout the region. In this Maya land of mystery and superstition nothing is quite what it seems, the line between the sacred and the secular is blurred – gods determined the routine of life, and art and architecture symbolised the universe. Thus pyramids were mountains, and doors and entrances were caves and passages into the underworld. In the peace of Palenque you could feel this other world. And I got ridiculously excited by seeing my first wild monkeys.

On the way back to San Cristobal I impulsively got off the bus at the junction to the Agua Azul waterfalls, which was a steep four kilometres descent away. On a bike I would probably have passed by, thinking of the tough haul to get back up to the main road and dismissing it anyway as a tourist haunt. I was enjoying this bus detour, enjoying the temporary novelty of being a backpacker and the ease of making spontaneous decisions. It brought a flexibility into my journey that I hadn't anticipated, hadn't even thought about, giving me the combined pleasures of having a break whilst getting to see parts of the country which I wouldn't otherwise have had time to do. I decided to do it again.

At Agua Azul I thought I was going to see 'just' a waterfall, but as I came down into the village I stopped dead in my tracks, stunned by the scene which lay before me. Rushing white waters tumbled over sand coloured rocks into numerous pools of the most vivid and translucent turquoise-blue. For several kilometres up and down-stream the river bounced and leapt over a series of large rocky steps. The waters roared and foamed, creating the most desirable and seductive (but potentially lethal) series of swimming holes I had ever seen.

I erected my tent in a quiet grassy area under the trees where a couple sat by the water. They shouted to me and I went over. It was then I saw that the man was stark naked. As we talked, a group of Indian women walked past, staring briefly in incredulous disbelief at the man before quickly turning their heads in embarrassment and rushing by.

"I am part Mexican," he told me. "There is nothing shameful about the human body. This is a beautiful place and I like to take my clothes off and be natural like the trees around me."

Yeah, yeah! What is it about these people? He wasn't the first of his kind I'd come across in Mexico, where 'being one with nature' was the cue to strip off and show their bits to all and sundry, and who show such a staggering disregard to the sensitivities of the cultures they impose themselves and their willies on. It must have been the same when the first tourists started baring their boobs in what were then the sleepy coastal fishing villages of the Mediterranean.

In the village the feeling that I had entered some kind of weird alternative reality continued when a young white woman in her mid-twenties walked by. Very tall and extremely thin, short hair, nothing exceptional except that she was walking down the street wearing a tiny bikini. She was very white and so skinny that every rib showed and her collar bones and shoulder blades stuck out sharply. Great, long, spidery legs were accentuated by the high cutaway leg of her bikini and heeled sandals as, with rounded shoulders, she loped along apparently unconcerned by the looks of disbelief, disgust and amusement she was getting from everyone; children giggled, women pointed and men spat. A couple of locals pointed to their heads and said:

"Chica muy loca." A very crazy girl.

Maybe there's something about sparkling blue water that makes people lose their senses.

I decided to move my tent to a little campsite I found in the village. There I met the naked man and his girl (now taking a public naked shower together), and Bikini Girl was also there (a German called Anna) still wearing her bikini.

When it was nearly dark, she told us she was going up into the hills to try and buy something at another village. We told her she shouldn't go up there so late, especially without clothes, but she couldn't be stopped; still in her bikini she set out along the darkening country lanes. None of us could believe it; even I, who had taken so many risks, was astounded by her stupidity.

Two hours later she was still away. By this time it was pitch black up the lane she had taken. Her chances of molestation in her state of dress on those black lanes were almost one hundred percent and I knew there had been attempted rapes of tourists in Agua Azul. The other guys wouldn't go in search of her.

"If she was stupid enough to go out dressed like that then she asks for all she gets."

"Yeah, but come on, she can't be quite right can she? I mean who in their right mind would go out like that in the dark?"

Just then two Mexicans from the site turned up. We explained.

"What! She must be totally crazy! We'll take our torches and try to find her."

We watched their distant torches moving up the lane in the blackness until they disappeared in the trees. An hour later all three returned.

"We met in the lane, she was on her way back."

Luckily, nothing had happened to her, and she couldn't understand our worries.

"What is wrong? Why do you worry so much that something bad has happened?"

The American lost his temper,

"I don't give a shit what happens to you if you're stupid enough to go out like that. Where the hell do you think you are, hey, a fuckin' naturist camp? You're in Mexico, man, Mexico. If these guys'd found you dead it would have been your own fault."

Everything went silent. Anna went to bed without saying another word and we all crept to our beds.

After a few days we all paid to be taken up to the main road to catch a bus back to San Cristobal; Anna stayed to wait for what we thought was her mythical Mexican boyfriend.

I left San Cristobal knowing that I had not got all I should out of it. In the town and its environs there were many things of interest which I had failed to visit, and when I saw other travellers busily planning their schedules I felt very guilty and lazy. (Although I had cycled up to a couple of outlying villages, blissfully luggage-free). But the reality was that they jumped off at towns with the aim of seeing what was there, whereas I stopped in a town to recover from the effort of getting there, and to pootle around. For me it was a great pleasure to do nothing, not to have to pack and unpack, to have a pillow, and to make my room my home for a day or two, laying out my things in cupboards and on shelves.

And yet, without any effort, I had learnt a very sad thing: in coming to Chiapas I knew I was coming to 'Maya country', and I thought that a Maya was a Maya, but in San Cristobal I learnt of the many divisions and resentments which exist between different tribes. It made me wonder if history would have been different if tribal peoples throughout the world and throughout time had always realised their strength lay in unity not division.

I also saw with amazement that even after five hundred years of struggle the Maya spirit still remained so powerful that not only was much of their culture intact, but they still had the courage to risk their lives against the military might of a belligerent government.

I was happy that I had finished my Mexican journey in the mysterious San Cristobal de las Casas. I felt as though my travels through Mexico had taken me on a spiral through history, or that I had dabbled in time. I had touched the Zapatecs and the Maya, the Tarascans, Aztecs and Tarahumara. I knew a little of rebellions and revolutions, of heroes and traitors and had learnt that the history of Mexico is both passionate and tragic, colourful and dark, full of joy and the most terrible things.

And I left knowing that I had been right in the matter of ghosts; they really did follow the old cobbled streets and hide in the crevices of yellowed stone, peeping and laughing at you as you walked by, vanishing just as you turned a corner; and sometimes, when the dark settled, they sat quietly by the temples of Palenque and dreamt of the old days. Their difference being that, unlike the American ghosts, these are urban based!

That night, in a secret roadside glade in the undulating mountains which border Guatemala, I celebrated having 'done' Mexico with an extra cup of coffee.

CONFUSED IN GUATEMALA

The Guatemala border guy tried to sting me for twenty dollars, instead of five. When I refused, he told me to go back to Comitan, in Mexico, for a visa – that was a day's ride back, uphill. I had the Lonely Planet guide for Central America so I pulled it out and showed him the five dollar visa fee. He was unmoved. Another official then entered the office and told him I was cycling; this had a good effect.

"Okay, I will accept nine dollars and we'll all be happy. Yes?"

"Yes!"

Guatemala doesn't mess about, it just heads straight up to the sky. Up and up into the highland cloud forests and damping mists which hide the few remaining oases of the Quetzal, the stupendous bird of Maya myth and legend which is the national symbol of Guatemala. The beautiful Quetzal has a magnificent red breast stained from the blood of past battles, and feathers of blue and jade which shine and shimmer with the light; the male has a long tail which trails inconveniently but splendidly through the wet forests of its rapidly diminishing homeland.

I was thrilled to be entering Central America at last. For ten long years I had been passionate about the terrible struggles of Guatemala, El Salvador and Nicaragua in their respective civil wars. I had studied their political complexities, knew who was fighting who and why, I knew who the bad guys were and went to demonstrations to show I was on the 'right' side!

During this time the greatest event I went to was a talk by a Guatemalan woman who told us of her personal experiences of the civil war which had murdered 150,000 of her people. In telling her own story she brought home to us the realities in a way that no book ever could; how we felt for her, how we empathized with the tragedies of her people. And now here I was, entering the very country of which I had heard and read so much. For reasons which were probably not totally rational I was expecting to be enveloped by a feeling of recognition and familiarity.

In spite of the dangers I had been warned of, I wasn't afraid. After all, I had spent the past months learning how to wiggle my way through the intricacies of daily bike life and by now it was second nature to quickly identify potential problems and deal with them. (Jung and I were old buddies by now, in fact I think I took him a little for granted.) I really believed that I could take a snap view of my surroundings in my head – identifying the characters and shadows, the murmurs of dissent. Of course, it could be that I had just been lucky up to now!

So as I rode with heightened awareness and curiosity past the small hill communities of Guatemala it was like a slap in the face to unexpectedly find myself the focus of their hatred, to several times be the target of stones which were thrown at me, spit that was directed towards me, a stick that was raised in my face, and women who, screaming, grabbed their children and ran away to hide from me.

What was this? Didn't they know that I was on their side? Didn't they know that I was the good guy here and that I really couldn't pluck their children off the road and pop them in my panniers even if I'd wanted to?

The whole thing was ironic. I'd spent months crossing Mexico, a country of which I had had absolutely no knowledge and certainly no expectations. It was simply a very large stepping stone hindering my way to Central America, but to my utter joy and surprise I had been completely entranced and captivated by it – eventually giving myself wholly to this fantastic, dynamic, and very handsome, though often infuriating, seducer. And now here I was in a place I'd looked forward so much to reaching, a place where I had really wanted to be, only to find that it really didn't want me.

Yet it was a fine lesson for me to realise that what one reads and learns in another form and place does not necessarily correspond to the reality on the ground. I was an unknown, unwanted alien, and

I saw how utterly simplistic were the assumptions I'd made; how naïve I had been to imagine that just because I was pootling along in a green left-wingy sort of way that everyone would know that I was an OK kind of girl. But that was me thinking about me, instead of seeing myself from their perspective – that is, from a background of superstition and persecution.

I thought of the contradictions the traveller is often confronted by when things are not as we think they are going to be. For example, touristy places are considered to offer a less 'authentic' experience, where encounters with local people can be brash and commercial, and visitors exploitable. Getting off the beaten track was what it was all about wasn't it, where the tourist was an enthusiastically received novelty. But it wasn't working that way in Guatemala! Here I was riding through bypassed communities where a single female cyclist such as I would be as rare as a visitor from Mars, but I was finding that the authentic experience I was having was not the one that I was supposed to be having, according to the norms of travel.

Deciding that I'd had quite enough of being the bad guy for a while I decided to give tourism a chance so, leaving my bike in Huehuetenango I jumped on a bus crowded with Maya women, chickens and pigs, for the slow grind up to the high plateau village of Todos Santos. This was until recently a distant unvisited place, but it is now becoming known as a tourist destination where the visitor can supposedly have the experience of visiting a real ethnic outpost without the accompanying sense of being voyeur. Or so I'd heard.

As we passed through ponderosa woodland into the cool misty heights the evidence of deforestation became increasingly evident; at times the sound of the chainsaw rose above the grinding low gears of the bus. Huge coffee plantations and cattle ranges have dispossessed the Indians of much of the lower land and forced them ever further into the marginal highlands, to farm land that should not be farmed, tiny plots on slopes so steep that they can only be worked on hands and knees. As these farmers may have too much land to starve on but not enough to live on, they also provide cheap seasonal labour to the plantations.

At the top of the plateau we came out beyond the trees onto a bare, harsh land where half-dressed children stood in the cold wind – bare-foot, silent, unsmiling; nobody seemed to notice them.

In Todos Santos I was greeted by women offering accommodation. They wore vivid pink and intricately pattered tops, huipils, whose design was specific to their village. It is believed that when a woman stops wearing her traditional clothes then she is no longer a true Maya, she has become ladino, but when she puts on her huipil, her head emerges at the very centre of a world woven from dreams, just as the tree of life emerges at the centre of the world.

Many women sat outside their small mud houses weaving for families and trade, but no one tried to sell me anything, no one stared, no men harassed me, no teenagers sneered. Even the many children, laughing, fighting and playing in the village centre, didn't bother me or follow me shouting gringa, gringa, palms open for money.

I think Guatemala was turning the old rules on their head – and what a relief it was after the past days to be able to just sit in the street and relax, to watch the village live its normal life.

I was aware of the temptation to idealise these descendants of the ancient Maya, and romanticise their culture, yet I could not help but be impressed by them – their quiet friendliness, their intelligence and self assurance. (It was sadly true though, that even in Todos Santos many young people wanted to leave, to go to America, to get rich.)

The peaceful face of Todos Santos was deceptive however, for in this calm laughing village I learned the awful truth that in March 1982, a brief occupation of the village by guerrillas gave the army an excuse to invade, and they burned 156 houses, raped women, systematically tortured and strangled 14 people in the church. Later they returned and killed another hundred; many only survived by fleeing to the hills and living on roots and wild plants until the army left.

But this was, after all, how it had always been, ever since the sadistic conquistador Alvarado had begun the habit of genocide here, and of which the priest Bartolomew de las Casas had written;

"The enormities committed… by him that was sent to Guatimala… are enough to fill a volume, so many were the slaughters, violences, injuries, butcheries, and beastly desolations which they perpetrate… like lightning from heaven he consumed these poor wretches…"

I walked up a nearby hill where I noticed signs of a small fire on a rock and evidence that some kind of religious ceremony had taken place. I was thrilled at finding evidence that the old religion was still alive in Todos Santos, and to learn that it still even has a cofradia, or spiritual brotherhood, which retains the traditional ways and beliefs of the Maya. I like to think that cofradias throughout the lands of the Maya have secret hoards of pre-Columbian artefacts and writings by which many still conduct their lives, away from the hot excited eyes of nosey gringos. I do hope so.

Before leaving I wandered into the little church where the murders had taken place in 1982. A statue of a conquistador stood near the altar, just as it had in San Cristobal. An elderly man had followed me so I asked him why the statue was there.

"It's just a statue," he said unconcernedly, and asked me for money.

In Panajachel I wondered why I was so knackered after only fifty miles. Then I looked at my map and saw that not only had I just ridden over the highest point on the whole length of the Pan American Highway, but it was also 3670 metres high. I hadn't given a thought to altitude effects!

This previously no-go area lies on the shores of Lake Atitlan, described by Hemingway as 'beyond the permissibly picturesque'. It was also here that the advice not to photograph or talk to Indian girls was obsolete because these were the very little girls that were sent out by parents to tout for custom. And they judged their customers well, as the children were so irresistibly beautiful, charming and intelligent that it was hard to refuse their hard-selling tactics.

At the beach I was joined by two little girls about ten years old. They asked if they could have my bracelet as a present.

"No, that was my mother's. Anyway, if you like jewellery so much, why aren't you wearing any?"

"We're not allowed to. Our religion won't let us. Our gods don't like it."

Mmmm... do I believe that?

"Then why do you want mine?"

"Oh, that's different. Tourist jewellery doesn't count."

Smart kids.

They then picked up my camera and asked if they could take a photo of each other – and so it was that I got a photo of Maya girls without having to touch the camera myself.

That night there was a brilliant storm, so I walked down to the beach and watched the lightning over the gunmetal grey waters, volcanoes silhouetted behind. I thought maybe the gods were putting an end to the fourth Maya world in a deluge of soaking blackness and that a new time of darkness was beginning.

Before leaving Panajachel I was surprised to bump in Bikini Anna again, now fully clothed thank god, and was amazed to find that her mythical Mexican boyfriend was actually real. When he went for a pee she whispered,

"I first met him in Mexico City and his parents have lots of money, but I've had enough of him, he's so boring and serious. Already he is talking about getting married, and he wants me to stay in Mexico with him. Next week I will fly back to Germany."

I imagine that someone who walks the Mexican hills in a bikini at midnight would soon get bored with a conventional boyfriend.

Guatemala was no different to anywhere else I had been in that I was constantly warned about how unsafe everywhere was, and maybe, both here and in El Salvador, 'bad things' were more likely to happen simply because there were people around who had been conditioned to kill. I didn't know. Certainly there was the odd occasion when I felt that a real threat existed and needed to be taken more seriously – either because something didn't 'feel right' or because the evidence was pretty overwhelming. But I doubted very much whether anything south of the border could equal the risk of hitching on the highways of America, which I had quite happily done with aplomb! The reassuring thing in Guatemala though was that, in contrast to Mexico or the USA, warnings were never given with any conviction, not even by the police. It was more of a casual 'Well, yes, I suppose a few people have been murdered/robbed/raped/pillaged, but it's the luck of the draw really. Just make sure you don't take your camera.'

This always made me laugh! Life was assured in the absence of a camera.

The fact is that all countries have some element of risk, neither bigger nor smaller, just different types from different quarters that's all – be it a bus or a bandido – and from the very beginning in Seattle I had probably made many stupid or foolhardy decisions. Maybe I did ignore real dangers, whilst imagining them where they didn't really exist. Who knows? But I totally believe there is more danger in life by always being careful, watching every step, always having safety as the prime concern, than in saying, 'what the heck' and just going for it and having only vigilance and common sense as protectors – so long, of course, that we leave our cameras behind!

Having said all that, there was one place where I was a little cautious. I wanted to take the coast road to El Salvador which meant travelling from the heights of Antigua, through Esquintla and down to the sea. I had been told that Esquintla was the place where the Canadian woman had been attacked so as I entered the town I remained alert to any vibes and kept my eyes very firmly away from any children. Maybe this was a place of imagined dangers but I didn't like the feel of it or the stares, so deciding that 'one against the town' would be a hell of a lousy deal if I got it wrong, I chose not to linger.

When I reached the coast I stopped and sat in the shade of a tree to have a break from the heat. As I did I saw three people in the distance walking slowly towards me – two men and a woman in their twenties; they looked worn out. When they reached me they greeted me solemnly and just stood watching. They said they were from El Salvador and had taken the mammoth journey to the United States but had been caught at the border and were now trying to return home.

No wonder they were exhausted. To take a journey of thousands of miles with no money, just on the off chance they may be one of the lucky few to get across the border, and then to have to come all the way back again, speaks volumes for the desperate plight they must be in back home. But maybe they were the lucky ones; there are thousands who make it across the border only to perish in the desert beyond – no warm clothes for the freezing nights, no maps or GPS, no rucksack full of food and drink – just T shirt, flip flops and a litre bottle of water. And a crap death!

I felt so sorry for them and though I didn't have much food other than bread and hard boiled eggs I handed them over. When they got up to go one of the men hesitated and hung back, and quietly, hesitantly, reluctantly, asked if I had a bit of money so they could get a bus some of the way home. I handed over ten dollars which was easily accessible and did not feel that I'd been an easy touch. Just then a bus came and they ran after it. When I think of Guatemala today, I think of those three youngsters from El Salvador.

By the time I came to my energy gap there were no opportunities for wild camping, everything was under plantations. I asked advice at a little store where a man said I could put my tent in his family's garden across the road. Everyone was so friendly and I spent the remainder of the day with a horde of children and adults examining everything I had. The grown-up son sat talking until midnight, impressing on me how friendly people were around there and how safe I was. I believed him.

PACIFIC WAVES

El Salvador's most horrific civil war raged up to and including the early 1990s, and left in its wake a brutalised society, including some who had become addicted to violence. It was a time and a place where 'bad things happened', and although it was now three years since the peace accord had been signed, El Salvador still felt like a country only just daring to lift its head above the ramparts. But if I had wanted a jolly holiday experience I could have gone elsewhere, and I was not going to try and contort this tiny country into a travesty which would make it fit a Thomson brochure. It was a dark country. I was just glad I could get out of it.

Although I had only just entered the country, and even though a brief glance would convince the motorised traveller that El Salvador was scenically, agriculturally, and culturally a continuation of the Pacific coast of Guatemala, it wasn't long before I began to feel a difference. I realised now that, in spite of its problems, Guatemala retains a feeling that the people and their culture are still intact and resilient. This feeling is entirely lacking in El Salvador, where there is everywhere a continuing undercurrent of tension and unhappiness, a real feeling that it is a society struggling to survive.

To lump together all the countries which straddle the gap between Mexico and Columbia, and give them the collective name of Central America is to deny them their differences, one of which is the contrast of personalities. Salvadorians are more vociferous and outgoing than their neighbours, and were the only people who did not ask the usual where, how and why questions to which I had become so accustomed. They couldn't care less about me; they had the more pressing issue of survival to cope with.

I went into a café. As I sat eating, a man stood at the door asking me for money until a sailor came by and cleared him off. He sat with me while I ate and I asked him what was happening in the country now the war was officially over.

"This is a very poor country, and many people have big psychological problems because of the war. Some of them are hardly more than kids but they have raped and tortured and killed. Now they are supposed to forget all that. Some have even learnt to like killing, while others feel terrible about what they have done – maybe they killed neighbours, family and friends. Sometimes different people in the same family were on opposite sides; brothers became sworn enemies. After the war, what happens to those families. How do they forgive or forget?"

Ironically, it was natural phenomenon which nearly finished me off.

The day's ride from Acajutla was short and pleasant. The road wound its way verdantly up and down, and round and round the rocky coast – following the thundering Pacific (and how it thundered) much of the way. A man retraced his direction on his motorbike to escort me through a dark tunnel. Everything felt good.

Fancying a night by the sea, and a swim in the cool, cool water, I found my way down to an idyllic isolated beach surrounded by woods. There was a man walking in the trees, so, knowing that the sea was lethal further up the coast (I had read that about two hundred drown there each year) I asked him if it was safe to swim. He said 'yes' so I took him at his word.

The sea was rough and the breakers were crashing down in a deafening roar. Wading up to my calves I could feel a very strong undertow so decided against swimming, thinking instead simply to immerse my body in the exquisite coldness. For not more than five seconds I lay down in the delicious water, but when I stood up I found to my horror that the sea was up to my chest, and I was in the grip of a powerful undertow.

I couldn't fight the pull of the current, the waves were breaking over my head and I couldn't swim in to shore as the seaward tow was stronger than the incoming waves. For the second time on my trip (the first being the encounter with the bull back in the States) I felt real fear. In those few seconds the thought came to me:

"This is it. This really is finally it. I am going to die!"

Luckily panic didn't take over. I couldn't wade towards the shore, so tried to reduce resistance by turning my body sideways against the undertow and shuffling in sideways – taking only tiny steps to maintain my balance. After a seeming lifetime of concentration I reached shallower water and emerged, shaking and frightened, amazed that I had got away with my life.

Sitting outside my tent – still in a state of shock and relief – a couple came over with their two dogs and talked awhile.

As they left the man said, "I'll leave one of our dogs with you tonight," and giving a sign to the large crossbreed, it remained happily by my side for the rest of the night. In the morning, as I packed up, it went on its way back home, its duty done. Incredible!

My 'near death' experience stayed with me for the rest of the week. I kept telling myself that by rights I should be dead, and I got the heebie-jeebies every time I thought about it. From now on, if I wanted to get wet it would be in a shower, or by remaining decidedly vertical in ankle-deep surf.

When I got to the run-down seaside town of La Libertad, I crashed out for three days. I liked the town very much, it felt comforting and womb like; I loved my simple, bare concrete room on the beach, looking out onto that deadly sea and had a romantic urge to stay there for a few months, dwelling on the meaning of life – or not. I was lulled to sleep by the sound of waves crashing against my wall. I spent hours talking to my lovely landlady, and walking along the little wooden pier, where fishermen fished and stallholders sold their goods. I sat in the beach cafe, and marvelled at the little boys, who, like seals, dived in and out of the surf (gentler here) like they'd been born in it.

The poverty of El Salvador showed in the market. Gone was the busy bustle and vibrancy of the Guatemalan and Mexican markets. Even in areas which had suffered heavy repression, the markets of Guatemala were happy affairs, but this was a depressing place of nearly empty stalls in a dark shed, one or two customers wandering around silently – and for some reason it saddened me more than much else I had seen. When a market is finished it is a sure sign that the heart and soul has gone from a community, and it seemed to represent all that had gone wrong in the country.

Just north of La Libertad was Santa Tecla, where I had a contact given to me by some Spanish cyclists I had met in Mexico. I decided to use it. I phoned and spoke to Armin, who said he would come to pick me up two days later.

Armin turned up with his Salvadorian wife Marie and baby son Juan. He was an amazing guy from Switzerland. High-energy, extremely intelligent and slightly intimidating, he was battling against all odds to promote cycling in El Salvador, both as a leisure activity and as a non-polluting mode of transport.

He made new parts for my cooker, helped me service my bike, and persuaded me that I should cycle round the northern Caribbean coast of Honduras before entering Nicaragua, rather than simply nip across the short Pacific strip which was only a couple of days ride at the most, and which I had planned to do.

The most special person Armin introduced me to was Alfredo. He was a native of El Salvador, married to Carmen, with two gorgeous and charming daughters of ten and twelve. They were a lovely warm and friendly family, and the new estate where they lived on the edge of Santa Tecla could have been any estate anywhere in the world; it sat surreally adjacent to the realities of El Salvador.

Alfredo was a graphic artist by trade; he had illustrated a cartoon book of the war – a sort of 'Revolution made Easy'. He gave me a copy, plus biker-friendly T-shirts which he had designed. His work seemed normal to me at the time, it was only later that I was able to appreciate his courage in openly publishing this work – during the war such activities would have made him a certain target for the death squads. In my little experience of El Salvador, Alfredo symbolised the courage of the whole nation. Thousands had been killed for no reason other than that they were there, that they were poor, that they were Indian; but thousands more were killed because they had dared to stand up, like Alfredo, and be seen –union reps, peasant leaders, teachers, priests, liberal politicians.

Alfredo was also a biker freak, but more than that he had built a tandem. With his encouragement I jumped on the back and we rode around town waving at the jeerers, and cheering with the well wishers.

Oh, how ridiculous and wonderful life is – the ability of people to bounce back. In this tiny, crowded country, where many were barely keeping starvation at bay, which had just come out of a horrendous war, here was Alfredo riding his homemade tandem through the streets of Santa Tecla, laughing with pleasure!

How wonderful and big hearted was this brave little country!

Santa Tecla was almost a suburb of the capital, San Salvador, so before setting off for Honduras I jumped on a bus and went to explore the city where, on the 24th March 1980, the people of El Salvador were brought to a standstill by the terrible news that their beloved champion of the poor, Oscar Romero, Archbishop of El Salvador, had been murdered while saying mass.

Throughout Latin America the church had done a U-turn. Whereas it used to preach that poverty was the will of God, by the 1960s Catholic priests were telling the poor that they no longer had to accept their fate in this world for the reward of a better one in the next. On the contrary, they encouraged them to take up arms and fight for justice. Romero had effectively signed his own death warrant when he proclaimed:

"When all peaceful means have been exhausted, the Church considers insurrection moral and justified." A month later he was dead. Right wing crusaders were soon calling: 'Be a patriot! Kill a priest!'

Romero's death hit world headlines, and the violence burst into a terrible civil war. Ten years later the headlines again went international with the announcement that six Jesuits priests and their housekeeper and daughter had been murdered by death squads.

The first event – the killing of Romero – marked the start of civil war, the second – the killing of the Jesuits – marked the beginning of a call for peace negotiations. Between the two events, 75,000 lesser-known El Salvadorians were murdered.

The capital, San Salvador, is reputed to be reasonably safe now. In the 1980s it became normal for children going to school to pass the mutilated victims of the previous night's death squad activity, and there are still the usual provisos that you don't walk around certain areas at night, but they say that about Nottingham too. But even walking round in daytime I couldn't shake off an almost overwhelming feeling that I was in a place I did not want to be; it was a city without a heart. I bought my necessities and returned to Armin's house.

As I was leaving, Armin fertilised my imagination by showing me a photographic record of the war; page after page of mutilated dead – young and old, men and women. He told me:

"They say that death-squads don't exist any more, but everyone knows they do. People are killed by them all the time. The civil war may be over, but the country is not at peace."

His advice to me was simple:

"Always keep some small money on you, so that you have something to hand over. That way you don't lose everything, and the person may be satisfied that he has at least got something from you. This is El Salvador, just accept that this is how it is."

In spite of the problems of El Salvador, I was often charmed by the downbeat friendliness of the people I met along the way. At the simple roadside cafes women laughingly entreated me to try one of the many different varieties of plantain cuisine. Pigs and chickens wandered round my table picking up any dropped morsels. It was no big deal that I was female, alone, and passing through a country where violent death was still a frequent occurrence. I was finding that the more dangerous the country, the less surprise there was at people doing dangerous things.

By now I had actually lost all desire to eat, other than lashings of cornflakes, but fortunately my Coca-Cola lust had been replaced by a craving for ice-cold plain or strawberry-flavoured milk – my body's attempt to get some nutrition I suppose – and I could easily down three pints straight off.

The heat and humidity were phenomenal and dominated my day and my schedule. I was now rising at around three-thirty in order to be on the road just as daylight was breaking. In Central America there is nothing unusual in this, the majority of the rural population worked as labourers and, like me, their working day started with the rising of the sun and (unlike me) ended when the sun went down.

Once on the road, my aim was to get as far as possible before that infernal red globe peered over the horizon, cycling like a mad thing as its vermilion rim crept steadily upwards.

I remembered the pleasure the sun had given me in the first few months in North America, now it had become a thing to be dreaded, a terrible burning furnace, malicious and evil, which shrivelled the juices out of all living things. I could easily believe that the Aztecs and Maya regarded it as a bloodthirsty being who could only be appeased by the sacrificing of throbbing young hearts. I amused myself by making up some 'Happiness is' phrases:

Happiness is a tree
Happiness is a shadow
Happiness is rain
Happiness is dusk

I was aiming for the Maya ruins at Copan in Honduras, which entailed briefly crossing back into Guatemala. At Jocotan, I resisted the temptation of a bus and sat by the roadside drinking the delicious strawberry milkshake I had scoured the town to find. Two young boys came over to talk to me, one with an open, friendly face and a personality to match, the other silent and glum. On impulse, and because he was trying to learn English, I gave the friendly one my spare dictionary. As I stood up to go, he said:

"You have no air."

"Sorry?"

He pointed to my tyre: "You have no air."

Shit! At least I now had a good excuse to catch a bus so, with a clear conscience, I stopped the next one that came by on the way to the border, where I spent the evening repairing my tyre to an enthusiastic audience of customs officials and locals.

RATS AT SARAH'S HOUSE

Honduras! As soon as I crossed the border I felt at home; me and Honduras went together very well. I felt a weight drop from my shoulders, the very air lightened, and I became the most relaxed I had been since Mexico. I realised how sombre El Salvador was by comparison, how the burden of its tormented history lies so heavily on its troubled soul.

Looking back now on those small Central American countries, in my mind the sun shines only on Honduras, and El Salvador sits under the darkest cloud. Of course, it could be that I was influenced more than I realised by the knowledge that Honduras had not recently had a civil war; and I was unlikely to be stoned. But I think it was more than this, and the more I experienced the country, the more it grew on me.

For one thing I liked its geography. The boiling, roasting Caribbean coast, with its massive American-owned banana plantations, moved down into lumpy mountains with pine forests, cosy wooded valleys and stony, bubbling rivers. Knobbly, bumpy hills fell around all over the place. Cattle grazed the grasslands, horses were a form of transport, and (best of all) there were my beloved rocky outcrops!

I realised that in excluding Honduras from my original route I had been guilty of the same error of which Hondurans constantly accuse the rest of the world: that no one thinks about including Honduras on their route. It seems that ever since Columbus relegated it to a passing prayer, it has remained a neglected backwater. Few even know where it is, and anything they do know is bound to be something to do with bananas.

In fact, you might even begin to get the idea that history didn't really happen in Honduras, it just existed in some kind of time warp. When eventually I found a whole book about the country, it was twenty years old, forty pages long, and the chronological history jumped from the conquistador landings in the 1520s to its independence from Spain in 1821. You can be forgiven for thinking that absolutely nothing happened for three hundred years.

Honduras, unlike Guatemala, El Salvador and Nicaragua, has not had the big nose of the USA sticking into its affairs and exacerbating bloodshed among its people. And the reason for this is simple: Honduras put on its best perfume, gently wiped away the tears of America's angst, smiled coyly at the dribbling fruit companies and said: 'Come on in! It's all yours!'

And come they did!

Today American fruit companies own most of the banana producing lands of northern Honduras, they still pay a lousy wage, and Honduras and its people are still dependent on America for their economic survival. Cooperating with the States has not done it much good, for, if I had been struck by the poverty of El Salvador, rural Honduras was in even worse straits.

Some statistics: Honduras is the poorest country in Latin America – 68% live in extreme poverty; illiteracy is around 50%; birth and child mortality is very high; 73% of under fives are malnourished and 34% of two to five year olds are stunted. AIDS and HIV are the highest in Latin America and there is high alcohol and drug dependency. Most of the population have no running water or sanitation facilities and a third of them have no access to health care; infectious and parasitic diseases are the leading causes of death. And on a grading of corruption from 1 to 85, (85 counts high) Honduras comes in 83rd.

But, for once, let's have some good news in Central America. Because it was more than the delights of the landscape which made me happy to be in Honduras; it was the people. Basically, Hondurans are wacky! And in spite of everything, they laugh! They are the eccentrics of Latin America; whether it is the laaaiid-back, black, Garifuna communities of the Caribbean coast, or the outgoing extroverts of the rural areas.

There was another thing: it was often the women who came to talk to me, who invited me to their homes, and who laughed uproariously as they told me about their useless, philandering men.

If the ruins of Palenque in Mexico are reminiscent of a cathedral, the ones at Copan are its intricately carved altars and fine-hued stained-glass windows. And where the spacious majesty of Palenque may instil a feeling that it is enough merely to wander and listen to its lost voices, Copan makes you get down on your hands and knees and work for your culture.

I was ignorant, and a three hour stint round the ruins with my Lonely Planet Guide opened at page 270 – 'Copan Ruinas'-- did little to help me get my head around kings with names like Smoke Jaguar, Eighteen Rabbit or Waterlily Jaguar, marvellous though they are. I just wandered round muttering to myself 'Amazing! Brilliant!'

That is until an off-duty guide decided to pluck me from my pleasant mental lethargy and give me a site tour in Spanish. It was a horrible shock for my comatose, heat-stunted grey matter cells and they threw their hands up in horror.

In the early days Maya life was far less bloodthirsty, and as Copan grew into a thriving kingdom, more and more people flowed into the valley to enjoy a fruitful, convivial life in the protection of a powerful developing state. But time passed and whereas war was once just a ritual pastime when people dressed up in silly costumes and knocked each other around a bit, gradually it grew into a brutal war of expansionism. As kingdom after kingdom turned upon its neighbour sacrifices were now in their thousands.

The whole thing was totally crazy; every Maya kingdom was frightened of its neighbour, and in the end, either directly or indirectly, they destroyed each other and their environment. This magnificent culture became reduced to a shambles, a self-inflicted disaster.

The Maya didn't perish however; all they did was strike out on their own again, just as they had been before the days of empires, tending their maize, weaving their huipils, and leaving small offerings for their gods.

As I left Copan I saw the saddest sight – an ocelot in a small cage. This medium-sized kitten-like large cat was probably the most beautiful living thing I had ever seen, a creature of the dripping forests and bird-drenched dawns and I could feel my heart breaking at its imprisonment.

"Why do you keep it here in a cage? Why isn't it in one of your national parks?"

"Oh, these cats are dangerous. You couldn't let it go."

How I wish I'd come back at night and set it free!

I was making no attempt at high mileage, my aim being simply to get to a convenient stopping place before mid-day, as by then cycling had become horrendous. Sometimes it got a bit silly, as I would reach my destination by eleven and then there was the rest of the day to be got through, holed-out in my room to escape the heat.

Although I hadn't considered giving up since Taxco, and that was the only time, nevertheless I did still question my reasons for continuing, and always my answers remained the same as they were the day I set off: I was addicted to the sheer simplicity of my way of life. I had none of the decision-making of a more complicated existence because there was usually only one viable option. With this responsibility removed from my hands, life became a tough but frequently beautiful thing where I cycled until I could cycle no more, I ate what was in my pannier, I slept wherever my bed was, and I watched the rest of the world. And that was it.

And even though I did my share of moaning, I liked the simplicity and straightforwardness of my difficulties – the wind, the heat and thirst, hills and exhaustion. I was living the enigma that my life of apparent freedom was actually one with none, because freedom usually involves choices, and I had few. It was a great life for a decision-avoider and a perfect way to expand time and live forever.

Anyway, however hard the day I always perked up very quickly and was always ready to go again in the morning! And every single time I thought of the millions in their offices and the zillions in their factories, how grateful I was. I really wouldn't have swapped my life with anyone!

I had been warned against staying in the dusty company town of La Lima which I was told was full of alcoholics, delinquents and no-goods who would strip the rings off my fingers at knife-point, cutting my fingers off if necessary. I had little choice but to stop there, as I was now entering banana territory and camping wild was out of the question. Besides, it was too hot to camp and with accommodation in pleasant and blissfully cool hospedajes costing only one or two dollars a night, I was happy to leave my tent in its bag.

La Lima was the town where I had the nicest social event of my whole trip. Dangerous or not, I liked this hot, dusty town, so after basking a while in the cool haven of my room I set off to explore.

As I wandered the streets I had a sudden lust for a cup of hot drinking chocolate. I entered a bar where half a dozen men lounged against the bar and others sat around the tables. They had no chocolate so I asked for milk. Suddenly a customer leapt up.

"No! No! You want chocolate. I will get it. No problem. No problem!" whereupon he dashed into the street, returning ten minutes later with a kilo bag of chocolate powder. Six hours later, in a state of considerable inebriation and after a noisy night of fun and silliness, (being assured by all that I would be slaughtered in the plantations of Honduras) I left the bar – unsteadily escorted by my equally inebriated chocolate provider.

I have never visited Jamaica but I imagine it to possess a similarly hypnotic, dreamy and relaxed approach to life as the coastal towns and villages of Honduras. In Tela I took a room at the well-known Boarding House Sarah – a large, rambling and quaint wooden house near the sea. Returning to my room after a walk I noticed my bag of porridge oats had been scattered around and knew that I must have company. I lay on my bed and waited. After ten minutes a black rat emerged from under my bed, soon followed by a bigger one; then, horror of horrors, a huge one emerged. The three of them pootled fearlessly around my room seeing what other goodies they could raid from this kind visitor's bag.

Now, I am most definitely an animal person. With animals I have no fear and, I used to think, no phobias; but everyone has one exception and in adulthood this has become for me rats. I can't even look at one on TV without getting panic symptoms and here I was having to share my bedroom with three of them.

On the other hand, these were black rats, which were infinitely less terrible than the skulking brown rat of Britain's sewers. I decided this would be a good chance to test my nerves so I threw a lump of bread under my bed in the hope they would gorge themselves and sleep the night away.

About that time the air suddenly erupted into such a blast of sound that I learnt my room was feet away from the local disco. The din was phenomenal. The old creaking boards of Boarding House Sarah shook and rattled until three o'clock, when hell finally ended and with it my rapid gravitation towards suicide. To reduce this inclination through those endless hours I kept telling myself that as sleep was not an option, at least I wouldn't experience the nightmare scenario of being woken by a rat running across my face, whereas if I were to slit my throat with my Swiss army knife, the black devils would have my eyes out before I was cold.

The night ended. I packed my bag and beat a hasty retreat to another place down the road. Before leaving I explained to the elderly owner that the rats and the disco were too much for me.

"The whole town is full of them – there's nothing we can do about it," he said. His only comment on the disco from hell was:

"Well. . . it does get a bit noisy."

The new place wasn't so quaint but my priorities had changed.

"Do you have rats here?" I asked.

"Oh, on the upstairs floors we do. Everywhere has rats. If you don't like them then you'd better have a room on the ground floor." I did.

The road curved inland through poor mestizo villages, past numerous rivers where children leapt and played in the pools and women stripped to the waist to wash themselves. At the small village of San Juan Pueblo there was a hospedaje and a nice river, so I stopped for the day, throwing myself on the bed of my cool, dark room and sleeping for an hour.

I became aware of whisperings, of people peeping into my room. Gradually my door was pushed open and half a dozen faces kept appearing and disappearing. A woman came in and stood looking down at me. She vanished and was replaced by another; a host of children were flitting around like moths. Then both women stood at my door discussing in rapid voices everything that lay about my room. Getting braver they began picking things up. When they got to my cooker it was easier for me to give a demonstration than explain. This caused such excitement that one of them rushed off to fetch a young man to see the functioning of my little stove.

So I had acquired my family for the day. I was bundled off and forced-fed chicken soup and tortillas, whilst being entertained by the tribe of delightful children, all of whom appeared to be the offspring of the two young women – two of the children were very blond.

Between five and ten o'clock every night Honduras was plunged into darkness. It was a little nerve-racking to walk the streets of a town in pitch darkness, every shadow scrutinised for its mugging capability, and I avoided it where possible. During this darkness I was marched by my little gang down a lane behind the hospedaje, where to my surprise I discovered that there was a whole village hidden away from the road.

"It is the feria!" I was told.

The whole village had turned out and the mood was festive in the darkness. I was taken to each of the identical stalls in turn by my small entourage, and through it all eight-year-old Sofi only let go of my hand when she could sit on my knee. How wonderful were these enchanting, warm and affectionate children!

In fact, children were everywhere and I was tripping over them wherever I went; they are bursting out from the country's seams. When I looked at the rudeness of the people's homes, and the tiny bean and corn plots of those lucky enough to have land, I marvelled how they could continue to provide their existing basic needs, even without the addition of so many more mouths to feed. But of course, they don't and many go hungry.

As I started my morning's cycling in the pre-dawn light, the landless, and those with insufficient land on which to survive, would already be in the fields for their long day of labour in the baking sun. From dawn till dusk they toiled for wages which allowed nothing but the barest of lives. Unless they left for the towns, this was the future for the laughing, beautiful bright-eyed toddlers – for as long as the whims of the multi-national fruit companies or the large farmers needed them. Honduras has long since spread her eggs between too few baskets and the people have to live in the fear that even these shabby baskets may be removed.

And yet, amazingly, the women laughed, the men made jokes, the children played. There were few down-turned mouths, and no obvious resentment of my comparative wealth – no begging or grumbling, just welcoming friendliness and hospitality, and an acceptance that this was their lot. I asked about husbands. Teresa emitted a hooting guffaw:

"Mine is gone, and he can stay gone. He was always with other women and never gave me money. I have to work hard to keep my children and I am very poor, but he was no good and I am better without him."

Maria continued the theme:

"I told my man to go. He only drank and hit me. All men are the same here; they do what they want. They all have other women, but we must stay home and do what they say. If he had found me with another man, he would have killed me. I never want another man – only if I find a kind, rich one."

It was a story I was to hear over and over. The men I met may have been friendly and amusing company to me, but it sounded as though they were all philanderers who abandoned their wives and children, and left the women as the sole providers.

Honduran women are seen as second class citizens, and (sadder still) that is also how they see themselves. A consequence of this is that they continue to perpetuate the situation by their treatment of their own children: girls have to wash their brothers' clothes, clean their pots and clear their mess, while the boys only play – girls are not given the freedom of their brothers and you rarely see them playing out, certainly not in the evening. It is easy to believe that Honduras (and indeed all Central America) produces only boy babies.

Yet I believe that throughout the whole region it is the women who hold together the families and communities. They are its ultimate strength, and it is their attachment to children, friends, family and life that enables them to survive the very worst that life throws at them. It was in Honduras where I most felt the power, and the potential for joy, of the women, and where I could see that it was a real tragedy that they were not truly appreciated.

DEEP WATERS

On the coast road I cycled in the shadow of the Pico Bonito National Park – the biggest in Honduras, rising two and a half thousand metres from the sea into mist-covered cloud forest. From the road I couldn't see the peaks or the waterfalls and pools which I knew were hidden there, only forest-covered slopes rising into the distance, but that didn't stop me feeling the thrill which can only come from encountering the primeval, knowing that jaguars and pumas prowled there leaving soft footprints in the spongy earth.

I wanted to visit a Garifuna village, so I headed off to the small coastal village of Sambo Creek and found the village hospedaje. The Garifuna, or Black Caribs, are the beach people of Honduras, desendants of shipwrecked slaves who 'integrated' with the Carib and Arawak Indians and produced a new, wild race free from the clutches of European slave traders and plantation owners.

It was not only blood that was mingled by the intermarriage of Amerindians and Africans – their religion, music, drumming, stories and dance have also become an inseparable mix of colour and vibrancy.

Sambo Creek is a simple but lively beach village of small thatched houses, dug-out canoes and children. It has an all-purpose creek running into it where pots, clothes and bodies are washed; bowel contents are deposited on the adjacent beach (unlike India, I didn't see any goats to eat it up), so you have to watch where you walk. The women were large and laid-back.

Fishing is traditionally the main activity that sustains these villages, and their dug out canoes lined the water. I thought how easy it would be to drift along here, and was surprised that the area had not been adopted as a hippie retreat. It was an ideal place for stringing up a hammock, listening to the sound of drumming carried on the sultry night air. The Honduran coast is a place to turn up for a day and stay for a month; a place where the metabolism slows down, and the mood becomes dreamy.

Apparently I was not alone in my thoughts, and it wasn't long before I began to hear about plans for hotels and tourist compounds, about foreigners buying up properties and land, and of the prospects for the arrival of a rampant holiday industry. Honduras was about to be 'discovered' again.

Ridiculously photogenic thatched red-ochre mud huts scattered the road to Trujillo where they blend with the hillsides and vegetation like no other dwelling can and offer a cool haven from the heat. I took a room in a beach hospedaje run by an aging Garifuna couple with two grown daughters. A fat coati-mundi was tied to a tree in the garden; it curled up in submissive, quivering delight when I stroked it. I wanted to lengthen its lead so it could climb into the tree.

That evening I began to realise there was a thriving sexual sub-culture in Trujillo. Sitting on the beach in the evening dusk, Rami came and sat with me. He was a young and very handsome Garifuna man, with a Rasta hairstyle. He really was absolutely gorgeous, with sleepy eyes, silky skin, and sultry mouth and I would definitely have been more inclined to put my trust in a second-hand car salesman. He was one of those fidgety, foot-tapping people who have the ability to make you feel incredibly boring because you're not boogying your way along the beaches of the world, stoned out of your brain.

Anyway, Rami was convinced that Alka Seltzer did great things for his health and it was now time for his 'fix', so would I come to the bar with him. I don't know if Alka Seltzer addiction is a common trait in Trujillo but there were dozens of boxes scattered along its shelves.

"Let's go to the cinema," he said.

The cinema was packed, and after no more than fifteen minutes he was again getting restless.

"Come on, let's go. There's a street party tonight."

Ready by now to go with the flow, intrigued where it would lead, I followed Rami to the upper town, where the streets were busy with crowds of people doing nothing in particular. There we met a friend of his, Miguel, and the three of us sat together in a bar overlooking the streets below. Suddenly Rami jumped up and said he would be back in five minutes. Miguel and I stayed.

Miguel was gay; he was also very camp, and with lots of wrist movement and head tossing he related his experiences in the world of men:

"I only go with foreign men, never Honduran men. Honduran men are so ugly – muy feo, muy feo – I could never fancy one. Anyway they are too poor. My favourite men are Italians. They are so handsome." (Lots of limp wrist movement and head-tossing here.) "So beautiful. Gorgeous! But Honduran men; agh, they are just ugly."

There was a disturbance in the street and we looked down to see Rami involved in a fight. A couple of policemen quickly appeared on the scene and escorted him away struggling. Half an hour later he turned up limping at our table, and with great drama explained that he had been beaten up by four men. He was unaware that we had seen his one-to-one combat.

We walked down to the beach, Rami limping whenever he remembered, Miguel busy greeting his many acquaintances. As we sat at a beach table, a beautiful black woman came and joined us. Slim and elegant, tight, black, leather trousers and waistcoat, hair shining with gel – totally out of place in this poor town. She greeted me like an old acquaintance, at which point I realised my mistake: she was a he.

Rami wanted to go to a bar along the beach, so the two of us went off. A car approaching on the sandy track suddenly crashed headfirst into the beachside ditch, so Rami stayed to drag the car out with several other men, whilst I went on to the bar. There I got talking to an American who was staying at my hospedaje – he was an artist living on the Bay Islands, and was over with his friend who ran a diving school there. He had just told me that they were returning at three the next morning and did I want to go with them when Rami reappeared on the scene.

It transpired that these two knew each other. A huge row broke out in which the American, Dan, accused Rami of swindling him in a dope deal, and blaming the swindle on someone else (who Dan had subsequently thumped). Rami swore innocence, but as he was increasingly developing as the guy most likely to steal from his own granny, I didn't put a lot of weight on his pleas. Eventually the two of them stomped off to track down the 'thumpee' and sort the business out.

Deciding the novelty of being a stand-in in a Monty Python sketch was wearing off I stayed on the beach in the company of a ten-year-old boy who, with an improvised can, gave me my own private Garifuna drumming concert. Later I strolled to another beach café near my room where I heard the hypnotic adult version; it was stupendous. Before sinking into a trance-like state I noticed that I was unable to tell the sex of three of the dancers.

I cycled along a nearby peninsula to Puerto Castilla, twelve kilometres east of Trujillo where I took a track to the eastern side. Gone were the cosy palm-fringed beaches; this was an untamed wind-swept place taking the full force of the Caribbean winds. I crossed to the sheltered western side and rode to the village of Castilla.

The village was predominantly Garifuna, and I liked its cosy single-storied wooden houses. Many people were employed by Dole, the big American fruit company which had a large plant nearby, others were fishermen. Juan came up to me:

"I saw you in Trujillo yesterday. I wanted to talk to you then." I remembered noticing him looking at me in the zocalo. After a while he said:

"Why don't you stay for a couple of days. I can take you out to the lagoon to see the monkeys, and we can go canoeing on the sea."

I hesitated.

"It's no problem. You will be my sister; I will treat you always as my sister," he told me, adding, "I've got my own house, with a fridge and toilet."

I weighed up the pros and cons. Of course, I didn't believe the sister bit, but I wanted to canoe on the lagoon and to experience a couple of days in this interesting village. Anyway, Juan was only small, so I reckoned I could easily get out of any trouble if he started to forget the 'sister' bit. I returned the next day with all my gear.

I should have looked at his house before I agreed to stay. It was a wooden, concrete-floored room with pieces of rough cardboard nailed up in some places and the old bare boards elsewhere. The only items of furniture were a double bed and a kitchen chair. There were no cooking facilities, no table, no utensils, nothing to indicate this was a home. By the looks of it the place had never even been swept, never cleaned, it was just the filthy den of an uncaring owner. There was no proper ceiling and dirt was falling through the gaps as I looked.

"Look; I have a fridge, and a toilet. The shower doesn't work but I go to my mum's for that."

That night, as I had expected, Juan needed reminding that I was his sister so he hung his hammock in the kitchen, I took the bed. Then the rats started; dozens of them scampered in the rafters over my head the whole night long, shaking cascades of dirt and dust onto me until the morning, when I rose as one emerging from the dirt of her own grave.

Anyone would assume that I would have been out of there first thing in the morning, but no, I actually stayed another night. For one thing I found the village interesting; for another I was still waiting for the canoe trip which did not happen that first day. This was partly because Juan was less motivated to please me since he had still not managed to adjust my status, and partly because a yacht came into shore. This was owned by an elderly American, Jim, who made his living by diving to old wrecks. Juan had a bit of shipping instrument and was trying to do business, so we canoed out to the yacht.

Jim was a cool but polite man. His cabin was all burnished wood – beautiful and warm. He told me that his son had died and his marriage had collapsed, so ten years ago he took to the sea and had been sailing the Caribbean and the Central and South American coasts ever since.

It is in places such as Castilla that you meet the misfits of white society, those who cannot adapt to white plastic, suburban life and a postage-stamp lawn. Some can handle the plastic and get as far as the beaches of the Baja in their RV's. Others freak out at the sound of a lawnmower, and they go to the forests, lakes and indigenous villages of Central and South America, take a local wife, and never return.

At the beach local men were up to their waists in water, encircling the fish with their nets. One held up a large bloated fish, like a football, and posed grinning for me. Four giggly little girls came to me and told me there was a white man living on the edge of the village

– another 'misfit'. Coincidentally, he then walked by and spotted me. He was a tall, white-haired Canadian of about seventy, who invited me to his house for a cup of tea. As we walked through the door we were leapt on by a small tethered monkey and Mike walked to the table and peeked in a box that lay there.

"Oh no," he exclaimed, "you just can't rely on these people."

I looked in the box. There lay the tiniest, cutest little baby coati-mundi, only the slightest tremor showing that it was still alive.

"I have told them that they have to buy fruit every day for the animals, and that this must be given milk every hour. But they have no feeling for animals, they don't care if they live or die. I have to be here all the time to see that they do what I ask."

The 'they' he was referring to was his very young and very attractive Honduran 'housekeeper', who then made an appearance. During our conversation he made it clear that he paid her well to keep him in whatever ways were required of her. This is another reason for old men to go to poor countries, where else could they get such smooth-skinned lovelies in their beds – and keeping their houses – for peanuts? I cringed at the thought of this girl sacrificing herself to this old man, but there are always two sides.

After a few drops of milk the coati made a miraculous recovery from death's door and within five minutes it was leaping around its box seeking freedom.

Two nights of being showered by the plague of two thousand rats was finally enough; I kept waiting for one to fall through the rafters onto my bed, and now Juan was sullen and grumpy. I had enjoyed my time there though. I'd had an insight into village life, taken a canoe onto the sea and watched the fishermen; I'd played with the children and talked with locals in the bar, I'd been to the homes of village women, visited two eccentric exiles, and seen that a man can happily live in a filthy rat-infested hole.

I had also learned that Dole paid its workers twenty-five lempira (about three dollars) a day. They worked for sixty days and then had to take ten days off – this kept them as continual temporary labour and got the company out of insurance, pension, holiday and severance payments. It was a shameful story, as was the fact that being laid off was the thing most feared by employees, for though wages were atrocious they were better than nothing.

In the happy capital of Tegucigalpa sexual boundaries continued to merge. The man in my hospedaje had breasts; the lovely vision on the street in white with long, sleek black hair, painted eyes and red lips was a man; the grey-haired lady waiting for a bus had a beard and moustache. When Columbus spoke of the 'deep waters' of Honduras he didn't know the half of it!

The Nicaraguan border was now only two days ride away. On the way I camped on a 'proper' lawn by a 'proper' restaurant (great rarities in Honduras), where I met Saccra, a waitress who worked there from 7am to 8pm six days a week. For this she was paid the grand sum of thirteen lempira a day, the equivalent of one and a half dollars, or one pound. She was another woman with no husband around, and four children and her elderly mother to support.

"But how on earth do you manage?" I asked.

"I have a small piece of land and grow beans. Every day we eat beans."

She took me to her house – overflowing with children, women and laughter – and in the darkness of the power cut we ate beans and tortillas. Again I was charmed by the women, and impressed by their ability to keep laughing under the phenomenal burden of their lives.

The ride to the border was the most enjoyable of my Central American journey. The theme was again pine-covered knobbly hills, with occasional rock-outcrops and a back-drop of mountains. They gave me a little nudge which I recognised as being a memory from the Caledonian pine forests of Scotland, I felt myself sink into it.

There was another thing which added to my contentment: it had become cool, it was cloudy; and it actually drizzled. Once more my body and brain could breathe. The coolness also brought with it a desire to eat once more, and I returned to my old fry-ups.

In Danli, unsurprisingly, the manager of my hospedaje was gay!

The fact that sexual minorities were able to be so open and so readily accepted in a part of the world renowned for its machismo spoke volumes for the character of the Honduran people. They are a people with a real penchant for happiness, constantly frustrated by poverty. As I crossed the beautiful border into Nicaragua I felt sad to be leaving a people and a country I had come to like and admire so much.

SANDINISTA COUNTRY

A nd so to Nicaragua, a country claimed for Spain by Columbus in 1502 when he sailed along the Caribbean coast on his doomed fourth voyage; he was mightily fed up:

"Eyes never beheld the sea so high, angry and covered with foam. . . there I was held, in an ocean turned to blood, seething like a caldron on a mighty fire"

It was an omen indeed for the Indians, for if Columbus feared for his own life, the storms accompanying him were certainly a black prophecy for those who watched his ships pass by. It wasn't until nearly five hundred years later, in the year of 1979, after fifty thousand had died, that the poor and oppressed finally and fantastically rose up against the corrupt Somoza government and their US backers. The new revolutionary government, the Sandinistas, aimed to create a healthy, sustainable country which could resist the efforts of North America to destabilise it.

Nicaragua nearly fell over itself trying to get the approval of the United States whilst still maintaining its political integrity; but nothing satisfied, because Reagan's government wanted nothing less than the downfall of the Sandinistas. To achieve this, the USA trained and armed a pro-Somoza army – the contras – to destroy the Sandinista government.

So ultimately, their brave attempt at building up a model of social stability and justice had to crumble. All efforts and resources had to be concentrated on fighting the enemy and rectifying the damage it caused. They were having to run just to stand still – social programmes had to be cut, environmental schemes abandoned. Eventually the

Sandinistas began to see contras under the bed and started to clamp down.

Finally – and tragically – the people had had enough. All they wanted were the Americans off their back and food on the table so in 1990 the moderate, US backed Violeta Chamorro, was voted into power and the tremendous hope and elation which the Sandinistas brought to the world in 1979 was over. And all of us who went to money-raising Nicaragua Solidarity events during the 1980s felt a great sadness.

Nicaragua was the first border to register my bike details diligently, and enter them as an independent item in my passport. In fact the process of leaving Honduras and entering Nicaragua was so precise and incomprehensible that I simply handed everything over to a young boy, and for a couple of dollars let him organise everything, while I sat drinking coke and absorbing another border.

These 'all-purpose boys' are everywhere in the third world, where they serve as anything from errand boys to bus touts and trinket sellers – they know everything there is to know about the infrastructure of a place and if these multi-skilled miniatures can't fix it, they know a man who can. I came to respect the incredible efficiency with which a twelve-year-old child was able to smooth the path of a frazzled tourist. Sadly, many tourists push them aside as pests whose only aim is to fleece them, instead of seeing them as hard working kids just trying to make enough to buy their supper.

El Paraiso was an ugly, dusty place, basically a junction, and the first stop over the border. I paused briefly to eat, and watched a small boy in a dirty ripped T-shirt being thumped by a larger one. They were arguing over a few cordobas, about ten pence worth; I gave the small boy one of the T-shirts I was given by Alfredo in El Salvador.

El Paraiso was also my first taste of overwhelming Nicaraguan attention. I had imagined the country to have been so flooded by do-gooding gringos during the aftermath of the revolution that they would be a familiar and un-noteworthy sight, but here more than anywhere else my every move was scrutinized, solemn children gathered around me silently, men with dull eyes stared and women with angry faces glared.

Elsewhere (apart from Guatemala) such attention had been curiosity, here it was something else; these people were not merely poor, they were also hungry and malnourished. They did not laugh, merely looked with unsmiling eyes at whatever was in my hand. I stopped eating in public.

It continued in Ocotal, where I felt like the first white person ever to have been in town. Everyone stared suspiciously as I passed, and no faces looked welcoming until I suddenly realised that I too (feeling cowed and intimidated) had put a dour expression onto my face. Why, oh why should I expect anyone in this country to smile at me anyway?

As it was my problem, not theirs, I decided it was up to me, the stranger, to make the effort. So I took the frown off my face, smiled at the children who stared and the women who glowered. If there was a chair by the door of the little shops I sat on it.

The effect was incredible; like the moment when the family dog enters a room of tension. Everything relaxed, just slipped into place, became normal. Women's faces suddenly opened and lost their suspicious expressions, children became normally shy, men stopped looking fierce; all that had been needed was for me to show I was happy to be in their town. I began to think that I would like this country after all.

Later in the evening, sitting on my bed in my six feet by four feet room – only wooden planks screening it from the other rooms – I heard a rustling sound coming from under my bed. Images of rats immediately stormed my brain and I sighed as I thought of the repacking and new search for a room. I would never share with rats again. I looked under my bed in trepidation, and there, hopping around under the boards from room to room were two large fluffy white rabbits.

Moving away from the border there was a change. Children would now run towards me with 'hellos' and after me with 'goodbyes', they looked better fed, happier, and it felt good. But I began to notice other less positive things – there were no chickens to cluck comfortingly in the small, muddy yards as they had in Mexico, no pigs to run between your legs like in El Salvador. I began coming across horses which were thin and out of condition, eyes dull and ribs projecting, many with saddle-sores and scars. And whilst larger towns bustled with activity, they looked neglected and uncared for – roofs needed mending, walls and windows needed painting, roads needed repairing. Zocalos were just bare, trampled patches of earth, dark and dismal in the evening – another victim of the war.

I expected to find anger in the town of Esteli as I knew it had been a steadfast supporter of the Sandinistas. I very soon noticed many legless or one-legged men around – a stark reminder of the heavy fighting which the town had undergone. Sitting in the plaza I got talking to a man in a wheelchair, he had one leg.

"I took part in the revolution in 1979. Somoza was evil, and only the rich and the corrupt were sorry to see him go. I was one hundred percent Sandinista, they were my heroes and I lost my leg for them; we all hated America for sticking its nose in our affairs. When they first came to power they did only good, they sent people out to teach us to read, built hospitals and gave people land. But eventually I got angry with them, they started doing bad things, and we were very tired of war, we aren't a war-like people, so in 1990 I voted for Chamorro. Everyone just wanted peace."

The vote against the Sandinistas in 1990 not only marked the end of a revolution which had begun with such fine and far-reaching ideals, but it also showed the faith of the Nicaraguan people in the ballot box, they still had hope that it could improve their lives. It was a triumph of unquenchable optimism over bitter experience!

As well as optimism the Nicaraguans have another characteristic which distinguishes them from their neighbours: in spite of years of civil war, and with every reason to be inward looking, they still have an insatiable curiosity about what is going on in the rest of the world, and what is more, they actually know what's going on. This is no mean achievement. I would find Nicaraguans selling ice-cream or running market stalls who could not only tell me who was the prime minister of Great Britain, but could give an intelligent analysis of Ireland's problems which would put most Britons to shame. Amazing!

I realised with incredulity that after nearly a year of cycling I was now within sight of my destination. Unfortunately neither my money nor my time could be stretched the extra week to Panama and my 'new end' was now to be Costa Rica. I knew that Nicaragua was an interesting, beautiful country with so much to teach me, and I had found the people extremely intelligent and admirable, so it was with much regret that I was visiting this very special country at the wrong end of my journey, when I was unable to give it the attention it deserved. But by now I was saturated with sights and sounds, I needed to speak my own language again and absorb all I had seen. And I did miss my tent!

When I reached the pleasant valley town of Dario I crashed out for two days in a cosy hospedaje in the company of twenty-four jolly Americans, where for a couple of dollars the son of the owner gave my bike a thorough strip and clean.

The thought of being surrounded by a party of do-gooding westerners could have been daunting in any other state of mind, but this was exactly what I needed right now; American Methodists of both sexes from twelve to seventy years of age, who were in Nicaragua to build a school in a nearby village, though I doubted whether many actually had any building skills. As they were clearly thrilled by their experience it was all quite heart-warming, and I knew they would quickly demolish any lingering myths about a communist Nicaragua back home.

"I couldn't believe it," said one woman after her first visit to a local home. "They had a mud floor and cooked on an open fire. It was unbelievable; it was just like the museum we visited which showed how people used to live. I didn't know people still lived like that in this day and age."

"And" said another "the natives are really friendly!"

What? They don't eat people anymore?

I liked these people. I felt particularly fond of the elderly members of the party – these silver haired ladies could not have been further removed from the toffee-nosed snowbirds of the Baja and the USA. As I sat in the courtyard drinking my morning coffee three elderly women sat around me, including me indulgently in their conversation. One leaned forward and said to me conspiratorially:

"We are all so proud of you, my dear!"

That inane little comment made me ridiculously happy. I

beamed.

As I stood in the shower on my last night, a girl of about fourteen undressed in the next cubicle. Her father stood outside.

"Have you got everything?" he asked.

"Yes."

"Have you got soap?"

"Yes!"

"Have you got a towel and a flannel?"

"Yes Dad! I've got everything!"

"Okay." A minute's silence. Then....

"Have you got shampoo?

The shower ended. The third degree didn't.

"Have you finished?"

"Yes."

"Dry yourself properly then."

"Okay, Dad!"

"When you're dry, get dressed and come out."

I don't think that girl is ever going to be allowed to write her own shopping list.

DOWN THE RIVER

By the time I reached Tipitapa I was down on the coastal flatlands. It was only eleven o'clock and I would have gone the extra fifteen miles to Masaya if I had known what dives were on offer in Tipitapa. On the edge of town the sour-faced owner of a hospedaje with a huge rough garden refused to let me camp, even though I offered a full room fee. In town I stopped a man and asked his help. He led me to a dark and dingy place where a smirking young couple sat behind the desk. I asked the price.

"You want it for the night?"

"Of course."

"Thirty cordobas."

"What!? Thirty? A room is usually about fifteen."

"You can have it for half an hour for fifteen."

"Why would I want it for half an hour?"

Ah....yes.

I tried the hospedaje round the corner. A woman of about sixty came towards me. I stood by my bike and asked the price.

"Do you want it for the night?"

"Of course I want it for the night."

"That's thirty cordobas."

"Thirty? That's much too much. I normally pay fifteen."

"Do you have a companion?"

"No. I'm travelling with my bike."

"You're alone?"

"Yes."

"You can have one for twenty-five."

Eventually I got one with crumpled stained sheets for fifteen and covered the gruesome details with my sleeping bag. Clearly there were things going on in this town that I hadn't come across anywhere else; or at least other places had been able to tell the difference between a hooker and a scruffy foreign cyclist. But still, I found it strange; why here and not elsewhere? And here was this apparent paragon of elderly respectability, with small children running around the place, allowing her premises to be used for prostitution.

Maybe she had no choice; and anyway in places like Nicaragua tens of thousands of people have to do what they have to do. And when sex trafficking is rife within and between Central American countries, then any question of pomposity becomes irrelevant.

I had started giving things away and it felt good. I wanted to have everything reduced to two panniers for the return trip by train and bus to Boston. It was a great satisfaction to cut my load down.

As I cycled towards Masaya I saw a small cardboard and polythene shelter in a field – this was a house. A woman stood outside, so I waved to her and she came over. As she did I held out my groundsheet to her and asked if she wanted it – it was just a piece of reinforced plastic about seven feet by five. The effect was incredible; gripping both my arms tightly, she smiled, rocking me back and forward.

"Gracias, gracias" she repeated.

As I left her she waved, and stood by the road gripping the sheet. That image stayed with me; even now when I start getting twinges of materialism, I think back to the lady for whom happiness was a piece of plastic!

In Granada I discovered, with a ridiculous sense of loss, that I had lost Charlie, my dog basher!

Granada lies at the top of the huge Lake Nicaragua, the biggest lake in Central America, with four hundred islands, and the only one in the world with fresh-water sharks (if there are any left). It is a nice old colonial town with a fantastic market, horse-carriages as taxis, and great hospedajes. It is also a place of extreme contrasts for, as I walked quietly along the street, a young man came up behind me shouting:

"Hey, you; you!" He grabbed my shoulder.

I turned round.

"You fuckin' motherfucker."

"What?!"

"You fuckin' motherfucker!"

What was going on here?

I didn't know, but I could see it was time to do a Clint Eastwood. I walked up close to him, looked directly in his eyes, and pointed my finger under his nose. Speaking slowly I said:

"Don't...you...ever...ever...call me a motherfucker again. Okay?!"

The effect was fantastic; a little voice answered:

"Okay. Sorry." And he vanished into the market.

Granada! After three days I didn't want to leave it. It was just what I needed at the end of my trip – town of buccaneers and conquistadors, pirates and filibusters, the oldest town in Nicaragua. A place to wind down and get quietly excited over the long ferry ride ahead which would take me across the huge Lake Nicaragua, nearly to the border of Costa Rica. Of course, this meant I would be 'leaping' across half of the country in idleness, but I no longer even tried to justify my laziness.

After three days of wandering the streets in a happy daze, I boarded the crowded afternoon ferry which runs the full length of the lake to the small town of San Carlos. I arrived twelve hours later, in the dark and pouring rain.

Wondering where to go, I met Christine, a woman from my hospedaje in Granada. She was accompanied by two Body-Beautiful males who obviously thought that she and they would be seeking out a place to stay together; she had other plans. Turning to me she said quietly:

"Come on. These guys are a pain in the butt. Let's go and find somewhere together."

Christine was an American woman from San Francisco. She had lived in El Salvador for six years during the civil war, when she had taken groups of Americans on 'educational tours' to the liberated zones. I really liked her; she was another of those admirable, single, female travellers one occasionally meets and was one of the most politically-informed I had ever met. We talked long into the night – mostly about Central American politics, on which she was an expert, and of which (because of its complexity) I kept getting confused.

We thought we should do something exciting so we jumped on a small boat and took the four hour journey down the beautiful San Juan River to El Castillo de la Concepcion. After three days in this exquisite eco-village (where I luckily got constipation when I realised the toilet was through a hole straight into the river where the children swam) I returned to San Carlos to find that the border crossing I was aiming for – ten miles away down a gravel track – was illegal, and I would have to take a boat to the border town of Los Chiles.

My Nicaraguan papers had to be sorted out in San Carlos, and the next boat went in two hours, or else wait three days. It is true that the bureaucracy in many parts of the world is totally ludicrous, and it can sometimes drive you crazy trying to do something as simple as posting a letter. So when, as in San Carlos, things are being done in little, disorganised, usually closed offices by a man in baggy jeans, you expect the worst. I stressed to the friendly but unhurried man:

"Excuse me, but the boat leaves at three."

"No problema; no problema."

I didn't believe it. I didn't know where the boat went from and I imagined another crowded ferry, revving its engines to be off on the dot of three, and me being stuck in this place, gradually getting as eccentric as the locals.

After ten minutes he handed me my passport with an easy smile.

"Okay, we can go now."

With that, he stepped out his door, walked two metres to the jetty side and called to a boy sitting alone in a small motorised rowing boat:

"Okay, Juan, we are finished, you can go now."

No big ferry, no crowds, no schedules; only my own personal boat, just big enough for me and my bike!

DRIPPING TREES

To enter Costa Rica after months in the poorer economies to the north is a bit like stepping into a fibre-glass boat after getting used to an old wooden one: the new one is nice for its clean, shiny efficiency, but the old one, with its warts and patches, is the one you love for its experience and character. Costa Rica is what Nicaragua would be if it had had fifty years of peace and a healthier bank balance, so I experienced a very real culture shock. In Costa Rica everything is different; you can feel the peace in the air and in the relaxed manner of the inhabitants.

New cars pass you on the road, and inside you can see families with neat haircuts and crisp ironed clothes, the horses are plump! And families actually go for Sunday picnics, something I had not seen since the Valle de Bravo in Mexico.

It all looks too good to be true, and a visitor who has entered via Nicaragua can so easily be dazzled by surprise and relief (oh, the relief!) that once again they can recognise 'a life lived'; that they don't have to feel guilty at putting food in their own mouth; that people are doing things they understand, and they are doing things the Costa Ricans can understand.

Well, that's probably not entirely true; this is still Central America, after all. But everything is relative and, like most of the rest of my fellow Britons, I always want the Ten O'Clock News to end with a happy story about a cat rescued from a tree. In Costa Rica the happy story is that the elite realised that giving people rights did not threaten their own positions of wealth and power. On the contrary, they saw democracy as the most intelligent way of keeping their country stable, as a stable country is more likely to be an economically successful one. So while other Central American countries freaked out at the first sign of any attempt by its citizens to improve life, and used thuggery as a tool to control social discontent, Costa Rica instead used reform and conciliation.

And one more thing, in 1948 President Jose Maria Figueres Ferror outlawed all standing armies, including his own. Costa Rica has had no army since then.

Of course, nothing is perfect, and there were also the usual warnings that murderous bands of thugs would be waiting impatiently for me to zip up my tent each night so they could rip both it and me to shreds and rob me of my worldly goods. But I couldn't take the warnings seriously. Neither, in Los Chiles, did the local priest, which was good enough for me. I camped on the village green next to the church.

As word of my arrival got round and hordes of horrible teenage boys descended on me, my optimism got a bit ragged round the edges. And when their increasingly cocky behaviour and offensive language became unbearable, I started the threats: 'Piss off or I'll get the police.' Even in Costa Rica this had a miraculous effect.

In the background through all of this stood a tiny little girl. This was eight year old Eva, with all the charm, worldliness and conscientiousness of someone five times her age. As the pests withdrew she came forward and took me in hand for the remainder of the evening, tidying my food, cleaning my pans, rearranging my bed, and always, always asking questions. Then, with eyes open wide she began to paint a gruesome picture of what was in store for me if I stayed where I was;

"Men will come in the night and stab you with a knife, and if they don't have a knife they will strangle you," she assured me. When I told her that I would take the risk, she had the solution:

"Then I will go and get you a candle from my house."

I meandered my way to Muelle, where a man cleared his cows out of a field so that I could camp down by the river. This was such a kind move that for a few seconds I was speechless. I set my tent up in the shade of a massive tree whose huge trunkal ribs and fantastic aerial roots were a sad reminder that his farm used to be part of a magnificent rainforest.

As I passed immaculate village greens, cute freshly painted clapboard churches and twee houses, I tried to develop a craving for something slightly more basic and less New England – for a bit of rough, unpainted wood, a roadside food stall of doubtful hygiene, kids with snot running into their mouths, pigs wandering the street – but I failed. In any case, what was I trying to resurrect – that old image of photogenic poverty; the romanticizing of hunger; those third world lives which we who do not have to live them can freely idealise?

The reality was that it actually felt good to enter a democratic country where the population was not traumatised by war, where fathers could play football with their children on undamaged legs, where people did not wake up under a cardboard roof and where chubby horses with neatly trimmed manes and tails, looked at me with big eyes and full tummies.

As I passed between two national parks the roadside vegetation became ever more riotous – thousands of species of plants, shrubs, trees, ferns, creepers, flowers, all jumbled together in an inseparable mass. I bathed under a waterfall and watched monkeys high up in the canopy, I saw the smallest humming-bird, the size of a bee.

As darkness fell I followed the beetles carrying their own personal torchlights, some shining green, some white, so bright that the darkness glowed. Choruses of birds bounced back and forth through the canopy, cicadas hummed, and water dripped in heavy plops onto my tent.

Apart from my 'jadedness' and the fact that I'd run out of time and money, there were two other things which made Costa Rica an appropriate place to end my trip.

Since leaving Seattle nearly a year before I had done a lot of moaning about hills. Now, belatedly, I realised how easy I'd had it – Rocky Mountain roller coasters, southern Mexican inclines, crumpled crusts of all descriptions, they all faded into insignificance. In Costa Rica the gradients are... well... sort of vertical!

After a year of cycling up mountains and down gorges, those absolutely final hills of Costa Rica, on that absolutely final day, presented me with an endless series of short, vertical slopes, totally impossible for me to cycle up. I counted it both a blessing and a fitting coincidence (er, synchronicity) that, on what was to be the last day of my ride, both me and my bike had finally come up against our absolute limit – where we gasped our last breath!

Since returning home, many people have dismissed my claims to low stamina as false modesty. How could I have low stamina when I had cycled up hill and down dale for seven thousand five hundred miles? In answer I can only say that I believe physical ability is a curious flexible thing partly controlled by the mind and which, in my case, adapted itself to whatever was on the menu for the day, so that even on an easy day I still felt, as they say 'physically challenged'. Certainly in the thick all-enveloping humidity of those south of the border days I was always cycling up to my limit, and often beyond it.

I had anticipated a victory ride down into the capital. As it was I gave up after a shattering sixteen miles, when the rain began to fall in a relentless sheet. San Jose would have to wait until the next day.

And that was another thing: the rainy season had started in earnest, and for the first time I had to put my tent away soaking. Consequently my very, very last night was, for the very, very first time, spent huddled – cold, wet and miserable – in a sodden tent in a dripping forest, squashed into a tiny clearing which I had managed to slash out of the undergrowth. My last night under nylon could hardly have been a greater anti-climax.

It was perhaps fitting that a continent which is so full of life and living, so vibrant and intelligent, but which has been made so shabbily less by its history, should in these last hours bring me to a mood as grey as the forest which was dripping on me.

As I sat in the glow of my candle only one thought came to me, it was a returning thought and I recognised it; it hung before me and wouldn't disappear. It reminded me that though the past is over, and the dead do not suffer, the truth will remain tragically unchanged forever: that whole worlds and fantastic cultures were grubbed out, crushed without thought, and left crawling in their own mangled remains. And an unimaginable potential for beauty was lost.

The next day I sailed the last downhill miles into the valley of San Jose.

eyeSight

Our greatest fear is not that we are inadequate, our greatest fear is that we are powerful beyond measure. By shining your light, you subconsciously give permission to others to shine theirs.
Nelson Mandela

Travel can be a liberating experience, as it was for me in 1990, when I was just one hundred yards from Nelson Mandela as he was released from prison. I watched this monumental occasion from on top of a traffic light, amidst a sea of enthralled onlookers.

This was the 'green light' moment that inspired the creation of Eye Books. From the chaos of that day arose an appreciation of the opportunities that the world around us offers, and the desire within me to shine a light for those whose reaction to opportunity is 'can't and don't'.

Our world has been built on dreams, but the drive is often diluted by the corporate and commercial interests offering to live those dreams for us, through celebrity culture and the increasing mechanisation and automation of our lives. Inspiration comes now from those who live outside our daily routines, from those who *challenge the way we see things*.

Eye Books was born to tell the stories of *'ordinary' people doing 'extraordinary' things*. With no experience of publishing, or the constraints that the book 'industry' imposes, Eye Books created a genre of publishing to champion those who live out their dreams.

Twelve years on, and sixty stories later, Eye Books has the same ethos. We believe that ethical publishing matters. It is not about just trying to make a quick hit, it is about publishing the stories that affect our lives and the lives of others positively. We publish the books we believe will shine a light on the lives of some and enlighten the lives of many for years to come.

Join us in the Eye Books community, and share the power these stories evoke.

Dan Hiscocks
Founder and Publisher
Eye Books

www.eye-books.com

At Eye Books we are constantly challenging the way we see things and do things. But we cannot do this alone. To that end we have created an online club, a community, where members can inspire and be inspired, share knowledge and exchange ideas. Membership is free, and you can join by visiting www.eye-books.com, where you will be able to find:

What we publish

Books that truly inspire, by people who have given their all, triumphed over adversity, lived their lives to the full. Visit the dedicated microsites we have for each of our books online.

Why we publish

To champion those 'ordinary' people doing extraordinary things. The real celebrities of our world who tell stories that celebrate life to the full, not just for 15 minutes. Books where fact is more compelling than fiction.

How we publish

Eye Books is committed to ethical publishing. Many of our books feature and campaign for various good causes and charities. We try to minimise our carbon footprint in the manufacturing and distribution of our books.

Who we publish

Many, indeed most of our authors have never written a book before. Many start as readers and club members. If you feel strongly that you have a book in you, and it is a book that is experience driven, inspirational and life affirming, visit the 'How to Become an Author' page on our website. We are always open to new authors.

Eye-Books.com Club is an ever-evolving community, as it should be, and benefits from all that our members contribute, with invitations to book launches, signings and author talks, plus special offers and discounts on the books we publish.

Eye Books membership is free, and it's easy to sign up. Visit our website. Registration takes less than a minute.

www.eye-books.com

eyeBookshelf

THE AMERICAS / ASIA

Book	Author	Region	eyeThinker	eyeAdventurer	eyeQuirky	eyeCyclist	eyeRambler	eyeGift	eyeSpiritual
Thunder & Sunshine	Alastair Humphreys	The Americas		•		•		•	
The Good Life	Dorian Amos	The Americas	•	•					
The Good Life Gets Better	Dorian Amos	The Americas	•	•					
Cry From the Highest Mountain	Tess Burrows	The Americas	•	•					
Riding the Outlaw Trail	Simon Casson & Richard Adamson	The Americas		•					
Trail of Visions Route 2	Vicki Couchman	The Americas	•		•	•			
Riding with Ghosts	Gwen Maka	The Americas		•					
Riding with Ghosts – South of the Border	Gwen Maka	The Americas	•	•					
Lost Lands Forgotten Stories	Alexandra Pratt	The Americas		•					
Frigid Women	Sue & Victoria Riches	The Americas	•	•					
Touching Tibet	Niema Ash	Asia	•						
First Contact	Mark Anstice	Asia	•	•					
Tea for Two	Polly Benge	Asia	•	•		•			
Baghdad Business School	Heyrick Bond Gunning	Asia	•	•					

AFRICA / EUROPE

Book	Author	Region	eyeThinker	eyeAdventurer	eyeQuirky	eyeCyclist	eyeRambler	eyeGift	eyeSpiritual
Moods of Future Joys	Alastair Humphreys	Africa		•		•		•	
Green Oranges on Lion Mountain	Emily Joy	Africa	•	•					
Zohra's Ladder	Pamela Windo	Africa	•						
Walking Away	Charlotte Metcalf	Africa	•						
Changing the World from the inside out	Michael Meegan	Africa	•						•
All Will Be Well	Michael Meegan	Africa	•		•			•	•
Seeking Sanctuary	Hilda Reilly	Europe	•		•			•	
Crap Cycle Lanes	Captain Crunchynutz	Europe		•	•	•		•	
50 Quirky Bike Rides…in England and Wales	Rob Ainsley	Europe	•		•	•	•		
On the Wall with Hadrian	Bob Bibby	Europe			•		•		
Special Offa	Bob Bibby	Europe		•	•				
The European Job	Jonathan Booth	Europe							
Fateful Beauty	Natalie Hodgson	Europe		•					
Slow Winter	Alex Hickman	Europe	•						

ASIA / AUS

Category	Jungle Janes (Peter Burden)	Trail of Visions (Vicki Couchman)	Desert Governess (Phyllis Ellis)	Fever Tress of Borneo (Mark Eveleigh)	My Journey with a Remarkable Tree (Ken Finn)	The Jungle Beat (Roy Follows)	Siberian Dreams (Andy Home)	Behind the Veil (Lydia Laube)	Good Morning Afghanistan (Waseem Mahmood)	Jasmine and Arnica (Nicola Naylor)	Prickly Pears of Palestine (Hilda Reilly)	Last of the Nomads (W J Peasley)	Travels in Outback Australia (Andrew Stevenson)
eyeThinker		•	•		•	•	•		•	•		•	•
eyeAdventurer	•			•		•	•	•	•			•	
eyeQuirky			•										
eyeCyclist													
eyeRambler													
eyeGift		•											
eyeSpiritual													

ASIA | **AUS**

EUROPE / CROSS CONTINENT

Category	The Accidental Optimist's Guide to Life (Emily Joy)	Con Artist Handbook (Joel Levy)	Forensics Handbook (Pete Moore)	Travels with my Daughter (Niema Ash)	Around the World with 1000 Birds (Russell Boyman)	Death (Herbie Brennan)	Discovery Road (Tim Garratt & Andy Brown)	Great Sects (Adam Hume Kelly)	Triumph Around the World (Robbie Marshall)	Blood Sweat and Charity (Nick Stanhope)	Traveller's Tales from Heaven and Hell (Various)	Further Traveller's Tales from Heaven and Hell (Various)	More Traveller's Tales from Heaven and Hell (Various)
eyeThinker	•	•	•	•		•		•					
eyeAdventurer		•	•		•				•	•			
eyeQuirky	•	•	•		•		•				•	•	•
eyeCyclist							•						
eyeRambler													
eyeGift	•	•	•		•		•		•		•	•	•
eyeSpiritual					•		•						

EUROPE | **CROSS CONTINENT**

Green Oranges on Lion Mountain
Emily Joy
£7.99

Dr Emily Joy puts on her rose-tinted specs, leaves behind her comfortable life and heads off for to volunteer at a remote hospital in Sierra Leone. There is no equipment, no water, no electricity, and worst of all no chocolate to treat her nasty case of unrequited love.

Despite this, the strength and humour of the Sierra Leonean people inspire and uplift her with their courage and vivacity. Her poignant and hilarious experiences remind us why volunteering is essential and rewarding for all involved.

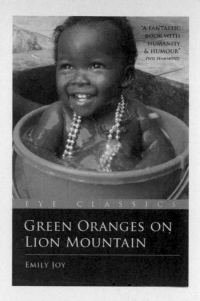

"A FANTASTIC BOOK WITH HUMANITY & HUMOUR"
PHIL HAMMOND

EYE CLASSICS

GREEN ORANGES ON LION MOUNTAIN

EMILY JOY

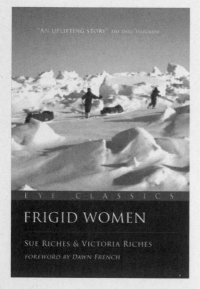

"AN UPLIFTING STORY" *THE DAILY TELEGRAPH*

EYE CLASSICS

FRIGID WOMEN

SUE RICHES & VICTORIA RICHES
FOREWORD BY DAWN FRENCH

Frigid Women
Sue & Victoria Riches
£7.99

Women wanted to walk to North Pole, the advert read. Sue & Victoria Riches, mother and daughter, never imagined how much one small article in a newspaper would change their lives.... Within two years, they were trekking across the frozen wilderness that is the Arctic Ocean, as part of the first all women's expedition to the North Pole. At times totally terrifying and at times indescribably beautiful, it was a trip of a lifetime. Having survived cancer treatment and a mastectomy it was an opportunity to discover that *anything* is possible if you put your mind to it.

www.eye-books.com

Riding the Outlaw Trail
Simon Casson
£7.99

A dramatic account of what it was like following the trail of the most elusive and successful bandits of the Wild West: Butch Cassidy and the Sundance Kid. An obsessive trouble-shooter and a cool-thinking, ex-Special Forces Marine Commando, with nothing in common but mutual suspicion, join forces for a gruelling, hazardous 5-month horseback journey across 2,000 miles of desert, mountain, canyon & high-plains wilderness through the 'Old West'.

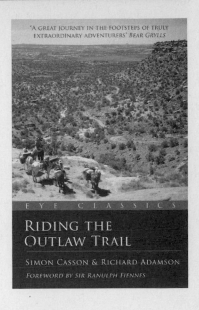

Triumph Around the World
Robbie Marshall
£7.99

At 45 Robbie Marshall had it all, or so it seemed. So what on earth made him trade his suit for leathers, his office for the saddle of a great British motorcycle, and his bulging appointments diary for an out-of-date world atlas?

The prospect of a new challenge held such overwhelming appeal that he was prepared to risk it all – his hard-won career, wealth and the love of a good woman – for life on the road, and a life-style completely removed from anything he had known before.

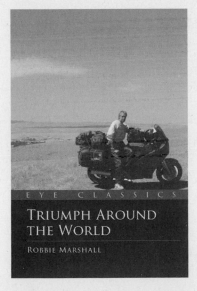

www.eye-books.com

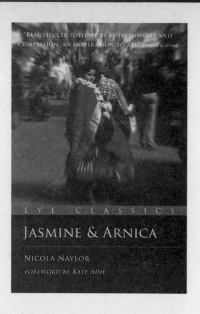

Zohra's Ladder
Pamela Windo
£7.99

Zohra's Ladder is a wondrous collection of tales about Morocco that immerses the reader in a world of ritual and deep sensuality. Pamela Windo chronicles her long love affair with the country and its people, peeling back layers of history and the finely embroidered fabric of daily life to find the truths in the mysterious and the exotic. Her stories describe the colours, flavours, sounds and textures of an almost dream-like place, told with extraordinary delicacy.

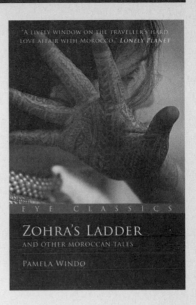

Eye Books are an inspirational choice for reading groups.

Fiction, fiction, fiction, that's all most book groups tend to read. Pick up an Eye Book and you will find that the truth is stranger than fiction. The spirit of adventure, intrigue and the pursuit of dreams described in our books provide inspiring reads that motivate lively discussion and debate. Eye Books offers a discount on purchases of five titles or more for reading groups. Please call for more details.

Eye Books are available through all good bookstores, online and directly from ourselves. To order by phone call: +44 (0)1903 828503.

If you would like to see a catalogue (available online or in print) of our titles with further descriptions of how our Eye authors have pursued their dreams, please contact us by email: info@eye-books.com

www.eye-books.com

Got a dream? Live it...

Eye Books champions the cause of 'ordinary' people doing extraordinary things.

These two books – *Ten Lessons from the Road* and *Blood Sweat & Charity* – have been published by Eye Books to help turn dreams into reality through the motivational insights of serial adventurer Alastair Humphreys and Nick Stanhope's insight into the planning and fundraising required to get the theoretical into practical application.

Special offers on these and all other books published by Eye Books can be found by visiting our website at: www.eye-books.com

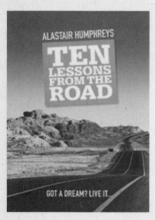

Ten Lessons from the Road
Alastair Humphreys
£9.99

Alastair learnt a thing or two as he cycled around the world. He learnt that big achievements come from big dreams, that they often start with big talk, and they guarantee some really big scares along the way. He also learnt that you only learn how far you can go by going too far.

Crammed with affirming quotes, insight and unique photographs, Humpreys asserts that the lessons he learned on his travels can be applied to any goal in life.

Blood Sweat & Charity
Nick Stanhope
£12.99

A guide for anyone undertaking a charity challenge – whether a 5km fun run or a year long expedition. Whatever your age, fitness or motivation, this guide will provide all that you need to achieve your chosen feat, hit your fundraising target and make a lasting difference to yourself and the world.

www.eye-books.com